CAREER SKILLS

Second Edition

Joan Kelly-Plate, Ed.D.
Career Educator
Madison, Connecticut

Ruth Volz-Patton, Ed.D.
Assistant to the Director
East Central Network/
Illinois Vocational Curriculum Center

GLENCOE
McGraw-Hill

New York, New York   Columbus, Ohio   Mission Hills, California   Peoria, Illinois

TEACHER REVIEWERS

Send all inquiries to:
GLENCOE/McGraw-Hill
15319 Chatsworth Street
P.O. Box 9609
Mission Hills, CA 91346-9609

ISBN 0-02-675680-3 (Student Text)
ISBN 0-02-675690-0 (Teacher's Annotated Edition)

7 8 96 95

CONTENTS

PART ONE
CAREER EXPLORATION

CONTENTS

CONTENTS

PART TWO
EMPLOYMENT SKILLS

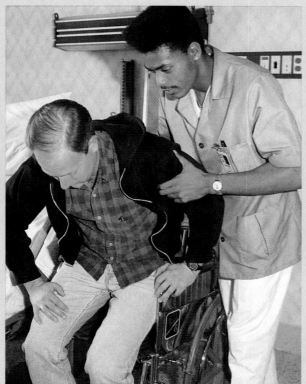

CONTENTS

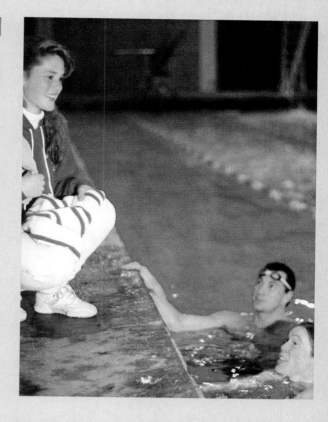

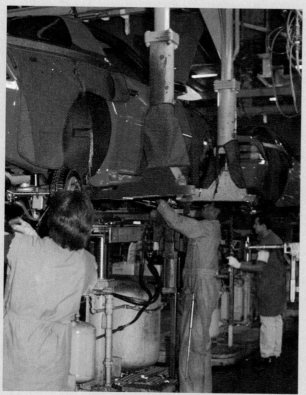

CONTENTS

INTRODUCTION

Career Skills is a book designed to help you plan your future. You'll like *Career Skills.* It's easy to read and is filled with interesting photographs and cartoons.

The best thing about *Career Skills* is that it is packed with ideas that will help you get what you want out of life. If you are not sure what you want, *Career Skills* can help you with that, too.

Career Skills is divided into two major parts. The first part helps you decide what you want by helping you to better understand yourself, your skills, and your interests. The second part shows you how to go after what you want and how to get it.

You've got your whole life ahead of you. Whether or not you are happy and successful will depend a great deal on the kind of work you do. *Career Skills* will help you learn the skills you need to find the right kind of work for you. *Career Skills* will get you started on the road to success.

CAREER EXPLORATION

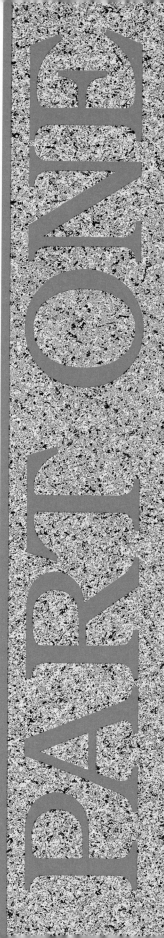

1

CHAPTER 1

THINKING ABOUT WORK

Have you thought about what you are going to do after you graduate from high school, or college, or trade school? Do you have any plans?

Many young people are unsure about their future in the working world. They know they want to be on their own. They want to earn their own money and live as adults live. However, when it comes to what they want to "be," they're confused and uncertain.

They may say, "Oh, I'll get a job *somewhere*. I'll just take whatever comes along." Once in a while one of them is really lucky and stumbles into a wonderful job.

Many people, however, are not so lucky. They find themselves doing work they hate for employers they don't like, eight hours a day, five days a week. They come home tired and grouchy and mad at the world.

Did you know that most people spend an average of 40 years in the work force? That's a long, long time to spend doing "whatever comes along."

A person's life is full of things he or she can't control. No one asked you when you wanted to be born, or where, or to which parents. You can't change the weather or the fact that you need to eat to stay alive.

You do, however, have something to say about how you spend your work life. You don't have to just take whatever comes along. You can find work you're happy with.

The World of Work

Work can be done by just about everybody, and there is a job somewhere to suit almost everyone. Let's take a quick look at the world of work.

Kinds of Jobs

The kinds of jobs available are almost countless. As you walk or drive down a street, look around you. Everything that meets your eye, from the stones under your feet to the clouds in the sky, is linked to some kind of job. For example, is there a billboard beside the road? How many jobs do you think have to do with a billboard? Here are some.

- **Landlord.** Owns the property on which the billboard is standing and collects rent.
- **Designer or architect.** Drew up the plans for the billboard's construction.
- **Carpenter.** Followed the designer's plans to make the billboard.
- **Electrician.** Installed lights so the billboard can be seen at night.
- **Advertising salesperson.** Sold the space on the billboard to an advertiser.
- **Advertising artist.** Designed the picture appearing on the billboard advertisement.
- **Advertising writer.** Wrote the words appearing on the billboard advertisement.
- **Sign painter.** Took the design from the advertising artist and writer and painted it on the billboard.

Everywhere you look, you see the results of people at work. What results of people at work can you see in your classroom?

So far our list names eight jobs directly connected with the billboard. How many other jobs can you think of that might be linked to the billboard? What about the advertiser? If there were no goods or services to advertise, there would be no need for billboards at all. Suppose the ad on the billboard was for chewing gum. What different kinds of jobs do you think are linked to a stick of chewing gum?

Following is a list of just a few of the jobs available today. By looking in newspapers or the phone book, by watching TV, or just by walking down the street, see how many you can add to this list.

- reporting the news
- teaching
- repairing cars
- solving crimes
- operating computers
- fighting fires
- waiting on tables
- designing houses
- farming
- playing professional sports
- studying the ocean
- raising fish
- nursing
- bricklaying
- playing a musical instrument
- chemical engineering
- photographing news events
- housekeeping
- selling clothes in a store
- writing scripts for TV shows

That's just 20 of the thousands of jobs people do in this country. Do any of these jobs sound interesting to you?

Places to Work

Have you thought about the places people work? Work is done in many different settings or locations. Some jobs, such as teaching skiing and forestry, are done outside. Librarians and dentists do their jobs indoors. Other jobs, such as those done on a submarine or spaceship, are performed in very tight quarters. Still other jobs require workers to go deep into mines or to climb mountains to study glaciers. Firefighters, police officers, and many construction workers find themselves in spots that can be dangerous.

Work is performed in many different settings. Can you think of any reason why this job might be a poor choice for many people?

Many things can affect a work setting. A writer works alone, and a tour guide works with people. Assemblers remain in one spot to do their jobs, while flight attendants must travel from city to city. A person may choose to work for a large company or to operate his or her own small business.

Some jobs offer a combination of settings. An airline pilot must stay in the close quarters of a cockpit while flying the plane but has a chance to see a different city or country after the flight is over.

Times to Work

Every hour of the day and night, someone somewhere is working. Sometimes a business must run 24 hours a day because of the type of service it offers. A hospital, for example, must be open and have a medical team available to treat emergencies at all times. Big hotels are staffed around the clock for travelers who come and go both day and night.

Other work is done at all times because of the work load. Some factories must work 24 hours to keep up with the demand for their product.

Many people prefer to work at night. Can you name an advantage to working at night rather than during the day?

Work is done according to the seasons, or whether it is day or night. Outdoor construction, for example, must be done during the warm months in northern states. Ski patrols, on the other hand, work only in the winter. Beach lifeguards are usually limited to daylight hours. Workers who clean office buildings do most of their work in the late afternoon and evening.

Work times also vary as to the number of hours put in. Most people work full time. **Full time** *means about forty hours a week*. The hours are usually broken up into eight hours a day, five days a week.

Work time influences the worker's daily schedule. The typical work days are Monday through Friday, and the typical work hours are eight to five. People who work a different time period find their free time is usually different from that of their friends and families.

REVIEW YOUR WORK

1. Give at least one reason why a person should not plan to accept just any job that comes along.
2. How many years does the average person work?
3. Name ten jobs, other than teaching, that have to do with your school.
4. Name three jobs done outdoors. Name three jobs done at night. Name three jobs that include travel.

Changes in the Work World

The world of work is constantly changing. Some business-es fail. New businesses start. Some products catch the public fancy. Others lose favor and disappear. For example, the field of electronics is changing so fast that a product can be out of date before it is in the stores.

While you are considering the type of work you want to do, the work world will be changing. All changes affect jobs. Being aware of the changes can help you choose a job with a more certain future.

The changes talked about in this chapter are only a few of those affecting jobs today. Keep in mind, too, that jobs can be affected by more than one kind of change.

Social Changes

Today young married couples are waiting longer to start families. Years ago, men worked to earn the family income, and women managed the home. Now most couples find it necessary for both the man and the woman to work outside the home.

By the year 2000, 12 million married and single women are expected to hold jobs. This means that 70 percent of all women will be working outside the home. Women will make up 50 percent of the work force.

Lots of young female students in high school do not expect to be working at age 35. However, they may find that they

DID YOU KNOW?

LONG DAYS

Most employees in the United States work an eight-hour day, five days a week, but this has not al-ways been the case. Up to the late 1880s, workers la-bored ten hours a day every day but Sunday. Wagon drivers and other transpor-tation workers put in 84 hours a week. Bakery workers were on the job as long as 120 hours each week!

The increasing number of women who work outside the home is an important change that has affected the world of work. Is this an example of a social change or a technological change?

cannot leave their jobs. Some experts predict that females will work an average of 35 years and that their pay will be more than what males earn.

Technology

Technology *is the use of ideas, processes, tools, and materials to get things done.* Consequently, as technology changes, the work world changes. These technological changes may involve new equipment, new materials, or new methods.

New equipment can affect many job areas. During the early part of this century, blacksmiths were needed to make and repair metal tools and objects, such as horseshoes. Today there is little need for blacksmiths since cars and tractors have replaced horses and metal tools, and objects are now made in large factories.

The space program has brought new materials to the building, clothing, food, and transportation industries. For example, a certain type of coating used on the space shuttle is now used by dentists to repair teeth.

In 1974 a small electronics firm made a personal computer in kit form. This microcomputer has affected our personal lives, created new jobs, and changed industrial systems and processes. It has affected the courses you take, how you enroll in school, and how the school keeps records. The computer is a development that cannot be ignored. Everyone who will work in the years to come needs to know about computers.

Technology also changes methods. It can help make the work place safer, more comfortable, and enjoyable. It can get jobs done faster. For example, workers in the clothing industry used to cut cloth by hand. Now cutters are power driven and computerized to adjust to the thickness of the cloth. A secretary who started working with a manual typewriter had it replaced by an electric one and probably now operates a word processor. The clothing worker and the secretary both had to learn new methods of working, but now they can do their jobs much easier and faster.

Technology can also replace some human workers with machines. Robots are now used in the steel industry for work that has to be done where temperatures reach 120 degrees. Welding that must take place underwater on an oil rig in the ocean can also be done by a robot. Laser technology is used in the construction business as well as in the medical profession. The workers who used to do these jobs must learn new skills.

CAREER Q&A

GET READY FOR THE FUTURE

Q: What can I do now to improve my chances of starting a career with good opportunities for the future?

A: Get a good education now. Keep up with the news and events that could affect your career. Do your best at work so you will be ready for any opportunities that come your way.

Technology in the form of computers has changed our lives. Do you think your future career will be affected in some way by computers?

Many jobs have also been created that deal with the aftereffects of technology. Such technological inventions as foam containers for fast-foods, hair spray ingredients, and toxic wastes are all troublesome by-products of technology at work. If not handled correctly, these products and substances can cause great harm to the environment. There are many important jobs that relate to their safe disposal.

Legal Changes

The Equal Employment Opportunity Act has made it illegal for a company or business to discriminate (treat people differently) because of race, color, religion, sex, or national origin. Other laws have made it illegal to discriminate against people for other reasons. These reasons include the person's marital status, family background, military discharge, physical or mental handicap, and age. Because of equal employment laws, people have a better chance of being treated fairly both when they look for a job and after they are hired.

Laws affecting product safety have also affected the work scene. Workers are needed to design and test products that must conform to these laws. For example, when the law required seatbelts to be placed in all cars, workers were needed to make and install them.

Thinking About Work

What is your attitude toward work? If you're like many young people, you probably haven't thought much about it yet. You've been too busy with your life as a student and teenager to think about working.

Work will be a big part of your life for a long time. You need to start thinking about it now. What kind of job do you want to do? How will you prepare for that job? What do you want to achieve in your lifetime?

You have a general attitude about work, whether you realize it or not. This attitude has been influenced by your parents or guardians and their adult friends. The chances are very good that your feelings about work are very similar to theirs.

What do your parents think about work in general? Do they talk about their jobs—either inside the home or outside the home—at the end of the day? If so, what kinds of things do they say? (You might try making a list.) Do they seem to enjoy their work—simply tolerate it—or despise it?

You probably know some people (hopefully not your parents or friends) who don't like to work and who hate their jobs. These people live only for weekends, holidays, and vacations. They go to work because they have to—not because they want to. They have a very negative attitude toward work.

If this is your attitude, change it! **THINK POSITIVELY** about work. You will spend many of your waking hours for 30, 40, or even 50 years *working.* You might as well try to enjoy it. Why

make yourself miserable? Besides, there are many things about work that you can enjoy if you have the right attitude.

One of the best parts of working is that you get to know lots of people. In fact, you will make many good, true friends at work.

Another positive part of work is that you will accomplish a great deal. You will do something useful—something that needs to be done. This will make you feel good about yourself.

You will also learn and grow as an individual. As you do different jobs, and more difficult jobs, you will become more knowledgeable and skillful. Again, this will make you feel good about yourself.

So don't start off on the wrong foot. Give work a chance—think positively about work. What have you got to lose?

Economic Pressures

In general, **economics** *has to do with money.* (Chapter 14 has more information on economics.) Many job changes are made for economic reasons. For example, the American auto industry suffered severe economic difficulties in the early 1980s. For a number of reasons, Americans began buying more and more foreign cars. The manufacturers had trouble making enough money to stay in business. As a result, many auto workers lost their jobs.

Sometimes the workers themselves put economic pressures on an industry. They may band together and demand that the company pay them more money. If the company is healthy and can afford to increase pay, the workers may win. If the company is already in economic trouble, it may have to shut down. In that case, workers will be out of both money and jobs.

Economic reasons may force companies to use different methods or materials in making products. Heating fuels are a good example. Because the fuels we commonly use are in limited supply, their price is very high. As a result, the field of solar energy has grown. People are needed to design, build, sell, and install the equipment that makes solar energy usable in homes.

Sometimes costs force companies to move to a less expensive location. They are sometimes forced to take their business to another country where costs are even lower. The clothing industry is a good example. Much of the clothing we buy today is made in the Far East—Hong Kong, Taiwan, and the Philippines.

This store is going out of business because it is no longer making enough money to pay its workers. Is this an example of legal pressure, social pressure, or economic pressure?

Why People Work

People have different reasons for working. Why will you go to work? As you think about the answer to that question, read about some of the reasons why other people work.

- **People work for money.** People need money to pay for the basics, such as food, clothes, and a place to live. They also want money for the things that make life better. Education, a car, travel, a cellular phone, a compact disc player, a VCR—all cost something. A lot of people look for the job that will pay them the most money.
- **People work to gain an identity. Identity** *is the way we see ourselves in our minds and the way we think others see us.* For many men and women, a job gives them part of their identity. They can see themselves as people who get things done, who are responsible, and who are capable enough to be paid for the work they do.
- **People work to feel good about themselves.** Everyone wants to feel important in some way. Being part of a busy, fast-moving world makes some people feel important. Wanting to feel important may make them work harder and longer than others. It also causes people to work at jobs that seem special to them.

  People also take pride in what they do. They like the feeling that comes with doing things well. They enjoy using their skills and talents and also enjoy working hard to improve those skills.
- **People work to be useful.** By working, people feel that they are doing their share. They may work to take care of themselves or their families, or they may work to help others in the community.
- **People work to be with others.** Most people like to spend time with others. They don't like being alone for long periods. Work gives them a chance to be with and talk to people.

Do any of the above reasons apply to you? Many people joke about working. They complain that they'd rather be doing something else. As you can see, however, work fulfills many important needs. Even many individuals who became wealthy overnight still work.

Of course, we all have days when we'd rather stay in bed longer or go to the beach. No job satisfies all needs. The right job, however, can be satisfying in a very special way. That's why it's important to think carefully about your own wants and needs. You don't want to miss out on what could prove to be a good time.

Many people work to feel good about themselves. How might being police officers make these two people feel good about themselves?

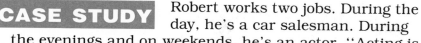

CASE STUDY Robert works two jobs. During the day, he's a car salesman. During the evenings and on weekends, he's an actor. ''Acting is what I love doing,'' he says, ''but it takes a long time to learn the craft. Right now I'm getting some good practice, but I am not making much money as an actor. I also have a job selling cars to pay my rent and buy groceries.''

Thinking About the Case Study

1. Why is acting an important job for Robert?
2. Why is selling cars an important job for Robert?

A Job or a Career?

A **job** *is a certain kind of work, such as building kitchen cabinets or selling real estate. A* **career** *is time spent in one type of job or area of interest.* A person might have a job selling lumber or a career *in the lumber business* doing many different jobs.

Work gives you an opportunity to meet and get to know many different people. Do you think this important social contact is a good reason for working?

Careers in Athletics

Ever since you first played a game of catch in your backyard, you have dreamed of being a big baseball player. Those players lead such a glamorous life, are so famous, and earn millions of dollars. What a life!

Are you still dreaming this dream? Are you working toward being a professional baseball player, or have you decided that you just don't have the skills?

Just because you might give up on being a player doesn't mean you have to give up being a part of the sports arena. For every player on the field, there are people behind the scenes doing interesting and important jobs.

Professional athletes attend training camps. At these camps, food service workers make sure that the athletes get the right foods. Sports doctors and trainers work to prevent and treat athletic injuries. Team personnel help to handle the team's business, as well as maintain the training and game facilities and equipment.

Athletes also need coaching. While many coaches and managers are former athletes, some are people who found that they have the skill to teach and help people with superior physical skills.

Maybe you would like to be involved in sports through the media. You could be a sports reporter for a magazine, a newspaper, a radio station, or television station or network. These people really get in on the action. Photographers, television camera operators, and technicians of all types also help to bring the games and events to the fans.

Professional athletes also need agents and business managers to help handle their money and their careers. Or perhaps you might choose a career in the advertising field working with athletes that endorse products.

You might choose to work in a ballpark or stadium. Ticket sellers, ushers, food service workers, maintenance people, referees, and security guards are all needed to help put on the big time events that pay the athletes' salaries.

All of these jobs and more are involved in professional sports. You can find similar jobs at the high school, college, and amateur levels.

To find out more about sports-related careers, you should talk to a career counselor and a coach or trainer at your school. By exploring other choices, you can still reach your dream and make it to the big leagues.

There is a big difference between a career and a series of jobs. Which would you prefer to have?

CASE STUDY   James wanted a career in transportation. During high school he had a part-time job picking up packages for a local trucking firm. When James graduated from high school, he worked as a dispatcher for the firm, sending trucks to different cities. Several years later he joined a postal service as an assistant manager. Finally, he started his own rapid freight delivery business.

Thinking About the Case Study

1. What did all of James' jobs have in common?
2. In what way was each new job James held different from his past jobs?

One career does not have to last for an entire work life. Many people have three or four careers. A career does not have to be with just one employer. Many people keep the same career but change their place of employment.

Some people do not bother to plan a career. They go from one type of job to something completely different. However, the happiest and most successful workers are those who do plan. The advantages of making a career plan are listed on the next page.

A career is part of one's lifetime achievements. Why is it important for you to start thinking about your career now?

- You can plan ahead and have some control over your life.
- Each job you hold will give you experience you can use for the next job in your career.
- The amount of money you earn will increase faster because you will not have to start at the bottom with each new job. Your growing experience and skill will be worth more money to your new employers.
- You will be able to look back on your life and see yourself moving each day toward what you want.

CAREER Q&A

CRYSTAL BALL

Q: How can I possibly make the right career choice for myself?

A: This book is designed to help you think about this question. Each chapter has information you can use now and in the future.

What's Next?

This book is divided into two parts. The first part will help you discover your own career needs and wants. In the next five chapters of Part One we'll be talking about

- **Your interests and skills.** What do you enjoy most? How can those things be part of your career plans?
- **Jobs that interest you.** What kinds of jobs are out there?
- **How to learn more about today's jobs.** Where can you get the information you need?
- **Making career decisions.** How do you make up your mind about what's best for you?
- **A plan of action.** How do you turn your career decisions into real-life steps to take?

Then, in Part Two, we'll discuss how you achieve success in your chosen career. The eight chapters in this part talk about

- **Where to look for a job.** How are jobs advertised and who can help you find them?
- **Contacting employers.** When they're ready to talk to you, do you know what to say?
- **Your experiences on a job.** What will your new employer expect of you?
- **Getting along with co-workers.** What's the best way to make friends on the job? How can you help make things run smoothly?
- **Basic skills and attitudes for success.** What if you need to brush up on the basics? What is it that makes a winner?
- **Health and safety at work.** How do health and safety issues affect you as an employee? What can you do to contribute to a safer work environment?
- **Working toward your goals.** How do you measure the progress you've made so far? How can you be sure you keep moving ahead?
- **The economic system.** How does our economy work? How does it affect your own life?
- **Your own business.** What are the different types of businesses you can start?
- **Managing your money.** How can you be sure you get the most from your paycheck?

When you've finished this course, you should know a bit more about yourself—your goals and strong points. You should also know more about what the world of work is all about and how you can be a success in it.

REVIEW YOUR WORK

1. What percentage of women will be working during the next ten years?
2. What is technology?
3. Name three ways computers have affected your own life.
4. What are economic changes? Give an example of how economics has changed an industry.
5. Name three reasons why people work.
6. What is the difference between a job and a career?
7. What are the advantages to making a career plan?

Chapter Summary

- There are so many kinds of jobs available that there probably is a job to suit almost everyone. There are also work times to suit everyone.
- The world of work is constantly undergoing social, technological, legal, and economic changes.
- The most common reasons that people have for working are: to earn a living, to gain an identity, to feel good about themselves, to be useful, and to be with other people.
- A job is a certain kind of work, while a career is time spent in an area of interest.
- There are many advantages to having a career plan.

Reviewing Vocabulary and Concepts

Write the numbers 1–16 on a separate sheet of paper. After each number, write the letter of the answer that best completes the following statements or answers the following questions.

1. What is an area of your life that you have some control over?
   a. where you were born
   b. the weather
   c. who your parents are
   d. how to spend your work life

2. How many kinds of jobs are there in this country?
   a. fifty   c. thousands
   b. hundreds   d. ten

3. Hospitals, fire stations, and police stations are three work places that have a staff on duty _____ hours a day.
   a. 24   c. 12
   b. 8   d. 16

4. One reason to keep a business running more than eight hours a day is because _____ .
   a. of the work load
   b. people like it
   c. it keeps everyone busy
   d. none of the above

5. Full-time work means _____ hours a week.
   a. 20   c. 60
   b. 40   d. 80

6. Some experts predict that in the near future, women will work an average of _____ years.
   a. 15   c. 35
   b. 25   d. 45

7. The use of ideas, processes, tools, and materials to get things done is called _____ .
   a. technology
   b. transportation
   c. artistic
   d. communication

8. The definition of a job is _____ .
   a. time spent in one area of interest
   b. a certain kind of work
   c. something other people do
   d. something nobody else will do

9. The definition of a career is _____ .
   a. a doctor's job
   b. a place to go
   c. time spent in one area of interest
   d. something not in your control

10. The happiest and most successful workers are those who _____ .
    a. work part-time
    b. plan ahead
    c. whistle a lot
    d. work at night

11. While you are considering the type of work you want to do, the work world will be _____ .

a. changing
b. getting smaller
c. going backward
d. hiring fewer people

12. Technology is responsible for changing _____ in the work place.
    a. equipment   c. methods
    b. people   d. furniture

13. The term *economics* usually means something having to do with
    _____ .
    a. the environment   c. science
    b. technology   d. money

14. Sometimes companies move to other countries because _____ .
    a. they want to help the people there
    b. the costs are lower
    c. there are more buildings
    d. there is more energy

15. Our identity is the way we _____ ourselves.
    a. see   c. like
    b. talk to   d. listen to

16. Wanting to feel good about themselves often motivates people to work at jobs that _____ .
    a. seem special to them
    b. are too hard
    c. are highly technical
    d. are not very special

Thinking Critically About Career Skills

Write your answers to the following questions on a separate sheet of paper.

1. Why do most people prefer to work during the day? What are some advantages of working during daylight hours? What are some reasons why some people might like to work at night?

2. What are some industries in which recent advances in technology have affected the work place?

Building Basic Skills

1. **Mathematics** Calculate the total number of hours you will work in your lifetime if you begin working full-time when you are 20; retire when you are 65; work an average of 40 hours per week; and work a total of 3,000 hours of part-time jobs before you turn 20.

2. **Writing** In a 50-word paragraph, write about why you think finding the right job is important.

3. **Time Management** Pretend that you were offered a job working ten hours a week either after school or on weekends. Write up a schedule for one week that includes time for school, work, homework, sleeping, and leisure activities.

Applying Career Skills

1. Across a sheet of paper make a list of five jobs you would like to try. Under each job list as many duties that relate to that job as you can. Then list the advantages and disadvantages of each job.

2. Talk to two adults you know who have had the same job for a number of years. Ask them questions about how they like what they're doing. Ask them if the job has turned out to be what they had in mind when they started. Ask if they have stayed in the same career field. If not, how difficult was changing careers?

CHAPTER 2

LOOKING
AT
YOURSELF

KEY TERMS

interests
interest inventory
skill
aptitudes
academic achievement
 tests
personality

OBJECTIVES

In this chapter you will
learn about
- how your interests
  can help you find a
  job
- measuring your skills
  and aptitudes
- work values
- how personality
  differences affect
  career choices

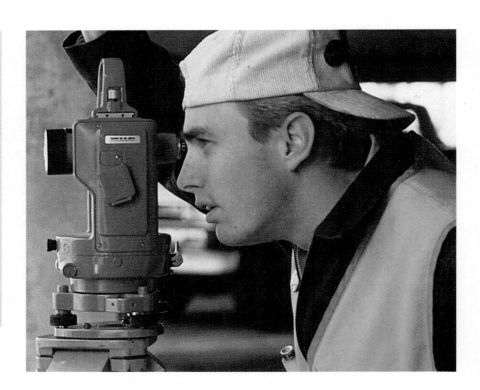

Most of us aren't geniuses. We don't have special talents or abilities that seem to say we're meant for a certain kind of career. In a way, we're lucky because we have more choices. However, if we have too *many* choices it's hard to know which way to go.

One place to start is by looking at what things you enjoy doing better than others. What you like doing, combined with your abilities and personality, will give you the most important clues to finding the right job.

How well do you know yourself? Do you know what things you're good at? Do you know what things you're *not* good at?

You may not know yourself as well as you would like. If so, you can gather information about yourself. You can find out what you are interested in and what you can do.

In this chapter you will learn how to collect information about yourself. After completing the chapter, you will know what to look for in a career. Then you will be more likely to find a career that will make you happy.

Your Interests

How do you spend your free time? Do you find yourself drawn toward some things more than others?

Your **interests** *are the things you enjoy doing.* They are the things you're curious about and like to spend time thinking about.

Some common interests are

- music
- different countries and cultures
- how cars are made
- animals
- the outdoors
- fashion design
- how sports are played
- how human beings think and act

Your interests influence the decisions you make. You choose the movie or book that sounds most interesting. You often choose friends who have the same interests you have. Your interests will also influence your career choice.

You need to identify your interests. Think about how you spend your leisure time and the things you talk about with your friends. Think about the TV programs you watch, the classes you choose to take, and the books or magazine articles you read. Try to identify as many interests as possible. Even romantic daydreams can give you clues. Do you dream about being an astronaut, a movie star, or a famous explorer?

Make a list of your interests. Then you can look over your list and decide which interests are really important to you and which ones are less important. Thinking about the things you do in the following categories will help you identify your strongest interests.

People, Facts, or Things

Which interests you the most—people, facts, or things? Which are you most comfortable with? Many people strongly prefer one of the three.

Your different interests and skills can lead to a career choice. What possible careers might an interest in music lead to?

**CONFLICT OF
INTERESTS?**

Q: Shouldn't peoples' outside interests be totally different from their jobs so they can
get away from what they do at
work?

A: People are more likely to
enjoy work if they are interested in what they are doing.
They can use their knowledge
about their interests to help
themselves on the job.

People who enjoy other people usually get along well with
others. They make friends more easily. They enjoy solving
"people problems."

Those most interested in facts like to collect information
such as baseball scores or famous dates in history. They
would rather work a math problem or read a book about
space travel than go to a party.

People who are interested most in things usually like to
work with their hands. They like to make things or fix
things. They might like doing jigsaw puzzles or working on
computers better than reading a book or meeting new people.

Are you usually more interested in people, facts, or
things?

Hobbies

A strong interest can develop into a hobby, which is an
activity you do regularly for pleasure.

CASE STUDY

Marta liked flowers. There were
lots of flowers in her backyard,
and she delighted in looking at the beautiful colors. One
day she cut a few flowers to make an arrangement for
the dinner table. Her family liked the arrangement so
much that they encouraged her to make more. She cut
pictures of arrangements she liked out of magazines.
She read books from the library on flowers. Marta became so good at flower arranging that her parents'
friends would ask her to make arrangements for birthday and anniversary parties. Almost without knowing it,
Marta had a hobby—and even some jobs.

Thinking About the Case Study

1. Could Marta's hobby lead to a career? What type of
   jobs could she do?
2. Is this the type of career that requires a college
   education?

If you have a hobby, take a look at what you have gained
from it. The knowledge learned from a hobby can be applied
to a job. A hobby can give you self-confidence in talking to
employers. The more you learn, the more career choices will
come to mind.

Television Programs

Do you spend much time watching TV? If so, think about the kinds of programs you enjoy. Make a list of the programs or what the programs are about.

After you have the list made, ask yourself *why* you enjoy the programs. See if some of them are about the same subject. If the TV shows on your list are about auto racing, then you are probably interested in auto racing.

Then think about the subject. What exactly about auto racing interests you? Is it the thrill of the race itself? Is it the way the drivers and crew all work together so well? Is it how the cars are put together?

If you watch TV just for the stories, that, too, may be a clue. Maybe you like to tell stories yourself. Maybe you're interested in the lives of other people. Such an interest could lead to many different kinds of jobs.

School Subjects

When school begins each year, it's common to hear statements in the hallway such as

"I like my French class best."

"Isn't history boring?"

"Chemistry lab goes fast. I wish we had more time to work the experiments."

"I love working on the word processor!"

"I like foods class almost as much as I like eating!"

You have probably had similar reactions to the classes you take. Think about your feelings toward each school subject you have taken or are now taking. Ask yourself, "If I could take any class I wanted to without worrying about grades, what class would it be?" List the subjects under the following headings:

* My favorite subjects
* The subjects I look forward to
* The subjects I dislike
* The subjects I like but find difficult

This activity will help you discover subjects that interest you. Try to keep the subjects separate from other likes and dislikes. For example, you may like the class because of the teacher but dislike the subject.

Use the list as a guide to select your classes for your remaining time in school. You have to take required classes, but you have the freedom to choose some other classes. Use your freedom of choice to develop your interests or explore and find new interests.

Looking at which school subjects you enjoy might give you a clue to a possible career area. Which school subject is your favorite?

Books and Magazines

Books and magazines, like TV programs and school subjects, can give you clues to your interests. What kinds of things do you read? When you read a magazine or newspaper, what do you turn to first?

Think of how your likes could be grouped. Do you like fiction or nonfiction? Pictures or words? When you read, do you prefer to read about food, animals, space encounters, danger, or history? If you were stranded alone on a desert island and could have only one book, what would the book be about?

Identifying your interests by looking at what you read is another way of getting to know yourself better. This will help you think of the kind of work you want to do.

Maybe you are one of those people who doesn't like to read. If so, that tells you something about yourself, too.

The books and magazines you enjoy can help you identify your interests. What magazines might someone who was interested in sports read?

Read each of the items below and indicate how you feel about the activity described by placing a check √ under

L (Like)	? (Uncertain)	D (Dislike)

	L	?	D
Write short stories or articles	___	___	___
Edit work of writers	___	___	___
Write reviews of books or plays	___	___	___
Teach classes in oil painting	___	___	___
Carve figures of people or animals	___	___	___
Design artwork for magazines	___	___	___
Direct plays	___	___	___
Perform magic tricks in a theater	___	___	___
Announce radio or television programs	___	___	___
Conduct a symphony orchestra	___	___	___

An interest inventory helps you identify your likes and dislikes. Who should you talk to if you are interested in taking an interest inventory?

Interest Inventories

So far you have been making your own list of interests. You may also want to take an interest inventory. *An* **interest inventory** *is a questionnaire that indicates your strongest interests.* Your school counselor can give you an interest inventory such as the one shown above.

Many interest inventories help you determine your interests by asking you to choose your favorites from pairs of items. For example, would you prefer working with numbers or working with words, helping people or fixing things, being alone or being with a group of people? The interests you identify are put into groups. Each different group of interests can then be linked to specific careers.

If you have not taken an interest inventory, ask your counselor about them. They are tests that don't require any studying beforehand. There are no right or wrong answers. The tests are just a tool for you to use in making up your mind.

REVIEW YOUR WORK

1. How do interests and hobbies differ?
2. How can a hobby help you with your career?
3. Name three ways to learn what your interests are.
4. What are interest inventories?

Your Skills and Aptitudes

A **skill** *is the ability to do something.* Some skills you already have. For example, maybe you already know how to swim, so swimming is one of your skills.

Aptitudes *are the skills you can learn to be good at.* For example, you may be able to swim well enough not to sink like a rock, but you may not really have an aptitude for swimming. Someone else who has never even tried swimming may have an aptitude for it. If that person were to take lessons, swimming would just *come naturally.* Just as people have different skills, they also possess different aptitudes.

You are more likely to be successful at a job if you already have the skills the job requires or an aptitude for developing those skills. Sometimes your aptitudes, skills, and interests go together.

Different jobs require different skills. In one job, you may have to know how to operate a computer. In another job, it may be important to know how to care for sick people. Some of the skills people use in their jobs are

- working with special tools
- operating machines
- drawing
- speaking in front of an audience
- writing
- working with numbers
- typing rapidly
- solving problems
- organizing schedules
- entertaining others

You probably know many of the skills you already have. You may also know some of your aptitudes. As we proceed through this chapter, try to identify other skills and aptitudes that you possess.

Judging your own aptitudes can be difficult because you may have an aptitude for something you've never done before. Looking at your skills now, however, can give you some ideas.

Because you already have so many abilities, it's easy to overlook some of them. The best way to become familiar with the things you can do, or might be able to do, is to write them down. When you can't think of any more, ask your family what they think your abilities and aptitudes are and add them to your list. You will look at your list again when you learn about skills required for different careers.

Air traffic controllers use advanced radar and communications equipment to help keep the airways safe. What aptitudes might be important for this job?

Take several sheets of paper and at the top of each sheet write one of the aptitudes given below. Then make a list of the things you have done that might show you have that particular aptitude. You will probably have several items on each list.

- **General.** You can understand facts, opinions, ideas, and reasons having to do with the things you study in school.
- **Verbal.** You understand words and ideas and their meanings. You are able to use words and ideas easily and clearly.
- **Numerical.** You are good at doing arithmetic and math problems. You work quickly and accurately.
- **Thinking About Forms.** You can see shapes, heights, widths, and depths clearly in your mind.
- **Observing Forms.** You notice detail in objects and drawings. You can distinguish shapes.
- **Clerical Accuracy.** You are good at observing all details and noticing errors in spelling, punctuation, etc. You are accurate in recording details.
- **Motor Coordination.** You are good at moving your eyes and hands or fingers together to do a job rapidly and smoothly.

- **Finger Movement.** You are good at moving your fingers quickly and accurately to work with small objects.
- **Eye-Hand-Foot Coordination.** You are good at moving your hands and feet together quickly and accurately.
- **Observing Color.** You are good at noticing differences and similarities between colors or colored shapes.

Now try to rate yourself according to these aptitudes. Of all the things you do, which do you do best? Put a plus mark (+) next to those things you seem to be better at. Place a minus mark (−) next to those things you do not seem to do very well. If you feel you are neither good nor bad at them, make no mark.

Count the pluses and minuses and write the number of each at the top of each page. On some pages you should have quite a few pluses. On other pages you may have a few minuses. The minuses may mean you have little aptitude in those areas.

CASE STUDY   Willis was tops in basketball, baseball, shop class, arcade games, and driving. He also liked to draw and paint. He counted the most pluses on the sheets labeled "Thinking About Forms," "Observing Forms," "Motor Coordination," "Eye-Hand-Foot Coordination," and "Observing Colors."

Thinking About the Case Study

1. What type of jobs do you think Willis would be good at?

Because it is difficult to judge your own aptitudes, your lists will give you only a general idea of where you stand. For the best results, you should take an aptitude test. When you finish the test, a counselor will help you understand what your scores mean. Aptitude tests are discussed on page 32.

How You Compare to Others

So far we have talked mostly about some of your skills compared to other skills. Now you must consider how your skills and aptitudes compare to the skills and aptitudes of other people.

Keep in mind that you don't have to be tops in a skill compared to everyone else. A range of abilities is usually needed. For example, if your best skill is math but your

All the World's a Stage

Ah, the theatre! The roar of the crowds! The smell of the greasepaint! What could be more exciting!

For many people nothing is more exciting and glamorous than the thought of a career as an actor or actress. Actors and actresses make their living by stepping into a character's shoes and bringing him or her alive for the pleasure of an audience. For many people this can be a high paying, glamorous, and wonderful career. However, for every actor who becomes a star, there are many more actors who cannot get work in their chosen profession.

Because there are so many people who wish to act for a living, acting is a very difficult business in which to work. Many people just never make it as an actor or actress. This does not mean that they have to give up their dream of working in show business. There are many interesting and exciting jobs in the entertainment field.

Any movie or television show you see is the product of many different people doing many different jobs. There are producers who arrange everything and make sure that there is enough money to pay the bills. There are directors who decide how the production will look and sound. There are writers who create the story the production will tell.

While the writers are writing and the directors are directing and the producers are producing, there are many other people busy at work. Camera operators work to get the best shots, and sound technicians record the performances. Lighting technicians work with set decorators to make sure the scenes look just right.

Costume designers, tailors, and costumers make sure that all of the clothes worn by the actors and actresses are perfect for their roles. Hair and make-up people make sure that the actors and actresses always look their best.

Stunt people take the falls and punches that are so exciting on the screen. Animal trainers work with the four-legged or winged actors to get the best performances out of them. There are extras who fill up street scenes, making the movies and television shows seem more real, while special effects people work to make them more *un*real. Publicists, secretaries, clerks, accountants, security personnel, and maintenance workers also contribute to every movie and television show.

These are just a few of the jobs involved with making movies and television shows. As you can see, there are many important jobs available for people who want to be involved in entertainment. So start planning your career now. There will be plenty of time to work on your Oscar acceptance speech later!

average grade is a C, you probably could not be an accountant. However, you might make an excellent file clerk for materials that are filed by number.

School Grades.

School subjects have already been discussed as a way of learning more about your interests. Looking at school subjects is also a way to learn more about your aptitudes. Which school subjects do you do well in?

Your grades can show how well you developed the skills required for certain subjects. However, there are times when a grade is not a real measure of your ability. A low grade may be due to other things. Perhaps you did not like the teacher, did not turn assignments in, did not pay attention, or did not study. Exploring the *reasons* why you received a grade is also important in deciding if you have the skills or can develop the skills.

Other Activities.

Your other activities outside of the classroom can also help you learn more about how your skills and aptitudes compare to those of other people.

Are you active in clubs? Are you often elected to office? Do others in the club look to you to get things done? Leadership skills are required in many career fields, such as law, education, and business. Student councils and vocational education clubs focus on developing leadership.

Participating in team sports, such as this game of flag football, is a good way to judge your athletic interest and ability. Can you name other reasons for participating in team sports?

Your activities outside the classroom might also help you to look at your interests. What types of careers might these yearbook staffers enjoy?

The yearbook and school newspaper are ways to try your skills in writing, editing, layout, film developing, and camera work. Do you get your name on the articles you write? Are your photos in demand?

Sports teams—tennis, swimming, football, baseball—help show your athletic ability compared to others. Are you on the first team? How accurate are your pitches compared to those of your teammates? Are you the fastest swimmer or the last one to finish?

Remember that all these skills can be affected by things other than aptitude. You may be the best football player your school has ever seen. However, if you don't show up for practice, sleep too little, and eat the wrong foods, you probably won't make the first team.

Measuring Your Skills

The guidance counselor gives tests to find out about your skills. You may have asked, "Do I have any skills? Am I better at some skills than others? How do I compare with other people? Is this the kind of job I'm suited for?" If you haven't taken any tests to help you answer these questions, ask a school counselor about them.

Tests.   Knowing the general kinds of tests will help you understand the purpose of each test. Your school counselor will probably have the following kinds to offer. Remember, these tests do not affect your school grades.

- **Academic achievement tests.** Can you spell? Do you work math problems quickly? What word definitions do you know? **Academic achievement tests** *measure your knowledge and skills in reading, science, math, and social studies.* Some tests also measure skills in chemistry, algebra, and American government. They may also measure your ability to handle ideas. Academic tests tell you what your present abilities are. It is possible to study for an academic test.

- **Aptitude tests.** Aptitude and skills tests are the same. Can you use a hammer, sewing machine, or computer? How fast can you type? These tests measure the skills you have and your natural ability to do something.

   The scores from aptitude tests are used to help tell how you *might* do on a job, in a training program, or in college. You cannot study for an aptitude test.

   A word of caution. These tests cannot tell you what you *should* do or *must* do. They provide only information for a wiser job choice.

Things to Keep in Mind.   Below are some things to keep in mind as you measure your skills and aptitudes.

- **Everyone is different.** Not everyone has the same skills. Even people who happen to be good at the same things want to use their skills in different ways.

- **Academic skills are not equally important for all jobs.** You should try to do your best in school because you will need math, English, and other such skills in your adult life. There are, however, many meaningful and worthwhile jobs to be done that don't require you to be the "brain" in school.

- **Just because you are strong in a skill does not mean you should sit back and relax.** Keep working to improve that skill just as an athlete tries to break his or her own records. You will be competing with large numbers of people for jobs. The better your skills, the better your chances for the job and for good pay.

- **Keep working to improve in areas where you do not do as well.** Just because you do not have an aptitude for math and don't plan to seek a job in which you'll need it, don't stop trying. You will need math to balance your

DID YOU KNOW?

BOY "WONDER"

Stevland Morris, who was born blind, began pounding on a tin pan with a spoon at age two. He attended special classes for the blind in a public school. By age ten, people would gather around whenever he sang. He had his first big hit, "Fingertips," when he was 12, and Motown Records called him Little Stevie Wonder. To date, Stevie Wonder has sold more than 25 million records!

Your school grades can show how well you learned the skills required for certain subjects. Why is it also important to look at the reasons why you received a particular grade?

checkbook, cook for yourself, pay bills, and measure a room for a rug. You will need all sorts of skills to survive when you are on your own.

- **Most people are more successful at the things they enjoy doing.** When they are having a good time, they just naturally seem to do well. If you do equally well at a number of things, or if you don't seem to be very skilled at anything in particular, let your sense of enjoyment guide you in planning your work life.

REVIEW YOUR WORK

1. Define skills.
2. Define aptitudes.
3. How does an academic test differ from an aptitude test?
4. How can looking at school subjects you have taken be useful in thinking about career choices?

Your Work Values

Values are what people believe are important or worthwhile. Values give direction to a person's life. They also affect career choices. For example, if you value money more than safety, you might choose a dangerous job that pays very well.

Following are some things people value that have to do with their work lives. Copy the list on a sheet of paper. Then rate the values from 1–10 as to which you want most from a career.

- high pay
- security (you don't want to worry about losing the job)
- independence
- creativity
- a regular routine
- a variety of things to do
- power over others
- a chance to help others
- making changes in society
- feeling important or recognized

Knowing and understanding your values helps you make wiser decisions, gain more satisfaction from work, and reduce conflicts between your values and the values of those with whom you work. For example, if you are a person who places a high value on money, you might not be happy in a job such as teaching or social work. Those jobs do not pay especially well. If you value fairness, you might not be happy working for a company that treats customers badly.

Each of the following statements shows how you could have a conflict of values.

- You want good grades, but you won't study or complete assignments.
- You are against war, but you take a job at an ammunition plant.
- Your home life is what you enjoy most of all, but you work as a traveling salesperson and are away from home for days at a time.

Most people don't think about their values a lot. We usually learn them from our parents and live by them automatically. You should give some thought to your values now.

Your school counselor can help by giving you values inventories to fill out. Afterward you will have a list of values that you have identified as the most important to you.

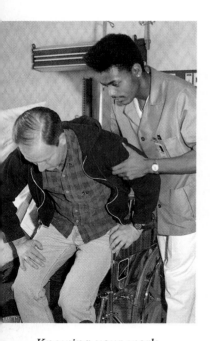

Knowing your work values can help you to find the right career. What type of work values might this person have?

Looking at Yourself

In this chapter you are supposed to be taking a close look at yourself. How is it going so far? Have you learned some things about yourself that you didn't know? Can you see how this process will help you choose a career that you will enjoy?

Maybe you're thinking, "This is a waste of time. I don't have any great interests, and I can't do anything anyone else can't do. I'm just a regular person like anyone else. I'll get a job someday, and it won't make any difference whether I like knitting or hanging out at the gym. Work is work! What difference does it make what I like to do or what I'm good at?"

It can make a big difference *if* . . . and this is an important *if* . . . if you make an honest, dedicated effort at really getting to know yourself better. That's the hard part—the *honest, dedicated effort.*

Looking at yourself is tough to do. It's tough to do because most of us are not satisfied with ourselves. Teenagers especially have a tendency to be too critical of themselves. They concentrate on their weaknesses and forget about their strengths. They tend to turn every blemish and lack of experience into a major catastrophe. If you are one of these people, you will have a hard time getting to know yourself better.

It's important to be honest with yourself. You need to be aware of your weaknesses, and you don't want to pretend you are interested in something you're not. It's probably even more important that you **THINK POSITIVELY** about yourself.

You do have strengths, and you do have interests. You can choose a career that will let you make use of your strengths and interests. If you approach the investigation of yourself with a positive attitude, you will find qualities to build on.

Some people make better use of their time than others, and these people probably have more interests than those who just "kill time." Even if you haven't developed any strong interests yet, you're still young. You have plenty of time to explore and try new things.

School courses are probably the best opportunities to find out what you like, as well as what you're good at. Think positively—if you're in school, you're in the best place possible for getting to know yourself better. Pay attention to who you are, and you'll increase your chances of getting what you want out of life.

Your Personality

"There goes the grouch!" "Sue has such a bubbly personality." "Eddie is an extrovert." Each of these statements is describing a personality. There are many types of personalities. *Your* **personality** *is the outward sign of your inner self. It is the total result of your attitudes, environment, and way of looking at life.*

Following are words used to describe people's personalities. Which words describe you? Are there other words you could use?

adaptable	"laid back"	quiet
aggressive	critical	impulsive
agreeable	confident	stubborn
shy	energetic	outgoing
friendly	trusting	happy
withdrawn	overbearing	

CAREER Q&A

PERSONALITY SAYS A LOT

Q: How can I learn more about my personality traits?
A: Ask your friends to write down all of the words that best describe you. This should give you an idea of how other people see your personality.

Your personality will have a lot to do with your happiness and success in a career. Your personality is important to the type of work you choose and the people you work with.

Do you like talking to people or helping them? Do you enjoy being in front of an audience? Would you almost always rather go to a party than be by yourself? If these things are true, then you probably have an *outgoing* personality. You would probably be happiest in a job that requires you to meet new people, or give speeches, or work with the public. You might enjoy being a salesperson, an entertainer, or a teacher.

Do you like being by yourself? Would you rather work in a room alone than be surrounded by people? When you spend time with your friends, do you say very little? If these things describe you, you probably have a *quiet* personality. You might be happiest in a job where you could keep to yourself, such as operating a computer or working in a library.

Keep in mind, however, that some people use their work to balance their personalities. Their work gives them a chance to bring out their hidden selves. Many actors, for example, claim they are really shy people. They never say much and prefer being alone. When they stand on a stage, however, all their shyness vanishes and they're the center of attention. On the other hand, some people are so much the center of attention in their families that they like a job that gives them peace and quiet.

People with outgoing personalities enjoy talking and spending time with other people. What is one way to find out more about your personality?

Don't be afraid to put yourself in different situations just to try them out. If you are usually pretty quiet, take a speech class or join a drama club. You may like it better than you think. It may even change your ideas about the sort of job you'd like.

What finally matters is not the type of personality you have, but the sort of job in which your personality is comfortable and happy. Everyone is different, and there are jobs to suit every personality.

As you might have guessed by now, your school counselor also offers personality inventories. The inventory can be like a mirror that helps you see yourself better. You may find out things about yourself you did not suspect.

By taking the personality inventories, you can also find out how similar your personality is to people in different career fields. For example, you might find out that your personality is like the personality of many scientists, office workers, or people who do church work. Then you will have one more clue to the kind of work you'd be happiest doing.

REVIEW YOUR WORK

1. Define values.
2. How can knowing and understanding your values be of help in choosing a job?
3. List ten words that describe personalities.

Chapter Summary

- Everyone has interests that are special to them.
- Areas of interest are divided into three categories: people, facts, and things.
- Interest inventories are questionnaires that indicate your strongest interests. You can usually obtain an interest inventory from your counselor.
- A skill is the ability to do certain things. An aptitude is a natural ability that helps you become really good at certain skills. Making a list of skills and aptitudes is another way to help you decide on a career.
- Comparing your skills and aptitudes with others' is a way of learning where you would best fit into the working world.
- You need to determine work values to help you decide where you would be happiest.
- Knowing your own personality is important to help you decide what kind of people you would like to work with.

Reviewing Vocabulary and Concepts

A. Write the numbers 1–16 on a separate sheet of paper. After each number, write the term from the word bank that best completes the statement.

Word Bank

interests   aptitudes
skill   academic achievement
personality   test
interest inventory

1. The things you're curious about and like to spend time thinking about are _____ .
2. _____ are skills that just seem to come naturally.
3. The outward sign of your inner self is _____ .
4. A way to measure your knowledge and skills in reading, science, math, and social studies is to take a(n) _____ .
5. A(n) _____ is the ability to do something.
6. A(n) _____ indicates the areas of your strongest interest.

B. After each number, write the letter of the answer that best completes the following statements.

7. Your _____ influence(s) the decisions you make about friends, hobbies, and a career.
   a. dog   c. hairstyle
   b. height   d. interests
8. People who are interested most in *things* usually like to work with _____ .
   a. other people
   b. animals
   c. their heads
   d. their hands
9. You are more likely to be successful at a job if you already have the _____ the job requires.
   a. skills   c. looks
   b. title   d. friends
10. It's a good idea to make a list of school subjects that you would like to take because _____ .
    a. you can be with your friends
    b. you like the teacher
    c. it will help you explore new interests
    d. the classes will be easy
11. Another way to get to know yourself better is to examine _____ .
    a. what you read
    b. your clothes
    c. the sky
    d. the newspaper

12. Eye-hand-foot coordination is
    _____ .
    a. not important
    b. hard
    c. considered an aptitude
    d. considered a skill
13. Comparing yourself with other students is _____ .
    a. not a good idea
    b. a way of determining your aptitudes
    c. too competitive
    d. not important
14. Activities outside the classroom should be taken into account because they help you _____ .
    a. compare your skills and aptitudes with other people
    b. stay away from places you don't like
    c. get into sports
    d. become popular
15. Values are what people believe are
    _____ .
    a. mistakes
    b. worth a lot of money
    c. important or worthwhile
    d. very entertaining
16. We usually learn our _____ from our parents and live by them automatically.
    a. values
    b. ABCs
    c. reading skills
    d. math skills

Thinking Critically About Career Skills

Write your answers to the following questions on a separate sheet of paper.

1. Why do you think it is so important for people to know their areas of interest? Do you think it is a good idea to turn a hobby into a career? If so, why? If not, why?
2. Across the top of a sheet of paper, make a list of many of your basic values. (An example might be that you believe in freedom of speech.) Then under those values list jobs that might conflict with each value.

Building Basic Skills

1. **Mathematics** Calculate your grade point average if A = 4, B = 3, C = 2, D = 1, and F = 0; and you have received an A in English, an A in physical education, a B in science, a C in metal shop, and a D in French.
2. **Public Speaking** Prepare and present to your class a speech about your main interest. Try to make your classmates understand why this activity or subject is so interesting.

Applying Career Skills

1. As a class, make arrangements with your teacher or counselor to take an interest inventory. When all are completed, have a class discussion about the differences in people and all the different jobs available for each person.
2. Go to the library and find books about aptitudes and aptitude tests. Research why certain aptitudes are important for certain jobs. Choose one aptitude and write a 200-word report about how it applies to a specific job.

CAREER CHOICES

The first time you stopped at an ice cream shop that featured dozens of varieties, did it take a long time to decide which flavor you wanted? There were probably many flavors you never even knew existed. How did you ever make up your mind?

Now imagine yourself in a different shop—a shop selling careers. There are more than 20,000 different kinds of careers to choose from. Do you know which one you will choose?

In this chapter you will get a "taste" of different occupations. You will start thinking about the type of work you want to do. Then you will be in a position to start shopping for an occupation that matches up with your interests, abilities, and values.

As you read this chapter, make a note of the fields of work that interest you. Then in the next chapter you will learn how to find out more about specific occupations.

Careers in Your Community

You're probably pretty familiar with the town you live in and the towns nearby. Does your community offer jobs that interest you? If you're not sure, why not take an occupational tour of your area?

Begin your tour at the bus station. What jobs are required to keep the bus station operating and to make transportation available? Who oversees workers who do the scheduling and maintenance duties? What about other jobs at the station? Notice the vendor operators who keep the machines filled with food, custodians who make sure the station is clean, and bus drivers who drive the buses.

The next stop on your tour is the courthouse where city business is conducted. City and county operations require managers for the various government offices. Each office needs workers. Examples of different departments include those for the water works, parks, public health, animal control, taxes, highways, and the court system. The jobs at the courthouse include public administration, safety, social, and nonprofit services. Many different types of careers are represented by the people who work in government buildings.

Continuing your tour, you see people working in specialty shops. The names of the shops give you a clue to the interests the owners have. The owner of a financial services firm likes' math and the challenge of completing customers' income tax forms. "Potter's Wheel" and "Wicker Basket" are owned by people who like creating objects with their hands. The owners of "The Pedal Shop" spend their free time discovering new bicycle trails and sponsoring races. They help customers purchase the bicycles and accessories that meet particular needs.

For lunch, you stop at a restaurant called "The Wharf." You tour the kitchen and watch the chef preparing the main dishes, the vegetable cook fixing the vegetables, and the pastry cook preparing the desserts. Other people are making salads and breads. One person is in charge of ordering supplies. Other workers are in charge of dishwashing and keeping the place clean. The waiters and waitresses serve the food and make sure you are comfortable and satisfied. A cashier takes care of the money. At night the restaurant

Take a look at the types of jobs available in your home town. How many jobs can you name?

offers entertainment and employs musicians. A valet (employee who helps customers) parks cars.

From your window in the restaurant you can see activities in the harbor. Fishing boats are arriving with the morning's catch. The crew includes workers who can mend fishing gear, handle the equipment to catch the fish, and operate the boat. A barge being towed by a tugboat passes. The barge crew operates and maintains the boat and equipment. One crew member is the cook and prepares the meals for the crew. A ferryboat is loading cars and passengers to transport them across the waterway.

A cruise ship at the dock will take passengers on vacation. The captain and crew operate the ship and move it safely through the water. This type of ship is a floating hotel, restaurant, recreation center, cleaning establishment, communications center, and doctor's office. The interests all of the workers share are a love for the outdoors, travel, and the sea.

After lunch, your tour continues. You pass a large construction project. Carpenters, electricians, excavators, and painters are all involved in getting apartment houses ready for sale. The workers have an interest in using and operating tools and equipment, working outside, and building new structures. After the apartments are built, other workers will become involved. An interior designer will select wallpaper, plumbing, lighting fixtures, and furniture produced by other workers.

Like sailors, these workers on a cruise ship have to make sure the ship sails safely and on time. How are these workers also like hotel employees?

You can even continue your tour by taking a look around your own home. Do you have a record or tape collection? How many workers were involved in producing and delivering these tapes and records? Songwriters, musicians, sound engineers, sound editors, directors, conductors, sound mixers, electricians, talent agents, secretaries, accountants, sales and advertising people, and truck drivers are just a few.

Obviously our tour was a quick one. We didn't get to many of the places in your community. Still, you saw many different kinds of jobs and workers—all representing different interests, skills, and abilities. Did any of the jobs strike you as one you might enjoy? If you took a *real* tour of your community, what other jobs would you encounter?

REVIEW YOUR WORK

1. How can you learn about different occupations by taking a tour through your town?
2. Name at least ten occupations your town offers.
3. Think about the kitchen in your home. How many jobs can you think of that might be represented?

Some Career Groups

In this section we will discuss careers in two ways. We will look at interest areas and occupational clusters. Looking at work in these two different ways will help you get an idea of the kind of career you might enjoy.

Career Interest Areas

Following is a list of career interest areas. **Career interest areas** *are categories of jobs that are similar according to interests.* They represent a general kind of work activity that takes place in many different career fields.

For example, one of the interest areas is selling. Selling is done in almost all fields. You can be a real estate salesperson or sell shoes. You can be a talent agent and sell the artistic abilities of your clients.

As you look over these interest areas, think of them as general types of activities you may or may not like to do. In the next section we will discuss actual job fields in which an interest might be put to work.

- **Artistic.**   Workers with artistic interests use their special creative talents. They express their ideas and feelings and use their skills through the many forms of art, such as painting or sculpture. Other workers make and decorate products. Some workers in this area perform before audiences.
- **Scientific.**   Workers with scientific interests do research on living and nonliving things. They do experiments on materials under controlled conditions. Some are scientists who test theories or discover new ways of doing things. Others develop useful ways of applying research.
- **Plants and Animals (Nature).**   People interested in plants and animals may like farming, forestry, and fishing. Others enjoy taking care of pets or houseplants. Many workers in this area do their work outside in non-urban rural areas.
- **Protective (Authority).**   Workers with protective interests enforce laws, regulations, policies, and standards. They protect people and property. Some enjoy adventure and excitement. Workers such as police officers and firefighters often face danger. However, not all workers are involved in such activities. Workers, such as fire inspectors, make inspections to be sure that laws are not broken.

This teen enjoys spending time working in her garden with plants and flowers. Which career interest area might she be interested in?

These dancers must train for years before being able to complete some of the more difficult and amazing dance steps. Which career interest area does dance fit into?

- **Mechanical**. Those with mechanical interests use tools and machines, or they apply the ideas and principles of machines and tools in their work. They may become highly skilled engineers, or they may operate simple machines.
- **Industrial**. Those with industrial interests enjoy the mass production of goods in a factory setting. Because many different kinds of products are made, workers may have many different kinds of duties. Some workers set up and operate machines, and some do hand operations aided by machines. Other workers inspect, test, weigh, or sort products. Some load and unload machines.
- **Business Detail**. Those who enjoy business detail are usually well organized. Some run office machines, type, or file. Others are responsible for bookkeeping and accounting.
- **Selling (Persuasive)**. Selling involves those who enjoy using their powers of persuasion to sell products or services. They usually like being with other people.

- **Accommodating.** People with accommodating interests provide a variety of services to people. Part of their work is to be pleasant and helpful. They try to make people relax and enjoy themselves. They also have a feeling of responsibility for the people they are serving.
- **Humanitarian.** People with humanitarian interests help people with personal problems. The problems might be mental (related to the mind) or spiritual (religious needs). They may be social (relationships with others), psychological (emotions), or vocational (a trade or job).
- **Leading-Influencing (Social-Business).** Those with leading-influencing interests like communicating ideas and information. Workers plan, direct, and manage the activities needed to organize and deliver programs and services. They have many business contacts with people. These workers may gain satisfaction from being recognized and appreciated by others for the work they do.
- **Physical Performing.** Those who enjoy physical performing may work in athletics, sports, and other events. They use physical skills and strength to entertain an audience. Workers may coach, officiate, or perform. Occupations in this area provide excitement, thrills, and the pleasure of competition for the performer as well as the audience.

Occupational Clusters

The large areas of work discussed below are called occupational clusters. *An* **occupational cluster** *is a group of occupations that are related in some way.*

Following are 15 clusters organized according to the nature of the work performed and the work environment. In addition there is information about working conditions and the type of education or training needed.

The descriptions included here are very general. They will give you an idea of what the cluster is like. Keep in mind that within each cluster are both simple and more difficult jobs. Each cluster also contains jobs in many different career interest areas. For example, if you have humanitarian interests and want to work in the field of agriculture, you might be a social worker who helps farm families.

Agriculture. Agriculture has to do with farming. Workers raise plants and animals. The work is performed in farm fields, orchards, barns, and storage areas. The cluster includes work on farms, services for farms, mechanics of farm equipment, and raising plants for home decoration. Typical

This worker's job is a part of the agricultural occupational cluster. Is most of the work in this cluster done indoors or outdoors?

occupations are livestock rancher, tree surgeon, general farmer, and soil conservationist.

Depending upon the occupation, the work could be supervising the farm operations, running or repairing machines, or providing advice and education to farmers.

Most of the work is done outdoors in all kinds of weather. Even if some agricultural workers have offices in the city, they spend time outdoors.

Production workers in agriculture can usually qualify with no more than on-the-job training. Jobs such as tree surgeon or conservationist can require four or more years of college. More advanced jobs require you to stay informed of technological developments.

Business and Office.   The jobs in businesses and offices range from administration to general clerical work. These jobs exist in both the smallest and largest companies. Some typical occupations are cashier, purchasing agent, typist, and complaint clerk. This cluster includes word processing, accounting and financial detail, management, personnel, and materials and product handling.

Most of the jobs are located in well-lighted and comfortable offices. The offices can be very large and noisy, or private. Although most jobs are done indoors, workers such as mail carriers and material handlers often work outside.

Many of the occupations—managers, accountants, computer analysts—require four or more years of college. Other occupations—secretaries and clerks—require at least graduation from high school. Secretarial jobs in the legal, medical, and executive areas require more schooling.

Communications and Media.
Jobs in communications and the media include those in radio, television, and telecommunication. (Telecommunication includes telephone, telegraph, and satellite systems.)

Work includes operating and managing the station or facility. It also includes designing, operating, and maintaining electronic equipment.

Occupations in this cluster may require indoor and outdoor work. Line installers and repairers work mainly outdoors. Disk jockeys perform in a studio.

Managers and engineers must complete four or more years of college. Operators can qualify with a two-year technical school degree. Telephone operators usually receive on-the-job training.

Construction.
The construction cluster jobs have to do with building such things as homes, roads, dams, and other structures from wood, metal, masonry, and stone. Work includes planning, designing, managing, installation, finishing, maintenance and repair, excavating, grading, and paving. Typical occupations are architect, carpenter, bulldozer operator, interior designer, and contractor.

Except for designing and planning, most of the work is performed outdoors. However, engineers, architects, and interior designers often visit outdoor work sites. Work conditions may be affected by weather, noise, and dangerous situations.

Architects and engineers must complete four or more years of college. Drafters and other technical people need a minimum of two years in a technical program. Contractors, who must estimate costs and manage workers, usually begin in a particular trade, such as carpentry, bricklaying, or plumbing. Workers in these trades may spend three to four years in an apprenticeship program.

Arts, Humanities, and Sciences.
The arts, humanities, and sciences cluster includes fine and practical arts, liberal arts, education, social sciences, physical sciences, and life sciences. Universities, research laboratories, libraries, concert halls, and newspaper offices are some of the work settings.

Drafters turn designs into blueprints that workers follow in the construction occupational cluster. What are the educational requirements for a drafter?

A botanist is a scientist who studies plants. Is most of the work in the arts, humanities, and sciences occupational cluster done indoors or outdoors?

Those who work in the fine and practical arts include musicians, composers, actors, and those who use voice, body, symbols, or instruments to express moods, ideas, and forms. Writers, linguists, and philosophers use language skills to express ideas. Social scientists explore human behavior. The physical scientists—chemists, physicists, and mathematicians—research properties of matter and use the findings to solve practical problems. The life scientists are botanists, zoologists, and biologists who study plants and animals. Through research they learn about living things, the environment, and disease control.

Most of the work in this cluster is done indoors. Formal education of fine and practical artists varies from a little to a lot. Most take some type of special classes at some period in their lives. The other occupations, especially those in the sciences, require a minimum of four years of college.

Home Economics.   Home economics workers are concerned about the quality of home and community life. The work is done in private homes and for community services and businesses.

The cluster includes jobs in child care, food and nutrition, clothing and textiles, housing and furnishings, and consumer affairs. Typical occupations are child care worker, dietitian, homemaker, and clothes designer.

Child care worker is an important job in the home economics occupational cluster. How do child care workers help to improve the quality of home and community life?

Child care workers may need to be licensed before they can supervise and care for children. A vocational program is usually required.

Nutritionists and dietitians must complete four years of college. These workers plan menus and supervise the people who prepare, cook, and serve food.

Fashion designers usually complete a four-year college or technical school program. Workers who cut and sew clothing complete high school and vocational programs.

The majority of work is performed indoors. Conditions range from hot kitchens and noisy factories to streamlined research laboratories.

Health.   Workers in the health cluster provide medical care and emergency services to people and animals in hospitals, clinics, and nursing homes. This cluster includes jobs in research, patient care, and technical and clinical support.

Pathologists, surgeons, and general practitioners look into the causes, prevention, and treatment of disease. Veterinarians are involved in the same type of work for animals. Dentists and orthodontists take care of the teeth, gums, and bones of the mouth.

Registered nurses and lab technicians aid physicians. Administrators manage hospitals and clinics. Other workers design and prepare special diets and take care of laundry, cleaning, and building maintenance. Paramedics provide first aid when emergencies occur.

Most of the work is performed indoors. Some workers deal with possibly dangerous X-rays, radioactive materials, drugs, and chemicals.

Typical schooling for physicians consists of four years of college, four years of medical school, and two years of residency. Nurses and technicians usually complete four years of college or a special program. Some types of technicians and nurses receive licensing after two- or three-year educational programs.

Hospitality and Recreation.   The cluster for hospitality and recreation includes jobs having to do with travel, food, lodging, entertainment, amusement, sports, and recreation activities. Typical occupations are professional athletes, club managers, fitness center directors, hotel managers, and flight attendants.

Flight attendants work in the hospitality and recreation occupational cluster. Can you name some of the tasks performed by a flight attendant?

Work is performed on planes, trains, and boats. Some workers prepare and serve food. Others run errands for guests and make them comfortable. Still others perform for the enjoyment of audiences.

The work takes place anywhere from luxurious resorts to amusement parks. Sports and recreation work may be done indoors in such places as bowling alleys or outside in a stadium where players are exposed to rain or snow. Baggage handlers must lift heavy loads and ticket takers may have to manage crowds.

Managers, recreation leaders, and camp counselors usually need a college degree. Most other workers need no special education beyond high school.

Manufacturing.   Workers in the manufacturing cluster process materials, produce goods, and develop or manage work activities. Typical occupations are welder, tool inspector, product assembler, and production superintendent.

The manufacturing cluster includes work with materials such as metals, wood, fabric, and food. It can involve electrical equipment and electronics, printing and publishing, industrial goods, and farm and transportation equipment.

The work is done mostly indoors. It may take place in a controlled room where precision instruments are made or in

This welder works in the manufacturing occupational cluster. Where did she probably receive her training?

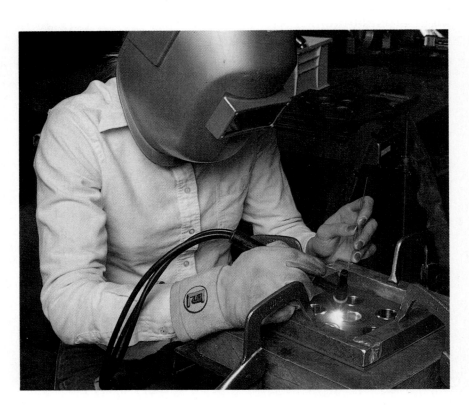

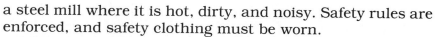

a steel mill where it is hot, dirty, and noisy. Safety rules are enforced, and safety clothing must be worn.

Managers must complete four or more years of college. Skilled industrial workers, such as machinists and welders, receive training in vocational and technical schools or apprenticeship programs. Most other workers receive on-the-job training.

Marine Science.   The marine science cluster includes research and fishing. Fish farmer, captain of a fishing boat, and net repairer represent jobs in this cluster.

Scientists observe lakes and oceans, life forms, and physical properties. Technicians collect and test water and mineral samples. Their work helps to find ways to improve weather forecasting and the harvesting of sea plants and animals. Other needed skills include photography, welding, diving, and instrument repair.

The scientists complete four to six years of college. The other occupations—net repairers, clam sorters, and fish farmers—are learned on the job or through vocational school programs.

Most work is performed outdoors where stormy weather can occur. Scientists and technicians may work indoors in laboratories.

On fish farms, workers raise the fish in tanks for sale to supermarkets and restaurants. Which occupational cluster does fish farming belong in: agriculture or marine science?

Marketing and Distribution.

The cluster of marketing and distribution occupations includes advertising and promotion, wholesale and retail operations, business and financial services, and maintenance and repair services. Jobs include vendor, salesperson, sales manager, and buyer.

Advertising and promotion workers promote the sale of goods and services, salespeople sell the good or service, and repair workers maintain the goods.

Most of the work is performed in an office, warehouse, or showroom. Some sales may be door-to-door or on street corners, such as at ballparks or fairs.

Advertising and promotion usually require four years of college. Real estate and insurance workers must be licensed. Repair workers receive training at a trade school.

Natural Resources and Environment.

Workers in the natural resources and environment career cluster are concerned about forests, minerals and chemicals, air, soil, water, and wildlife. Typical occupations include fish and game warden, soil conservationist, and pollution control technician.

Forestry workers manage, develop, and harvest forests. Miners' and chemical workers' responsibilities range from the designing of equipment and processes for removing minerals from the earth to transporting them. Air, soil, and water workers are involved in controlling air pollution. Wildlife workers preserve and improve wildlife populations throughout the world.

Most work is outdoors. Foresters, loggers, and wildlife workers are exposed to all kinds of weather in remote areas. Miners, oil and gas workers, and environmental technicians work in areas that can be dangerous.

Engineers and scientists complete a four-year college program. Technicians complete two or more years of college or technical training. The other jobs require completion of high school, and some vocational training may be helpful.

Personal Services.

Workers who help improve people's appearance and provide comfort and convenience work at jobs in the personal service cluster. Typical occupations are housekeeper, chauffeur, and funeral director.

The work is usually performed in clean, pleasant surroundings. Domestic service is done in private homes. Personal grooming takes place in shops, spas, or salons.

Most domestic workers need formal training and education. Funeral directors, cosmetologists, and barbers must complete training to become licensed.

CAREER Q&A

IN DEPTH

Q: How can I find out more about some of the jobs in an occupational cluster?

A: The *Career Handbook* on pages 325-355 describes some of the positions in each cluster. The reference section of the library has other books telling about different jobs.

Hair stylist is an example of a job from the personal services occupational cluster. Do hair stylists need special training?

Public Service. The public service cluster includes jobs in public administration, public safety, social services, and nonprofit services. Typical occupations are fire chief, sanitary engineer, and parole officer.

Administrators manage local, state, or national agencies. Public safety workers dispose of waste, fight fires, enforce laws, or operate the water/sewage systems. Social service workers help people meet their physical, mental, social, or spiritual needs. Nonprofit workers provide help through charities and emergency services.

Most work is indoors. However, police and firefighters work both indoors and outdoors. Administrators and managers need four years or more of college. Government workers must take a civil service test. Police and fire workers complete technical training. Most social workers need four years of college, while technicians must complete a two-year technical program.

Career Choices

It's easy to feel lost and confused when you try to sort through all of the career possibilities. There are more than 20,000 different occupations, with entirely new jobs being created every day. With so many careers to consider, you probably feel as though you're missing or forgetting something important. You may feel that the one career that would be just right for you is the one you'll never even know exists.

Many people give up at this point. They figure that they are too young and inexperienced to ever choose from all those careers. They think it would be much simpler to just take whatever job happens to be there when they start looking for a job. They think, "It would take forever to explore all those careers, and I probably wouldn't be able to get the job I wanted even if I did find one I liked. Why bother?"

Whatever you do, don't give up. **THINK POSITIVELY.** Yes, there are thousands of careers to choose from. Yes, it does take some time and trouble to explore all of them. You shouldn't give up, however. A little time and trouble now can mean the difference between a lifetime of happiness and a lifetime of frustration and drudgery. The people who take whatever comes along are rarely as happy as those people who *choose* their careers.

It wasn't that long ago that young people in our country had little or no choice in the kind of work they would do. Most young boys went to work on their fathers' farms or worked in an

apprenticeship chosen for them by their family. The girls got married and raised a family. Very few women worked outside of the home.

Even today, in many countries around the world, young people do not have a choice. They are told by their parents or by government officials what jobs they will do. In these countries, it doesn't matter if a person has a strong desire and special talent for art or music or sports. If that person is told to work in a factory or on a farm, the decision is made.

So if you feel overwhelmed and confused with all those career possibilities, think positively. Unlike your ancestors and millions of young people around the world today, you are free to choose which career you think you would enjoy. Don't you think that you should take full advantage of this freedom?

Transportation.   Workers in transportation help design, operate, and maintain systems and equipment for moving people and freight.

Managers and coordinators direct the operation of transportation services. Inspectors and mechanics maintain the equipment and systems. Material handlers move materials and products and load and unload equipment.

The work setting may be an office, the cabin of a ship or plane, highways, runways, or dry docks. Materials handlers may work outside in yards and docks, or inside the warehouses and storage areas.

Airplane pilots and ship captains must have a federal license. Managers complete a two- to four-year college program in transportation or business management. Drivers must qualify for a chauffeur's license. Maintenance workers receive training in high school vocational programs.

You can learn more about each of these career clusters in the *Career Handbook* on pages 325-355.

This train engineer works in the transportation cluster. Is it more important for train engineers to be good speakers or to be safety conscious?

Job Trends

An employment trend shows which jobs are most "popular" with employers. **Employment trends** *tell whether the need for certain work will grow or shrink over the next several years.*

Now, while you are learning about careers you might be interested in, you must also consider how trends will affect them. Will the job you want be available in several years? Will the demand for that type of work lessen to such a point that competition for the job will be very great?

As you will recall from Chapter 1, many things can affect the kinds of jobs available. Today, technology is having an impact on almost everyone's career. For example, when the wooden biplane designed by Wilbur and Orville Wright flew successfully for a few minutes, no one had any idea of the impact it would have on the job market. Who would have thought then that just a few years later thousands of people

This is a robotic assembly line in the automobile industry. Experts that can help set up and maintain these robots are increasingly in demand. What skills could you work on now to prepare yourself for such a job?

would be working in the air transportation and space exploration industries. New careers were born that did not exist during the Wright brothers' lifetime.

In other fields, the demand for workers is steadily growing. For example, some of the new jobs appearing in the automobile industry are

- CAD Engineering Software Specialists
- CAD Product or Systems Inspectors
- CAD/CAM Software Coordinators
- Industrial Robot Production Technicians
- Robot Programmers

Who knows? In a few years we may be mining on the planet Mars or at the bottom of the ocean. Maybe someday you will apply for a position as "psychologist of advanced robot behavior."

At this point, as you look over different career fields, be thinking about these questions:

- Is the industry growing or shrinking?
- If growth is taking place, in what direction is it moving? For instance, if you are interested in owning your own restaurant, what kinds of restaurants are popular now? What kinds might be popular ten years from now, and *why?*
- If the industry shrinks, in which direction will shrinkage take place?
- Are you interested in only one area of the career field or in the field in general? A more general interest means you might enjoy more than one kind of job in that field. You will be able to make changes more easily.

No matter what career you select, there will be some shifts in employment patterns. You will have to be informed of the job market, learn the new names of jobs and what they mean, and be willing to change and learn for the rest of your life.

DID YOU KNOW?

FAST WORKER

Modern electronic computers can accept up to 100 million instructions per second and retrieve information in 250 billionths of a second. As for computer printouts, 6,000 lines per minute have been issued by top-speed printers.

REVIEW YOUR WORK

1. What does an employment trend show?
2. Why should you be concerned about employment trends?
3. Name three questions you should keep in mind while learning about trends in a career field.
4. Name three new things you learned as you read through the occupational clusters.

A Career in Public Safety

You've seen them in their shining vehicles around your town, and you and your family have counted on them for your safety and protection. They are police officers and firefighters. They have dangerous and exciting jobs that are vital to your community's well-being.

Many children dream of being police officers or firefighters when they grow up. Some of these children go on to fulfill that dream and serve their communities in one of these important public safety jobs. However, these are very tough and demanding jobs, and many of those children go on to look at other careers. Others decide that they are interested in public safety but do not want to work as a police officer or firefighter. For these people there are still many opportunities for a rewarding and important career in the public safety field.

Some related jobs that are essential to public safety are 911 operators and emergency dispatchers who answer calls for help and see that the police and firefighters are on their way. The operators and dispatchers have very exciting jobs that also include such life-saving acts as giving first-aid instructions over the phone. Rushing to the scene of many emergencies are paramedics and ambulance personnel that provide often life-saving first aid and transportation for injured people.

Traffic officers and fire inspectors work to prevent problems before they occur by making sure that safety and parking laws are obeyed. Police and fire department lab technicians help solve crimes and determine the sources of mysterious fires. These high-tech detectives are armed with an advanced edu-

cation, a microscope, and some of the most sophisticated equipment you are likely to see anywhere.

Secretaries, clerks, accountants, and maintenance workers also are instrumental members of police and fire departments. In addition, both police and fire departments depend on mechanics to keep all emergency vehicles in top running condition.

The field of public safety is a vital and interesting one, filled with jobs to fit almost anyone's skills. If you would like to become a part of this exciting field, talk to your guidance counselor today.

Chapter Summary

- For every product developed or service performed there are many "hidden" jobs.
- Career interest areas are categories of jobs that are similar in interest.
- Occupational clusters are groups of occupations that are related in some way. Fifteen clusters organized according to the nature of the work performed and the work environment are: agriculture; business and office; communications and media; construction; arts, humanities, and sciences; home economics; health; hospitality and recreation; manufacturing; marine science; marketing and distribution; natural resources and environment; personal services; public service; and transportation.
- Employment trends tell whether the need for certain work will shrink or grow over the next several years.
- It is worth the time and trouble to explore all the job possibilities available to you.

Reviewing Vocabulary and Concepts

Write the numbers 1–15 on a sheet of paper. After each number, write the letter of the answer that best completes the following statements or answers the following questions.

1. There are _____ different kinds of careers to choose from.
   a. 10,000   c. 40,000
   b. 20,000   d. 100,000
2. An animal control officer usually is an employee of _____ .
   a. NASA
   b. county or city government
   c. U.S. government
   d. a private company
3. A(n) _____ represents a general kind of work activity that takes place in many different career fields.
   a. employment trend
   b. protective authority
   c. occupational cluster
   d. career interest area
4. Workers in the protective fields protect people and _____ .
   a. pets   c. plants
   b. property   d. the environment
5. Physical performers are workers who use physical skills and strength to _____ .
   a. entertain an audience
   b. build high-rise structures
   c. lead and influence people
   d. sell products
6. _____ is a general term for occupations that are related in some way.
   a. Agriculture
   b. Communications and media
   c. Arts, humanities, and sciences
   d. Occupational clusters
7. An architect would be considered a member of the _____ occupational cluster.
   a. arts, humanities, and sciences
   b. communications and media
   c. construction
   d. home economics
8. Writers, linguists, and philosophers apply _____ to express ideas.
   a. language skills
   b. to radio stations
   c. to newspapers
   d. leadership skills
9. Workers in the natural resources and environment career cluster are concerned about _____ .

a. interest areas
b. weather forecasting
c. recreation
d. forests, air, soil, water and wildlife

10. A hairdresser is considered to be part of the _____ occupational cluster.
    a. health
    b. hospitality and recreation
    c. personal services
    d. public service

11. A tree surgeon belongs in the _____ occupational cluster.
    a. health
    b. natural resources and environment
    c. public service
    d. agriculture

12. A truck driver is a member of the _____ occupational cluster.
    a. transportation
    b. manufacturing
    c. personal services
    d. marketing and distribution

13. An employment trend tells which jobs are most _____ employers.
    a. popular with
    b. threatening to
    c. trouble for
    d. challenging for

14. The demand for workers is _____.
    a. steadily growing
    b. steadily declining
    c. remaining the same
    d. not important

15. The people who take whatever job comes along are rarely as happy as those who _____ their careers.
    a. are given
    b. choose
    c. change
    d. inherit

Thinking Critically About Career Skills

Write your answers to the following questions on a separate sheet of paper.

1. Many people in protective interest jobs feel a sense of responsibility for others. Do you think they are the only ones who should feel this way? What other kinds of workers should feel a sense of responsibility? For example, should salespeople feel this way? Why or why not?

Building Basic Skills

1. **Research** Use news broadcasts on television and radio and reports in newsmagazines to determine employment trends. What new jobs are being created? What old jobs are disappearing?

2. **Mathematics** Calculate the number of people in your community who work full-time. Suppose that 35,000 people live in your community. You just read in the local newspaper that 55 percent of the people in your community have full-time jobs. How many people work full-time?

Applying Career Skills

1. Go to a commercial area near your home, look at the businesses there. Select three businesses that interest you, and write down all the jobs needed to keep those particular businesses running. Don't forget all the duties the public usually doesn't see, such as accounting and ordering supplies.

RESEARCHING CAREERS

Which career areas in Chapter 3 "turned you on?" Was it construction because you like to build things? Perhaps you were interested in the health field because you like working with people. If none of the areas discussed interested you, try reading the chapter again. This time, try to be more aware of your reactions to each career area as you read.

In this chapter you will look more closely at the areas that appealed to you. You will compare these areas with your own skills, interests, aptitudes, values, and personality traits. You'll be asking yourself how your skills and interests can be applied to the career areas you like.

Career research is not difficult to do. However, it does take a little time and effort on your part. Remember, however, that you are doing research that will affect the rest of your life. The more careful and thorough you are now, the happier you will be later.

The following sections will help you research the career areas and clusters that interest you most. These sections are organized in the order in which you should work. First you must think about the sort of information you need to know. Then you must learn where to find it.

What Do You Want to Know?

Before you start your research, you should gather your lists of skills, aptitudes, values, and other personal facts. Keep these lists handy as you work. Refer to them whenever you need to refresh your memory about your needs. Remember, you are doing this research to find a career that fits *you*.

Next, take out several sheets of paper. At the top of each sheet write the name of a career field that appeals to you. Then divide each sheet into sections and label the sections with the headings below.

As you gather information about a career area, make notes under each heading. For example, if some of your skills are mechanical, you should make a note in the section labeled "Skills."

Now is your chance to use all those lists you've been putting together. Which list from Chapter 2 helped you rate what you believe is important or worthwhile at work?

- **Skills**—Do you have the skills? Are there any ways your aptitudes or abilities can be used?
- **Education and Training**—What education and training are necessary? Is the training you will have when you graduate from high school enough to get the job? If not, what additional education or training is necessary? Keep in mind that the jobs of the future may require education and training beyond high school.

  The expense and time needed for additional schooling and training may be something you can't afford in the near future. If so, try to be realistic about what may or may not be possible for you to manage. However, keep in mind that financial help is available.
- **Work Environment**—What is the work environment like? Some work places are fancy; others are plain. Some are clean; others are dirty. Often the type of job will affect the way the workplace looks. For example, an auto repair shop will smell of gasoline, and there will be grease on the floor. Give some thought to the type of surroundings in which you'd be most comfortable.

Age	Work Rules
18 and over	● Can work at any job, hazardous or not, for any number of hours
16 and 17	● Can work at any job which is not hazardous for any number of hours
14 and 15	● Can work only at certain jobs and only outside of school hours. Jobs cannot be in manufacturing or mining and must not be hazardous. Work hours are as follows: — no more than 3 hours on a school day — no more than 18 hours during a school week — no more than 8 hours on a day of no school — no more than 40 hours during a week of no school
Any age	● Can deliver newspapers or work in movies, theatre, TV, radio; can work in parent-owned business

Unless you are already 18, your choice of jobs is restricted by government regulations. What do you think the purpose of these regulations is?

If you plan to work before you reach the age of 18, you may not be able to work in some environments. Above is a list of rules that affects the jobs you can do.

- **Hours**—What hours will you spend on the job? As you know, not all employees work a normal calendar week. Some must work weekends or during hours other than eight to five. How much time do you want to spend on the job? What sort of free time do you want to have?

- **Duties and Responsibilities**—What responsibilities will you have? Would you enjoy these responsibilities?

- **Personality**—Do you have the sort of personality that will help you become successful? For example, if you like to be up and moving, you will probably not be happy at a desk job. If you are quiet and withdrawn, you probably wouldn't enjoy a sales job.

- **Location**—Where is the work located? Does your city or state offer the jobs you are interested in, or will you have to move? If you like living in the country, will you be able to do so?

- **Advancement**—Is there room for advancement? When you look at a career area, look at the *levels* of jobs available for someone with your abilities. Will you be able to move ahead?

- **Job Outlook**—How plentiful are the jobs? You have already learned about job trends. How will they affect the

CAREER Q&A

TOO MUCH?

Q: Why should I do all of this work to find out more about careers?

A: You'll get a much better idea of what a career field is like if you look into it carefully. After all, you probably don't want a lot of surprises when you make a career choice.

Having special skills, such as being able to operate heavy equipment, may mean higher pay for the worker. What other types of jobs usually involve higher pay?

career area? Will there be enough jobs to go around when you're ready to work?

- **Pay**—How much do the jobs pay? Is a high rate of pay important to you? How did you rate pay on your values list? Look for information about income levels so you know what to expect. If there is a lot of danger involved with a job, the income is usually higher. If only a small supply of qualified workers is available, the job may pay well. Education and training also affect income. Generally, the more education and training needed, the better the pay.

    Fringe benefits may be considered part of the pay. Sometimes housing and meals come with the job. In such cases the actual paycheck may not be as large.
- **Rewards**—Will you receive the rewards and satisfactions you require? Do you remember reading in Chapter 1 about the reasons people work? You must consider the main reasons why you will be working as you research each career. Does the career provide the things that are most important to you?

REVIEW YOUR WORK

1. Why is it important to take the time to research a career now?
2. Name at least three questions you should be asking while researching a career area.
3. How will the lists of your interests, skills, and values help you in your research?

Where Do You Find Information?

Finding out about careers is easier than you might think. You can gather information by reading, by talking to people, and through your own experience.

Reading Resources

Printed materials, such as books, magazines, occupational briefs, and government publications, are excellent ways to find more information about specific jobs. Take time to become familiar with three valuable government references: the *Occupational Outlook Handbook, Dictionary of Occupational Titles,* and the *Guide for Occupational Exploration.* You can also find several other reference books in your local libraries. Be sure you have the most up-to-date edition of whichever source you use.

Occupational Outlook Handbook.   The *Occupational Outlook Handbook* is the best source of general information about occupations. If you want to know what workers do in each job, how much the pay will be, and the future prospects of the job, check the *Occupational Outlook Handbook.* The *Handbook* covers about 250 occupations and is reprinted every two years. For each of the occupations there is information about job duties, working conditions, levels and places of employment, education and training requirements, advancement possibilities, job trends, and average earnings.

The *Handbook* is easy to use. First read the section titled, "How to Get the Most from the Handbook." Then simply look through the Table of Contents and find the area of work that interests you. A page from the *Handbook* is shown on page 68.

Your public library is one of the best sources of career information. Who can you turn to for help in understanding how to best use the library?

Dictionary of Occupational Titles.   The *Dictionary of Occupational Titles (DOT)* is published by the U.S. Employment Service. The *DOT* lists 20,000 different kinds of jobs. It is a big book that classifies jobs in different ways. Using the *DOT* helps you learn about jobs that you didn't know existed and jobs that focus on your interests.

Reading the information about a specific job will help you decide if the job really interests you. The *DOT* includes a detailed explanation of the job responsibilities. It does not tell you about education and training requirements.

The *DOT* can be confusing to those who don't know how to use it. Be sure to read the instructions before trying to use the *DOT.* Ask the librarian if you need help.

The Occupational Outlook Handbook *contains information on approximately 250 occupations. The* OOH *is revised every two years to make sure that the information is current. Why is current information important in career research?*

Dental Occupations

Proper dental care is an integral part of overall health care. This section focuses on the dental profession and the three dental auxiliary occupations.

Dentists examine and treat patients for oral diseases and abnormalities, such as decayed and impacted teeth. Most dentists are general practitioners, but some specialize in certain areas of dentistry, such as orthodontics or oral surgery. Other dentists are employed in teaching, research, or administration.

Dental hygienists are the only dental auxiliary workers required by each State to be licensed. They scale, clean, and polish teeth, expose X-rays, and instruct patients in proper oral hygiene.

Dental assistants help dentists while they are working with patients. This assistance includes tasks such as handing the dentist the

Dentists
(D.O.T. 072)

Nature of the Work

Dentists examine teeth and other tissues of the mouth to diagnose diseases or abnormalities. They take X-rays, fill cavities, straighten teeth, and treat gum diseases. Dentists extract teeth and substitute artificial dentures designed for the individual patient. They also perform corrective surgery of the gums and supporting bones. In addition, they may clean teeth.

Dentists spend most of their time with patients, but may devote some time to laboratory work such as making dentures and inlays. Most dentists, however—particularly those in large cities—send their laboratory work to commercial firms. Some dentists also

cial teeth or dentures); endodontics (root canal therapy); public health dentistry; and oral pathology (diseases of the mouth).

About 5 percent of all dentists teach in dental schools, do research, or administer dental health programs on a full-time basis. Many dentists in private practice do this work on a part-time basis.

Working Conditions

Most dental offices are open 5 days a week, and some dentists have evening hours. Dentists usually work between 40 and 45 hours a week, although many spend more than 50 hours a week in the office. Dentists often work fewer hours as they grow older; and a considerable number continue in part-time practice well beyond the usual retirement age.

Places of Employment

Guide for Occupational Exploration.   Remember the career interest areas discussed in Chapter 3? The *Guide for Occupational Exploration* (GOE) focuses on these interest areas. For each interest, work groups and subgroups are listed.

The *GOE* gives a definition and explanation of each interest area. The work groups are then listed. The following information is given for each work group.

* The kind of work done
* The skills and abilities needed
* How to know if you would like or could learn to do this kind of work
* How to prepare for and enter the job area
* Other factors to consider about the jobs

Career Publications.   Many schools and local libraries have career resource centers with pamphlets, newspapers, and magazines on file. These publications provide occupational briefs, occupational outlooks, and trends. They contain the most current information about the job market. The Department of Labor makes much of this information available on a weekly or monthly basis.

Books, Magazines, and Audiovisuals.   Books and magazines can tell you a lot about the jobs that interest you. Your school or local library will have some that you will find helpful. Most can be borrowed and taken home if you have a library card.

What areas are you interested in? Selling insurance, diesel mechanics, government relations—whatever the area, you can probably find several books about that area.

Researching Careers

What comes to mind when you hear the word *research?* Have you ever had to read lots of books and write information on note cards in order to write a research paper? Did it seem as though you could have spent the rest of your life filling out those cards and still never gather all the information you need?

Research means hard work, and it means time. It's like looking for a needle in a haystack. You can search through hundreds of pages of books and magazines just to find one paragraph that you can use. If you think doing research is frustrating and unproductive, you are not alone. Many people feel the same way.

Career research is different. If there was ever a research project worth the time, the effort, and the frustration, this is it. The career research you are about to do may be the most important research project of your life. **THINK POSITIVELY** about your career research. It can help you avoid years of unhappiness working at a job you don't enjoy.

Although good research takes lots of time and hard work, your career research can be interesting. You may even enjoy it.

Your career research differs from other research projects. This isn't just another school assignment—this is your life. Every minute you invest in career research is a minute that will increase your chances of being happy and successful for the next 40 or 50 years.

Career research is also different from other research projects because career research isn't done solely at the library. You will gather much of the most valuable information by talking to workers and working at part-time jobs. The best way to find out whether or not you might enjoy a certain career is to actually work at a job in that career area. You will meet lots of interesting people, learn a lot about the world of work, and move closer to a decision.

Your teacher and librarian will help. They know which books and magazines will help you the most. They want you to ask questions when you are confused. They want to show you how much valuable information is available.

Your parents and friends will also help. They can help you obtain leads for interviews and part-time jobs.

So think positively when you hear the term *career research.* It's going to lead you to a satisfying, successful career.

You can also read about careers in magazines. Are there any special magazines devoted to covering careers and getting and keeping a job?

You can also read about careers in magazines. *Career World* and *Real World* are magazines about getting and keeping a job. Now and then, magazines such as *Motor Trend, Auto Body,* and *Seventeen* also feature articles on careers.

Films, filmstrips, slides, and videotapes are excellent ways to learn about jobs. Since they offer photographs of the real work world, it is easy to imagine what the work environment is like. You can see what the workers wear and what skills and equipment are used. This will help you decide whether or not you would enjoy the work.

REVIEW YOUR WORK

1. Name the three main government resources that you can use to learn about jobs.
2. Which resource focuses on interests?
3. Why are visuals a good resource?
4. Which resources contain the most current information?

Guidance Services

Your school has a guidance counselor to help you with career questions. The counselor can help you find information on education and training programs, including their costs. Private career counseling firms do the same thing. They all help people select and plan a career. If you decide to choose a private counseling firm, be sure to check its reputation with the Better Business Bureau in your town.

Computerized Guidance Programs

Your school, local library, or guidance center will probably have computerized guidance programs. **Computerized guidance programs** *provide information about the job world.* The programs are helpful and often fun to do.

Computerized guidance programs operate in different ways. More and more, the information is contained on a disk that is inserted into a personal computer. You sit at the computer and go through the program at your own pace. Most of these programs are "user friendly," which means you can use them even if you have not used a computer before.

Computer programs can be fun ways to learn about careers. Do you have to know a lot about computers to use a computerized guidance program?

Ask your vocational teacher, director, or counselor about the computerized guidance programs available in your school. If none is available, check your local library. You might also check into the vocational guidance organizations that exist nationwide. Each state has a different occupational information system. Someone at your school can put you in touch with the vocational guidance organization offering computerized career information.

Computer-assisted guidance in the following areas is available:

- self-assessment
- occupational information and exploration
- educational information and exploration
- test practice and preparation programs
- financial aid exploration
- pre-employment and job seeking preparation
- career development
- special needs career guidance
- skill building (problem-solving, decision-making)

In Chapter 2 we discussed values. Computer programs are also available to help you identify your values and tell how your values can affect job choices. Other programs help you group your skills and write about them for a possible employer. These are just a few examples of the many ways you can use computer programs in your career research.

Most computer programs are designed to be used on your own. When you have completed the program, your counselor or teacher can help you put the information to use.

Talking to Others About Their Work

You are surrounded by working people. Sometimes the people you know and others in your community are the best sources of information about working and the different career fields.

Family and Friends.   Before you bought something that cost a lot of money, did you ever talk to your family or friends about it? Perhaps getting their ideas gave you more confidence in investing your money. The same is true about careers. The more information you get from your family and friends about the work they do, the better you are going to feel about the decision you make about your own career.

For example, do you really know what your mother does at the travel agency as a reservationist? She spends long periods of time on the phone talking to clients and operating

Talking to your parents about what they do can give you a good idea of their work routine. Who else can you talk to about work?

the computer. She has to find the right flight connections to get the client from one airport to another. She locates price rates for ground transportation and hotels. She must know about foreign currency rates and customs regulations. She is asked about the weather and what it is like in different parts of the world.

Talking to people about what they do can give you a pretty good idea of their work routine. A more complete work picture can be had if you find out about the general interests and functions of their work.

Each of your friends and relatives has different thoughts, feelings, and reactions to work. Their experiences can give you unique work information. They can tell you different "things" about a certain career, or work in general, that you might not have thought about before. Whenever you have the opportunity, ask your relatives, friends, and acquaintances about their jobs. Most people enjoy talking about their work. You can gain valuable information by asking questions and listening.

Other Workers or Employers.   Maybe you don't know anyone who works in an area of interest to you. Then ask your friends, relatives, teachers, or counselor for suggestions. Otherwise, you may have to plunge ahead on your own. The occupational tour discussed in Chapter 3 might give you some ideas. Making an appointment to ask about a job is easier than you think.

CASE STUDY   Carol was thinking about becoming a short order cook in a restaurant. Her teacher suggested she call a few restaurant owners. Perhaps one would agree to talk to her. The teacher warned her that employers were busy and she might be turned down a few times.

After four tries, Carol succeeded. When the restaurant's secretary answered the phone, their conversation sounded like this:

"Hello, my name is Carol Strauss. Could you please tell me the owner's name? . . . Thank you. May I please speak to her? . . . Hello, Mrs. Gonzales, this is Carol Strauss, a student at City High School. We are studying careers in school, and I think I'd like to be a short order cook. My teacher suggested I call restaurant owners like you and ask to visit with you about becoming a cook. I know you're very busy, but would you have a few minutes one day to see me? . . . No, I'm sorry, I can't come tomorrow. May I come the next day, Thursday, at 4 p.m.? . . . Thank you very much. I'll see you Thursday, in your office, at 4 p.m."

Thinking About the Case Study

1. Other than the owner, who else might Carol want to talk to at the restaurant?
2. What type of experience will Carol gain from such an occupational tour?

Notice that Carol was careful to introduce herself and explain why she wanted the appointment. Before the interview she made a list of questions to ask so she would be prepared. She included those given in this chapter under "What Do You Want to Know?" and a few others, such as

• What do you like most about the restaurant business? What do you like least?

A Flight to Your Future

People used to say that if we were meant to fly, we would have wings. Today air travel is a common part of our world, and there are few professions as glamorous and as demanding as being a pilot. Maybe you have always wanted to be a pilot.

Becoming a pilot demands a great deal of training and education. Especially needed is a strong mathematics background. In addition, you need to spend many hours in flight school as well as actually training in a helicopter or plane.

While not everyone who dreams of being a pilot becomes one, that does not mean that they have to abandon their love for air travel. There are many other jobs available that are related to air travel. You could become an air traffic controller. In this job, you could use your interest in air travel and your ability to work with high-tech radar and communications equipment to help keep the skyways and airports safe.

You could combine your love of air travel and your people skills to become a flight attendant or travel agent. As a flight attendant you would make sure that the passengers on airlines are comfortable and safe. You would help to serve food, answer questions, and provide safety instruction. As a travel agent, you would help people plan both business and holiday trips by securing travel tickets and hotel accommodations. Many travel agents get to travel free or at greatly reduced rates.

Just as airplanes need pilots, they also need airport support workers. Without people filling the important jobs of airline mechanics, baggage handlers, ticket agents, and airport security, all of the planes would be grounded. Airlines and airports, like all businesses, also need administrators, secretaries, clerks, and other office-related workers.

As you can see, there are many exciting and interesting jobs related to air travel. Your guidance counselor can help you explore these professions. With the right planning, you might discover that the sky's the limit for you!

- Do you have much contact with other people?
- What types of jobs exist at your restaurant and in our city?
- Do any of the jobs require talking to customers?
- Do all the jobs require standing all day or lifting heavy things?
- Can I become a cook right away? Would working part-time as a waitress help?

Talking to those who work in a job field can give you a lot of useful information. They can also be a source of job leads, which will be discussed in a later chapter.

REVIEW YOUR WORK

1. Name three types of information available through computerized guidance systems.
2. How can your family help you learn about careers?
3. What would you do to make an appointment with an employer in your neighborhood to acquire job information?

Work Experience

One of the best ways to research and learn about different occupations is to get an after-school or weekend job in a field that interests you. You may not be able to get the sort of job you think you would like best. However, you may be around others who do that job so that you can see what the job is like. At the same time, you get paid!

While you are working, you can be finding the answers to all the research questions, such as "Will I need additional skills?" and "Will the pay be right?"

There is an additional bonus to researching careers by having a job. The bonus is experience. All jobs give people experience. Experience means you have worked at a job long enough to learn how to do some type of work. Most employers want to hire workers who have had some experience. If you already have some part-time experience in a certain field, it will be that much easier for you to get a full-time job in the same field.

Cooperative Education Programs.   If you are interested in a job while you are still in school, you might look into cooperative education. **Cooperative education programs** *give students a chance to go to school and work at the same*

DID YOU KNOW?

EARLY CHOICE

Among some groups of people in Thailand, a baby boy is expected to choose his future career on his first birthday. Various symbols of different occupations are placed in front of the child. The first object he grabs determines his life's work.

Cooperative education students can get class credit for time spent at work. Do these students also have to attend any classes?

time. Part of the day is spent at school, and part of the day is spent on the job.

While in school, cooperative education students take regular school subjects plus the cooperative education class. In the cooperative education class, a training plan is created for each person. The plan describes the work the student will do on the job. The plan also lists classroom activities. The skills stressed in the classroom and on the job help students learn about the job and how to be better employees.

On the job, students have a chance to prove themselves. The job helps them use a lot of the information they have learned in school. It is a chance for students to try their skills and to see how they are doing. It is also a chance to continue to learn new things that can help in future planning and jobs.

Creating Your Own Job.   When jobs are hard to get, try going into business for yourself. Look around to see what needs to be done—that no one is doing. Stop in local stores or businesses. Start with those that interest you most. Do windows need cleaning? Is someone needed to make local deliveries? Then ask to speak to the manager and offer to do the work.

Perhaps you can work for your neighbors. Maybe you could babysit or take children to the local swimming pool. You might take care of yards, water plants, and feed pets for people on vacation.

Creating your own job is one way to find work. How can creating your own job help prepare you for the world of work?

It's even possible to get a group of your own friends together to do housecleaning around the neighborhood. Offer to wash windows or clean garages, basements, or attics. You might gather unused items for a garage sale. Profits can be shared with those who gave the items. There are always jobs that need doing, and you may be just the person to do them.

Creating your own job helps you get ready for other jobs. You learn how it is to organize a small business. You learn what employers look for. You may even learn something about a field you are interested in.

Part-time and Temporary Jobs.   Part-time and temporary jobs are excellent ways to research careers and gain work experience.

A **part-time job** *means you work a portion of a workweek.* You may work a couple of hours each day or one or two days a week.

A **temporary job** *is a part-time or full-time job that lasts only for a couple of hours, weeks, days, or months.* For example, department stores hire temporary employees during the heavy Christmas shopping season. Lifeguarding at the pool or beach is another temporary job since it is done during the summertime only.

Volunteering.   Most people would rather be paid for the work they do, but a job in a career that you'd like to research may not be available. **Volunteers** *are people who work without pay.* If you volunteer to do work for an organization, the job may tell you what you want to know about a certain career. Hospitals, for example, often use volunteer workers. If you are interested in learning about the health care field, volunteering may be an excellent way to test its appeal.

The YMCA, YWCA, Red Cross, and other community groups also offer many programs that depend on volunteer help. Your city or town may have an office that lists volunteer jobs. Newspapers often list them, too.

REVIEW YOUR WORK

1. Give three reasons why having a job is a good way to find out about various occupations.
2. What are cooperative education programs?
3. What are some advantages of creating your own job?
4. How can work experience now help you get other jobs later?
5. What is a temporary job?

Chapter Summary

- It is important for you to start career research right now.
- There are many points to remember when reviewing career possibilities.
- Finding out about careers is relatively easy. You can do so by talking to people, reading, and through your own experience.
- Three reading resources on careers are the *Occupational Outlook Handbook*, *Dictionary of Occupational Titles*, and the *Guide for Occupational Exploration*.
- School guidance counselors, private career counseling firms, and computerized guidance programs are three additional ways to find out the most suitable career possibilities for you.
- Another way to do research is to talk to family and friends about their jobs.
- There are several ways to get work experience while still attending school. They are cooperative education programs, part-time or temporary jobs, volunteering, and creating your own job.

Reviewing Vocabulary and Concepts

Write the numbers 1–10 on a separate sheet of paper. After each number, write the letter of the answer that best completes the following statements.

1. Career research is _____ to do.
   a. difficult
   b. not difficult
   c. boring
   d. for someone else
2. The more thoroughly and carefully you research careers now, the _____ you will be later.
   a. happier
   b. unhappier
   c. more exhausted
   d. bossier
3. A(n) _____ job is one that lasts for only a couple of hours, weeks, days, or months and then ends.
   a. part-time
   b. full-time
   c. permanent
   d. temporary
4. A(n) _____ job is one that lasts indefinitely, but in which you work only a portion of each week.
   a. part-time
   b. office
   c. after-school
   d. evening
5. A way to create your own job is to look around and see what _____ there are in your neighborhood.
   a. friends
   b. problems
   c. street signs
   d. needs
6. If you work as a volunteer to an organization, you're working without _____ .
   a. recognition
   b. supplies
   c. pay
   d. satisfaction
7. _____ is a term that means you have worked at a job long enough to know how to do some type of work.
   a. Work experience
   b. Education
   c. Temporary
   d. Part-time
8. A _____ provides computer-based information about the working world.
   a. data base
   b. satellite program
   c. computerized guidance program
   d. career publication
9. *Career World* and *Real World* are _____ about getting and keeping a good job.
   a. books
   b. magazines
   c. computer programs
   d. films
10. If you decide to go to a private career counseling company, it's a

good idea to check its reputation with _____ .

a. your friends
b. the Better Business Bureau
c. television
d. your favorite magazine

Thinking Critically About Career Skills

Write your answers to the following questions on a separate sheet of paper.

1. Why do you think keeping lists is an important part of career research? Do you think that writing things down helps you think more clearly? Does making lists help you remember details better?

2. Why is it important to have more than one career choice? Do you think the demand for your chosen career will be as great in the future as it is right now? Why or why not? Will the job duties change?

Building Basic Skills

1. **Writing**   Write a letter to a trade association, union, or large company requesting information about a career that interests you.

2. **Mathematics**   Calculate the effect of different starting pays over a period of time. Suppose beginning workers in Occupation X have a starting pay of $12,000 a year, while beginning workers in Occupation Y start at $14,000 a year—a difference of $2,000. If workers in both occupations receive a 5 percent raise in each of the next five years, what will be the difference in pay at the end of five years? (Round off all calculations in dollars and cents, to the next highest dollar.)

Applying Career Skills

1. Go to your local library and see how many job research reference books they have. Look up a career you are interested in and photocopy the pages that give information about it. Bring to class the information you have found and share it with the other students.

2. Make a list of jobs that you feel you could do as part of a cooperative education program. Note which of these jobs would give you work experience that you would be able to apply later.

MAKING CAREER DECISIONS

KEY TERMS

decisions
alternatives
evaluate
outcome

OBJECTIVES

In this chapter you will learn about
- making decisions
- the steps in decision-making
- special points to keep in mind about career decisions

Every day you make lots of choices—from the time the alarm goes off in the early morning until you crawl into bed late at night. You choose such things as where to go, what to do, and whom to see. Life is a series of decisions. **Decisions** *are situations requiring you to make a choice.*

No decision is more important than your career decision. This chapter will help you understand decision-making: what it is, the things that can get in its way, and the methods. Most important, you will learn how to apply decision-making to choosing a career.

Making Decisions

Have you ever seen the domino effect? Thousands of dominoes are arranged to form a pattern. Then the first domino in line is pushed over. This domino hits the next one, and on and on, until all of the dominoes have been knocked down.

The domino effect is a *chain reaction*. The action of one domino affects the action of the next domino. The first domino has an impact on the hundreds of other dominoes.

In this way, decisions are similar to dominoes. One decision affects the next decision. Your present decisions affect future decisions. The decisions you are now facing will have an impact on your life for many years.

Why Study Decision-Making?

You might be saying to yourself right now, "I have been making decisions all my life. It's no big deal. Why do I have to learn about something I already know how to do?" The answer is very simple: you want to do it better.

Decision-making is a skill. As with other skills, some people are more successful at it than others. Most of your decisions affect many areas of your life. It is to your benefit to make decisions as skillfully as possible.

Some decisions are much easier to make than others. For example, do you want eggs or cereal for breakfast? That decision should be fairly easy to make. Other decisions are more difficult. You have only enough money to pay for one movie, but there are three movies in town you want to see. All are leaving town at the end of the week. Which one do you choose? The more things you must consider, the more difficult a decision can become.

As you have learned, a career decision means considering a large number of factors. You will be investing many years of your life in the career you choose. Although many people change careers several times, you want all your choices to be happy ones.

Steps in Making Decisions

Almost all decisions require the same steps. By spending time with each step, you will make more careful decisions. However, these steps are only guidelines. You may find that the steps overlap or that you need to spend more time on one step than another. Adjust them as needed so they work best for you.

As you grow older, many of the decisions you make will become more important. How can studying decision-making help you in making these important decisions?

Making a decision means making a choice. How is making no decision actually a decision?

Step 1. Define Your Need or Want.   The first step in the decision-making process is to define the need that requires a decision. Be as specific as possible. Narrow the area of the need so you can focus on one need.

Step 2. Analyze Your Resources.   Analyzing your resources is what you have been doing in the last three chapters. By now you should have a good idea of your aptitudes, abilities, values, and so on. In other words, what do you have or what can you obtain that will help you meet your need?

Step 3. Identify Your Choices.

At least two choices or alternatives exist whenever a decision has to be made. What are those choices? The information in Chapters 3 and 4 made you aware of existing career choices. From what you have learned, what occupations interest you?

Step 4. Compare the Choices.

Based on the information you have about each choice, try to imagine as clearly as possible what it would be like to carry it through. Look at the advantages and disadvantages of each choice. Try to learn which choice seems to have the best chance of meeting your need, which choice is second best, which is third, and so on.

Step 5. Choosing the Best Alternative.

An **alternative** *is a choice.* After the alternatives have been examined and compared, choose the one that seems to meet your needs the best. Keep in mind that none of the choices may stand way above the others. In the end, the differences between the two top alternatives may be small. Do not be discouraged. No decision has to be final, and you may find you want to change your mind after you have gained a little work experience.

Step 6. Make a Plan to Get Started.

The decision-making process is not complete unless you know how you will get from where you are now to where you want to be. Planning does that for you. Chapter 6 will discuss in detail how to develop a plan of action.

When you are having trouble making a decision, try writing down all your choices and comparing them. What else might you do when having trouble with a decision?

Step 7. Evaluating Your Decision.

When you **evaluate** *something, you judge its worth, quality, or goodness.* Once your plan is put to use, you will begin to see if your decision was the best one. You will evaluate it. If the outcomes are good, you will continue. If the outcomes aren't good, then you will need to make a new decision.

An outcome should not be confused with a decision. *An* **outcome** *is the result of a decision and happens after the decision is made.* You have control of the decision but not the outcomes.

Each step in the decision-making process may require some back-tracking. Your goal may not be clear enough, or you may discover a new alternative that meets your needs better.

CASE STUDY

As an example, let's look at Jeff, who had mechanical abilities and could work with his hands. He enjoyed repairing small engines. The career areas that interested him were hospitality and recreation and tranportation.

Step 1. Define Your Need or Want. Jeff's need was to select a career that suited him.

Step 2. Analyze Your Resources. After all his research, Jeff decided he had proven abilities in small engine repair. His grades in school were only average, except for shop class. He often got Bs and As on shop projects. He also did well in math when it was used in the shop, but not otherwise. Jeff was also good in sports and was on wrestling, baseball, and swimming teams at school.

Step 3. Identify Your Choices. Jeff was interested in transportation because of his mechanical abilities. He also chose to learn about hospitality and recreation because he liked sports and working with people.

After Jeff talked to people in his community and used his library resources, he identified three possible careers: a pitcher for a softball team sponsored by a large company, a sports activities director for a resort, and a welder.

Step 4. Compare the Choices. Jeff reviewed his choices. He made a list of things both for and against each choice. All three jobs paid enough. The pitching job was seasonal, and he would have to do other work for the company off-season. As he got older, his value as a player would be less. The activities director job would be year-round as long as the resort offered winter sports. He wouldn't, however, have much chance to play himself. He enjoyed welding, but he would not be working with people. He would have to go to vocational school to earn a welding certificate.

Step 5. Choosing the Best Alternative. Jeff's first choice was sports director. His second choice was welder. He wished he could somehow combine the two, but at this point he saw no way to do it.

Step 6. Make a Plan to Get Started. Jeff was in his junior year of school. He made a plan for the coming summer and the next school year. He would try to get a resort job in the summer, and he would sign up for as many sports as possible during school. He selected those a resort might offer. Just in case he changed his decision, Jeff also took advanced shop classes his last year in high school.

Step 7. Evaluating Your Decision. Jeff worked as a caddy at the resort the following summer. Whenever possible, he observed the sports director and tried to imagine himself doing the same work. He noticed the director spent more time in an office than he did working with people.

Then one day, when Jeff was hunting for a golf ball, he discovered a machine shop at the back of the resort behind some trees. The resort had its own repair crew to maintain equipment. After work, Jeff returned to the shop and talked to the supervisor. He asked if he could work in the shop on days when he didn't caddy. The supervisor agreed, and Jeff soon had two jobs.

When the summer was over, Jeff made a new career decision. He decided that one day he would have his own repair shop in a resort town. He would specialize in sports equipment, such as boats and snowmobiles.

Jeff believed his new career plan would meet his needs even better. His best skills—mechanical ones— would be put to use. By running his own shop he would work with customers every day. His work would put him in contact with sports. Additionally, working in a resort town would mean he was near sports activities he enjoyed and could take part in during his free time.

Thinking About the Case Study

1. Did Jeff go through all of the steps in the decision-making process at one time?
2. Can you think of decisions other than career decisions where you could use the decision-making process that Jeff used?

The decision-making process helps you to plan for what will happen. However, events can cause you to change your plans. Again, it is important to remember the domino effect. If the outcomes are not satisfactory, another decision needs to be made to bring you closer to satisfying results.

REVIEW YOUR WORK

1. What is a domino effect?
2. List the steps in making a decision.
3. Why might a new decision be necessary for you at a later time?

When a Decision Gives You Trouble

With practice, you can become quite skillful in using the decision-making process. Sometimes, however, your surroundings, family, friends, and the way you feel about yourself affect the decisions you make. If you are having trouble, it may be for one of the following reasons. Most of these "reasons" are actually a lack of self-confidence in disguise.

* You think you can't do something because of your age, gender, or race. For example, you can't do a certain job because "you're too young."
* You expect too much of yourself. You think you must be able to do a thing perfectly or you can't do it at all.
* Your family expects too much of you.
* Your family's finances can't support what you want to undertake.
* Your friends pressure you to do what they want to do.

CAN'T DECIDE?

Q: What can I do if it's hard for me to make a decision?
A: Go through as many of the decision-making steps as you can. Write down your choices. Then talk with a parent, a teacher, a friend, or your employer. Another person may help you look at things differently.

You have been making decisions almost all of your life. What type of decisions did you make as a child?

- Your friends or family make fun of what you want to do.
- You're afraid of failure.
- You're afraid of change.
- You do not feel sure of yourself in new situations.
- You put things off.
- You expect too little from yourself. You think you can't do something and won't even try.

Identifying things that can get in your way will help you avoid them. Keep in mind that there is usually a way around problems. For example, money may stand in the way of your attending college. Instead of giving up, however, you can explore your chances for financial aid, such as student loans or scholarships.

Hints for Making Better Decisions

You want to become the best decision maker possible. The following hints should be helpful as you choose the career for you.

- Be aware of the decisions you make every day. If a decision did not turn out well, try to figure out why. Did you follow the steps?
- Practice the decision-making steps. The more decisions you make using the steps, the better you will become.
- Recognize the obstacles that get in your way. Are they things you could have overcome if you had tried a little harder?
- Check your way of looking at things. Do you look for good things to happen, or do you tend to have a "sour" outlook?
- Accept the outcome. If you made the best decision you could and things did not work out, accept the facts and start over. Next time will be better.
- Be willing to change your decision. Decisions aren't set in concrete. Sometimes the conditions for a decision change and a new decision is necessary.
- Remember, most decisions have both a positive and a negative outcome. However, a satisfying or positive decision has more good than bad results. Decisions that are satisfying are the ones that get you closest to what you want.
- Try to limit your need to depend on luck as much as possible. The idea is to get control of your life and of what happens to you. The more thorough you are in getting the facts you need and in planning ahead, the less you will need to rely on lucky breaks.

Making Career Decisions

It's time to make a career decision. You've looked closely at yourself. You've looked at the thousands of occupations available, and you've researched the careers that you thought you might like. There's no reason to postpone your decision any longer.

You can probably come up with lots of excuses for not making a decision.

- "I'm too young to make such an important decision. Besides, I've still got plenty of time. I'm not even out of school yet."
- "I need to think about it some more. A person shouldn't make this kind of decision overnight. It takes time."
- "Nothing sounds good to me. No career really interests me."
- "I don't think I'm smart enough or talented enough to do what I want to do. I'd never make it. Somewhere along the line I'd fall flat on my face."

These are just a few excuses for not making a decision. You can probably think of several more. People have always invented excuses for not making decisions.

In this case, however, you can make a career decision and you will! One way or another you will find yourself working at a job of some kind, and you will continue to work —either at that same job or at others —for most of your life. Even no decision is a decision. If you keep postponing your decision, you will eventually end up taking whatever job comes along . . . and that will be your decision . . . whatever comes along.

Therefore, you might as well **THINK POSITIVELY** and make a good, wise, firm decision now. Once you've made your decision, you will have something to work toward. You'll have a purpose in life. You'll feel as though you are making progress.

You have all the information you need, or, if you don't, you know how to get it. In this chapter you are learning a decision-making strategy that will guide you and help you make the best decision possible. That's all anyone can do, you know—make the best decision possible. Nobody can predict the future—nobody knows for sure what the right decision is. All any of us can do is make the best decision we know how to make.

So, go ahead! Think positively and make the best decision you can make.

Career Decisions

Have you seen the paths in cities, towns, or parks that are designed for people who want to exercise? The paths have stopping points along the way. Posted at each point are instructions for a particular set of exercises. A person follows the path until he or she has finished a complete workout.

A career decision path is similar to an exercise path. The path has points along the way. Each point has different things you must do that require certain information and actions.

When the path is completed, a final decision is required. If the final decision isn't satisfactory, the process is repeated. You return over the path until a satisfactory career has been chosen. The career decision path is shown on the next page.

Remember, the guidance counselor is at school to help you. If you don't know the answer to a career question, talk to the counselor. He or she may be able to point out a new way of looking at the problem.

With careful decision-making, you reduce your need for lucky breaks. Once you have made a decision, should you ever be willing to change it?

Keep Asking Questions

Don't think that just because you have decided on a career you should stop asking questions. Job fields constantly change. They may differ somewhat from state to state. A job may seem less satisfying than you thought it would be. Why is this? Some questions to keep in mind might be

- Is the work boring? Will it always be?
- Does it give me a feeling of accomplishment?
- Do I want to do this type of work for 15 or 20 years?
- Am I interested enough to spend the time and money for education and training?
- How am I better off choosing this career rather than another?
- Are my skills being put to good use? Do others in the field think I can handle the work?

There are many more questions you can think of. Try to think ahead to several years from now as you answer.

Keep Things Moving

A plan of action is especially important when choosing a career. It gives you some control over what happens to you. You also have a sense of accomplishment when you reach a certain goal.

The Career Decision Making Path

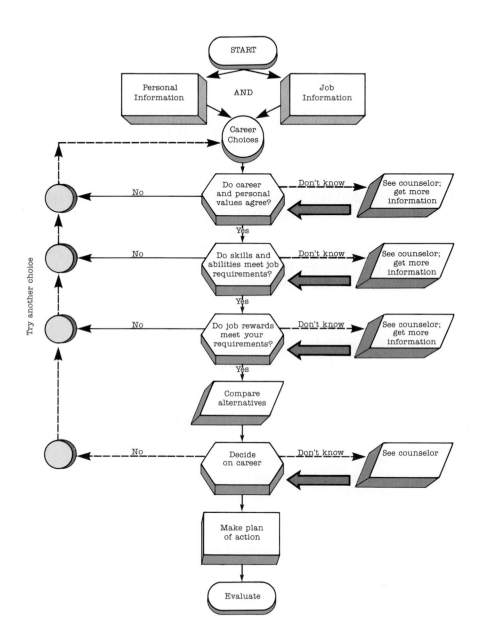

This career decision-making path gives instructions for each step of the way. What should you do if you find you don't know the answers at any step on the path?

Even if you make some mistakes, it is better to make them than to do nothing. Mistakes help you learn. They are also less serious at this time of your life. You have many years ahead in which to grow and change. Now is the time to jump in and try the water. Plans of action are discussed more fully in Chapter 6.

Your parents can help you to make important career decisions. Who else can you turn to for good career advice?

Evaluate, Evaluate!

Evaluation is an ongoing process. You do it all of the time. When you experience something you think, "that was good, that was bad, or I guess it was okay." Take a good look at the information about the career you choose. Is it really what you want to go after? Do you feel committed to achieving it?

At each point on the career path, you must evaluate new experiences and information. You are making a serious decision which deserves serious thinking.

Like Jeff, you may make a change very early in your career plan, or you may spend several years on a job before you realize it's not what you want. Sometimes you have to try a thing before you can tell how it's going to work. Don't wait until you're miserable before you evaluate. If it's a wonderful job and you're happy, evaluating will give you a chance to pat yourself on the back for all the things you've done right.

Starting Over

Never be afraid to start again. Never let anyone tell you that you are stuck with your first try. You have special dreams or needs that not every job can fulfill. Hang in there. Keep going back until you start to see some progress.

REVIEW YOUR WORK

1. Name four reasons why a decision might be giving you trouble.
2. Name three hints for making good decisions.
3. Why is it important to continue to ask questions while on a career path?
4. Name two advantages to having a plan of action.

Is There a Doctor in the House?

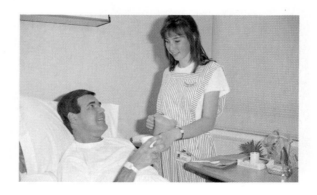

A life hangs in the balance as the doctor confidently strides into the operating room. The silence in the room is interrupted only by the hums and beeps of the patient's life support systems. Looking around at the other faces and checking the life support monitors, the doctor knows that the moment to begin is now. "Scalpel," she says.

With the pressure of life and death situations and the needs of ill or injured people, there are few professions that seem as exciting as being a doctor.

Becoming a doctor is a difficult and time-consuming achievement. Doctors follow four years of college work with as many as four or more years of medical school. As each step along the way becomes more difficult, more and more people drop out of the profession.

Doctor, of course, is not the only career available for those who want to be part of the health field. Registered nurses, licensed vocational nurses, and nurse practitioners also play an absolutely vital role in providing medical care.

If doctor or nurse isn't right for you, you could become a physical therapist who helps patients recover from illnesses, surgery, or accidents. You could become a phlebotomist who draws blood from patients for testing.

If you have an interest in technical equipment or chemistry, as well as medicine, you could become an X-ray technician or a laboratory technician. If you want to put your people skills to work in a medical setting, you could become a medical social worker. Medical

social workers help people to adjust to the changes in their lives brought on by illnesses, surgery, or accidents.

Because hospitals combine the worlds of business, medicine, and hospitality, there is an array of other important jobs needed to keep things running smoothly. Food service workers, maintenance workers, and security personnel are vital parts of any hospital's staff. Making sure that all the paperwork is processed and the bills are paid requires office personnel such as secretaries, accountants, bookkeepers, and file clerks.

In addition, as more and more hospitals become interested in being profitable, there is an increasing need for business administrators and public relations people who have an interest in and knowledge of medicine. These people work with the medical staff to see that the hospital runs efficiently and maintains a good public image.

Many of the careers in medicine have specific educational and training requirements, so you will need to begin your planning today. Talk with your guidance counselor about a career in medicine.

Chapter Summary

- Life is a series of decisions. Decision-making is a skill. By studying and applying proven techniques, you can improve your skill.
- There are seven steps in good decision-making.
- The "domino effect" refers to the way each decision affects another.
- When a decision seems to be giving you trouble, it's a good idea to examine closely the reasons.
- Decision-making is a skill that gets better with practice.
- It's okay to change your decision if new information comes in, or the condition changes.
- Evaluation is an ongoing process. At each point on the career path, you must evaluate new experiences and information.

Reviewing Vocabulary and Concepts

Write the numbers 1–10 on a separate sheet of paper. After each number, write the letter of the answer that best completes the following statements.

1. Making a decision means _____ .
   a. making a choice
   b. quick thinking
   c. going in another direction
   d. leaving town
2. The _____ is a chain reaction.
   a. decision-making process
   b. outcome
   c. domino effect
   d. alternative
3. Good decision-making is a _____ .
   a. hard thing to do
   b. skill
   c. no big deal
   d. natural talent
4. Alternative is another word for _____ .
   a. choice
   b. decision-making
   c. outcome
   d. analyzing
5. Outcome is the result of _____ .
   a. an alternative
   b. skill
   c. a decision
   d. an evaluation
6. When you _____ something, you judge its worth.
   a. buy   c. analyze
   b. decide on   d. evaluate
7. Writing down choices and comparing them on paper is a(n) _____ in decision-making.
   a. waste of time
   b. helpful tool
   c. not important
   d. exercise
8. It's _____ to depend on lucky breaks.
   a. not a good idea
   b. a decision-making process
   c. a shortcut
   d. a quick way to the top
9. Identifying things that can get in your way will help you _____ .
   a. use them   c. avoid them
   b. analyze them   d. be satisfied
10. Job fields _____ change.
   a. never   c. constantly
   b. may   d. rarely

Thinking Critically About Career Skills

Write your answers to the following questions on a separate sheet of paper.

1. Do you think the seven-step decision-making process will work for you? Have you tried it before? Do you know anyone who has? Do you think you can take shortcuts and still achieve the same results? Why or why not?

2. What do you think the saying "not making a decision is a decision" means?

3. Why is it a poor policy to depend on "lucky breaks"? How does being thorough in gathering facts and planning ahead lessen your need for lucky breaks?

Building Basic Skills

1. **Writing** Apply the seven steps in the decision-making strategy to a decision that you have faced recently.

2. **Public Speaking** Prepare and present to your class a two-minute persuasive speech about the importance of using a decision-making strategy. Assume that your audience will not want to make decisions.

Applying Career Skills

1. Go to your local library and research other sources of information on decision-making skills. Make a list of the book titles you find. Choose one book and read it, then write a 100-word book report. Ask the librarian about other resources, such as government informational booklets and organizations that help people develop decision-making skills.

2. To exercise this skill, think of something you need to make a decision about—perhaps what to do with your free time this weekend. Using the seven-step decision-making process, decide what you will do. Be sure to evaluate the outcome. How did you feel during and after your free-time activity? Were you satisfied with the outcome? If not, was there some way you could have improved your chances for a more satisfactory outcome?

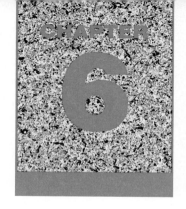
YOUR PLAN OF ACTION

KEY TERMS

procrastinator
G.E.D. certificate
apprentice
goals

OBJECTIVES

In this chapter you will learn about
- why you need a career plan
- what things you should plan for
- what goals to set
- how to make your own plan

In the last chapter, you learned about making career decisions. In this chapter, you will learn about the next step in pursuing that career—making a career plan.

A career plan can save you time, money, and effort. In this chapter you will learn how to make a career plan. As you read, think about how planning might help you in other ways as well.

Why You Need a Plan

Planning is important for several reasons. The major reason is that it helps you remember what needs to be done and when.

- A plan organizes your activities so you don't miss out on things. Even with a good plan you can't always fit everything in. Without a plan it's even harder.
- A plan prevents you from being a procrastinator. *A **procrastinator** puts things off*. Putting things off can be a bad habit to get into. Before you know it, you've run out of time and missed an opportunity. A plan helps you do things when they need to be done.
- A plan forces you to sort things out in order of importance. For example, perhaps you want to earn money toward college and go on a vacation. In the long run, which is more important? A plan doesn't mean you have to give up the vacation. It just means you get the job first. *Then* you plan for some time off.
- A plan gives you a feeling of accomplishment and satisfaction. As each activity is completed you can say, "I'm that much closer to my goal." That's why writing out a plan can be fun. You get to cross things off as you finish them. Soon, the completed activities pile up!
- A plan helps you learn how to manage your other activities, time, and energy. Sometimes you might feel as if you don't have enough time to do what you want. Perhaps you have enough time but not enough energy. Planning helps you get more done.

What Should Your Plan Include?

A career plan should take several factors into account:

- Education and training
- Ongoing career research
- Money you may need for education or equipment
- Personal duties, such as family business or responsibilities that might affect your work life
- Jobs leading to your ultimate career goal

Education and Training

While you are in junior high school and high school, there may be courses you can take that will get you started toward your goals. After high school, additional education and

Vocational schools offer training for specific jobs. Do vocational schools also offer advanced training?

training can help you meet the qualifications for your career. Going back to school in mid-career can be a good way to advance on the job. You can learn new skills or improve the ones you have. Due to rapid changes caused by technology, you might need to take courses once in a while just to stay on top of your job.

The following ways to get more education may be a part of your career plan.

- **Adult high school courses.** High schools offer courses at a time when working adults can take them, such as in the evening. The courses offered are high school level, based on popular demand, and not expensive.
- **Vocational education.** Vocational schools offer such courses as auto mechanics, welding, child care, and food preparation. The programs may provide basic skills for a job or advanced training. Most courses are offered during the day as well as in the evening.
- **Armed services.** The armed services offer a chance to learn a skill. A person chooses a job area and attends classes, which may include college.

    For people who choose certain careers, such as helicopter mechanics, the armed services can be an excellent way to earn a living while you learn.

- **Workshops.** Workshops are offered by schools and other organizations. A workshop is a short-term course. A workshop may last for a few hours, a day, or several days.
- **Private schools.** Many different private schools offer courses in such subjects as driving semi-trailer trucks or styling hair.

  Check the reputation of the school with the Better Business Bureau in your town. Some cannot do what they advertise. For example, they might say they guarantee you a job if you take the course. The job you get, however, may not be the same job for which you were preparing.
- **G.E.D. certificate.** If you must leave high school before graduation, you might want to plan on getting a General Educational Development (G.E.D.) certificate. To get the certificate you must pass the G.E.D. tests. *A **G.E.D. certificate** says that you have learned the things that are needed to get a high school diploma.*

Community colleges or junior colleges offer two-year education programs beyond high school. What type of degree can you earn from a community college?

There are five G.E.D. tests. They are in the areas of writing skills, social studies, science, reading skills, and mathematics. All five tests must be passed before the certificate is issued.

- **Technical-vocational centers and junior or community colleges.** These schools offer two-year programs of learning beyond the twelfth grade. When the program is completed, you have earned an associate degree. Technical vocational centers offer courses similar to those in vocational schools. The institutions have entry requirements.
- **Colleges and universities.** A college program takes an average of four years to complete if you attend full time. Course requirements include so many hours of English, math, and other basic subjects according to the career area you choose. Entrance requirements differ, but all require at least a high school diploma.

Career Research

Career research should be an ongoing process. This course is only one part of your career exploration and research. Even if you never change careers, you must remain aware of new opportunities. You must protect yourself as much as possible from trends that may work against your plans.

At different stages in your work life, plan to do some career research. Check your research against your career needs.

Money Needed

If you plan to continue your education or training, you will need money to pay for it, or a scholarship, or both. If you are lucky, your family may be able to pay the cost. If not, you will have to earn the money yourself. Do you know how you can do this?

Some professions require you to provide some of your own equipment. Hair stylists, for example, must provide their own scissors. A good pair costs between $65 and $75 and lasts only about a year. Theatre light technicians often own their own spotlights and reflectors. A full set costs several thousand dollars. Where will the money come from?

Even if you are able to get a loan from the government or a bank, you will have to earn some money, if only to pay the loan back. If you make a careful career plan, you will consider your needs for money. You may even be able to earn the money while you learn.

OPPORTUNITY

KNOCKS

COMPUTER SUPPORT ASSOCIATE

Modern business relies on computers and computer technology. Your interest in computers could lead you to many interesting careers like this.

COMPUTER SUPPORT ASSOCIATE

Large company offers outstanding opportunity to advance your career. Skills needed are:

- 2–3 years work experience
- Maintain database system
- Maintain computer software and publication libraries
- Provide in-house computer software support on many personal computer systems

Excellent benefits and generous salary.

Do you think there will be more jobs like this in the future than there are now?

Personal Duties

Do you have personal duties to attend to that might affect your career plan? If you are already working after school, perhaps you must give part of your earnings to your parents toward family expenses. Setting aside money for school may take you longer.

Perhaps personal duties might force you to delay your plans. Jim worked for the family business so his sister Karen could go to college. When Karen graduated and came home to take her own place in the firm, Jim was finally able to get his college education in a different field. When you make your plan, remember to consider all the things that might affect it.

Jobs Along the Way

Very few people reach their job goals in one or two steps. They may work at half a dozen jobs from the time they enter the work force until they achieve their goal. Your career plan should include all the steps between.

For example, while you are still in school, you may want to get a part-time job in the field. The experience will give you a chance to see if you like the field well enough to continue or if you should adjust your goal.

Keep in mind that jobs along the way may not meet all the requirements of the job you want most. The jobs may not pay as much. They may not be for a company you want or give you the responsibilities you feel you can handle.

This teen has a part-time job in a clothing store. Do you think her experiences here will help her in later jobs if she does not work in the retail or clothing industry?

CASE STUDY   When Raul planned his career he wanted to be a master plumber. When he finished high school, he looked for a job as a plumbing apprentice. *An* **apprentice** *is someone who learns an art or a trade by working for a set period of time in that field.* The job he found paid only $8 an hour. A friend of his, who got a job in a factory, was being paid $10.50 an hour.

After a year Raul's friend was making $11 and Raul was still making only $8. Raul got discouraged. He knew it would take him at least five years to become a master plumber. He would also have to take classes, pass several tests, and get a license. He quit his job and went to work in the factory.

Raul did well in the factory. In five years he was earning $12 an hour. He hoped to become a foreman one day and earn $15 an hour. In the meantime, however, master plumbers were earning $25 per hour!

Thinking About the Case Study

1. Why did Raul quit his job as a plumbing apprentice?
2. In the long run, which job will be better for Raul?

Remember, jobs along the way are like rungs on a ladder. Use them for where they can take you. Do not expect them to be something they're not.

Your work plan may include the following types of jobs.

Part-time Jobs.   Part-time jobs may be for 10, 20, or even 30 hours each week. If you are going to school or have other things you must do for most of the day, you might be able to do part-time work.

Temporary Jobs.   A lot of students look for temporary jobs for the time they are not in school, such as during the summer or the Christmas holiday. Temporary jobs may be full-time or part-time, but they last only a short while.

Many students take temporary jobs without giving any thought to how the job relates to their career choice. If you can, use a temporary job as a step in your career plan.

Some people ask to do temporary jobs to prove to an employer they can do a certain kind of work. For example, if you wanted to be a newspaper reporter, you might ask the editor to let you write one story. If the story is good, the editor might assign you others.

DID YOU KNOW?

DINO

Singer Dean Martin's first job was as a gas station attendant, but he later turned to boxing. By the time he was 20, he fought as a welterweight and won 24 out of his first 30 fights. A broken nose caused him to quit boxing and turn to card dealing in a gambling casino. When his gambling customers noted how well he sang, Dino then tried a new career in show business.

Full-time jobs are usually career jobs. How many hours does a worker in a full-time job work?

Full-time Jobs.   Full-time work amounts to about 40 hours a week. Full-time jobs are usually career jobs. As mentioned earlier, most people hold more than one full-time job in the field of their choice before reaching the job they want most.

REVIEW YOUR WORK

1. Name three good reasons for having a plan of action.
2. Name three different types of advanced education you can plan for.
3. Why might you have to plan for financial needs or personal duties?
4. What types of jobs may be included in your career plan?

What Goals Will You Set?

Goals *are the things you want to accomplish.* They are your reasons for doing something. Setting goals helps you move from where you are to where you would like to be. Your goals are your purpose for having a plan of action.

Some goals, such as receiving an A on tomorrow's assignment, are simple and can be reached quickly. Others are more difficult and take longer to reach.

Since goals are targets you're aiming for, they give direction to your life. Goals provide a focus for your energy, resources, and time. Because you are reaching for a goal, such as an A in class, you set aside time to study each day. Goals give meaning to each day. Goals are challenging, also. When you accomplish a goal, you feel good about yourself.

The previous chapters helped you identify your values. Values play a major role in deciding on your goals. How firmly you believe in the goal and how badly you want to achieve it will determine the amount of time, energy, and resources you will give to it. If security is one of your values, you will devote time, energy, and resources toward achieving goals that give you security.

Goal setting is easier if you use the following guidelines:

- **State your goals as clearly as possible.** Be specific. So you want to be a doctor. What kind? Doctors specialize in dozens of different areas. Maybe you can't be sure yet just *exactly* what your goal is, but get as close as you can.

Being specific is one of the important guidelines for setting goals. Why do you think being specific is so important?

- **Make the goals your very own.** Make your goals what *you* want, not what someone else wants for you.
- **Know the importance your values play in setting your goals.** Think about your values before you decide what you want.
- **Write down your goals.** Writing the goals helps you remember them. It also helps make them seem closer and more real.
- **Set a due date for your goals.** Some goals require little time and other goals require lots of time. Setting a date reminds you that you must set aside time to get the job done. It also gives you a day on which to celebrate another accomplishment!

    Goals can be short-range, middle-range, and long-range. Sometimes the time you have to reach a goal is beyond your control. For example, if an application is due February 1, then that's your due date. Sometimes goals must be reached in a certain order. For example, graduating from high school might be your short-range goal, finishing junior college your middle-range goal, and getting a job in an office your long-range goal.
- **Be sure your goals are realistic.** You want to aim high, but not so high that the goal is almost impossible to reach. If you can't reach most of your goals, you'll get discouraged. If necessary, set two kinds of goals. The goals you try for first should be sensible and down-to-earth. When those goals are accomplished, you can try for their more difficult versions.

    For example, C.J. wasn't doing well in English class. His first goal was to get a C. With his teacher's help, however, C.J. improved rapidly. His teacher agreed he should aim for a B instead.
- **Change your goals when needed.** Goals are targets that may be made larger, smaller, or done away with completely. Don't be afraid to change your goals.

REALISTIC . . . YES OR NO?

Q: How will I know if my goals are realistic?

A: Reread each goal. Ask yourself, what resources do I have to help me reach this goal? Have I done anything like this before and succeeded? Are there goals I need to accomplish before I can do this?

Making Your Own Plan

By now you may be tired of making lists and writing things down. Your other lists have helped though, and so will your plan. Writing down a plan helps you make it clear to understand. You can also refer to it anytime you need to.

You can use a plan for your weekly, monthly, or yearly goals. However, the information discussed below focuses on one target—your career goal.

Careers That Make Headlines

Extra! Extra! Read all about it!

What could be more exciting than the life of a reporter? They globetrot around the world to uncover the big stories and send back the news that people need to stay informed. In fact, many aspects of a reporter's job are exciting and glamorous. As members of the press, newspaper, magazine, radio, and television reporters often *seem* to be as important as the stories they are covering.

These jobs, however, require a great deal of hard work and are not always easy to find. The truly glamorous jobs for big newspapers or magazines or for television network news are few, and there is much competition among those individuals who want the jobs.

Even the less glamorous reporting jobs can be difficult to acquire. A person needs a college education and strong writing and communication skills to be considered for a career as a journalist. Many reporters then will spend years covering the less important and less glamorous stories before getting a shot at the type of story he or she might have always wanted.

Reporters, however, are not the only workers involved in keeping you and me informed about the important and interesting events of our world. Newspaper staffs include photographers, artists, and paste-up artists who make sure that the paper looks good and is easy to follow. Newspapers also depend on workers in the pressroom who handle the complicated jobs involved with printing a paper and workers in distribution who see that your paper arrives on your doorstep on time each morning.

Television and radio newscasts strongly rely on camera operators and sound engineers to make sure that the broadcasts are clear. Television news also requires the services of many other technicians, such as videotape editors, computer graphics specialists, and Tele PrompTer operators.

Workers are also needed to sell advertising to support the efforts of both newspaper and magazine reporters as well as radio and television reporters. Support staff members, including secretaries, clerks, accountants, and business managers are also vital to these operations.

As our world becomes more technologically advanced, our need for fast, accurate information also grows. Careers in journalism will become increasingly important. If you think you might be interested in this field, see your guidance counselor. Together, you can start on your way to the career you want.

MAKING CHANGES

Q: If you have to make changes in your career plan, what's the point of planning?
A: You have to make some adjustments in any plan. It shows you are thinking about what you want to do. As new events happen, you can make changes that will help the plan work for you. Remember, without a plan, you may not get anything done.

Take out the information you gathered on the career of your choice. You got this information by following the suggestions in Chapters 4 and 5. Then follow these steps.

1. At the top of one sheet of paper, write down your career choice. On the same sheet, note any special wants related to that choice, such as a certain salary or list of responsibilities. For example, Gali wanted to be the manager of a fast-food restaurant. He wanted the restaurant to be a member of a famous chain with high standards.

2. Next, take out three more sheets of paper. At the top of the first sheet, write "High School." At the top of the second sheet, write "Advanced Education or Training." At the top of the third sheet, write "Work Experience."

   On the first sheet, make a list of all the courses or activities you have to complete to get your diploma and prepare for what you must do after graduation.

   On the second sheet, list any training or education you plan to get after graduation. Be specific. Don't just write "graduate from college." Try to list the kinds of courses that will prepare you for a particular kind of work. If your only advanced training will be on the job, make a note here that the places you work must give you the type of training you want.

   On the third sheet, list the jobs you plan to get that will lead you toward your ultimate job goal. List all of them, including part-time work and volunteering. Don't worry about putting the lists in order yet.

3. Go over each list and assign dates. For a long-range goal, you may be able to estimate only the year. If some of your goals seem to get in the way of one another, make adjustments. For example, if you want to be able to leave school early for a part-time job, be sure the courses you need are taught in the morning. If no adjustment can be made, you may have to decide which goal is more important.

4. Next, using a new sheet of paper, write your plan of action. List all your goals according to the dates when you must get things done. On the next page is a sample plan for Gali, whose job goal is manager of a fast-food restaurant. Notice that his short-range goals are very specific and have exact dates.

   Remember, your plan should contain short-, middle-, and long-range goals. You are giving a date to each goal because it helps you keep track of your goals, gives you a sense of accomplishment, and reminds you of when you should reach the next goal.

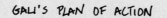

GALI'S PLAN OF ACTION

JOB GOAL: MANAGER OF FAST-FOOD RESTAURANT

	GOAL	BEGIN BY	COMPLETE BY
19—	TAKE BUSINESS MATH	SEPTEMBER 10	DECEMBER 15
19—	CONTINUE RESEARCH ON SPECIFIC RESTAURANT CHAINS	NOW	JANUARY 15
	CONTINUE WORKING AFTER SCHOOL AT HAPPY SAM'S HAMBURGER JOINT		JUNE 1
	TAKE BUSINESS ENGLISH	JANUARY 8	JUNE 6
	GRADUATE		JUNE 8
	REGISTER FOR BUSINESS COLLEGE		AUGUST 15
	BEGIN BUSINESS MANAGEMENT 101 (NIGHT SCHOOL)	SEPTEMBER 8	
19—	FINISH BUSINESS MANAGEMENT 101		JANUARY 5
	BEGIN BUSINESS MANAGEMENT 201 (NIGHT SCHOOL)	JANUARY 10	JUNE 5
	FINISH SAVING TOWARD BUSINESS COLLEGE		AUGUST 15
	QUIT JOB AT HAPPY SAM'S		AUGUST 17
	REGISTER FOR FULL-TIME CLASSES AT BUSINESS COLLEGE		AUGUST 18
	START BUSINESS COLLEGE FULL TIME	SEPTEMBER 6	
19—	COMPLETE BUSINESS MANAGEMENT COURSES		JUNE 7
	GET JOB AT FAST-FOOD CHAIN (BEGIN APPLYING IN JANUARY)		JUNE - JULY
19—	CONTINUE RESEARCH (AM I WORKING FOR THE BEST COMPANY?)		
	ENTER RESTAURANT MANAGEMENT TRAINEE PROGRAM		
19—	COMPLETE RESTAURANT TRAINEE COURSE		
	BECOME ASSISTANT MANAGER FOR RESTAURANT		
19—	BECOME MANAGER FOR RESTAURANT		

Don't let your long-range dates put too much pressure on you. They should be guides, not do-or-die deadlines. For example, Gali might not become a manager until after 1999. The chain may not have openings, or other things may get in the way. The date is a target to aim for that will increase his chances of reaching his goal.

5. Revise your plan as needed. Remember, your career plan is not carved in stone. Make it flexible, but try not to change it for foolish reasons. Think about what you are doing. Your career plan is a plan for your own future life.

CASE STUDY One day when Gali was working at Happy Sal's restaurant, it suddenly got very busy. Gali was asked to help the cook. He had never liked cooking for himself at home, but in the restaurant it was exciting. After that, whenever he could, Gali volunteered to help prepare the food. After a year, he carefully made a new career plan. Instead of going to business school, he went to a chef school. Today he is a successful pastry chef at an expensive restaurant. This was quite different from his original plan!

Thinking About the Case Study

1. Since he changed his career plan, did Gali waste his time by making the first career plan?

Now that your goals are set and your career plan finished, you are ready for action!

In the second part of this book, you will learn the steps to take in finding and keeping a real job. You will also learn more about what you need to do to be successful and happy in your career.

REVIEW YOUR WORK

1. Define goals.
2. Give five guidelines for setting goals.
3. Why is it helpful to set due dates for your goals?
4. What is a procrastinator?

Your Plan of Action

Be honest. Have you ever made a plan? Have you ever decided that you wanted something very badly and then planned carefully how to get what you wanted?

You're not alone if you answered no to the questions above. Many people live their entire lives without ever planning anything, even something as small as a weekend trip to the country or a picnic in the park. These people "play it by ear;" they believe in doing things spontaneously; they take things as they come. They think planning is silly. They say, "No one knows what tomorrow will bring. Why bother? Live for today."

From time to time, these people think of expensive items they'd like to have, faraway places they'd like to see, and feats they'd like to accomplish. However, nothing worthwhile comes easily. When they realize that time, effort, and planning are necessary, these "one-day-at-a-timers" give up on their dreams before they've even started.

You will not give up. In fact, you have already taken the first and most difficult step in creating any plan—you've made a decision. So **THINK POSITIVELY.** Having made a career decision in Chapter 5, you are already on the way to a successful career plan.

The biggest obstacle to success for most people is indecision. Many people don't know what they want. They drift from one job to another waiting for a lucky break or a flash of inspiration that never comes. They can't

plan how to reach their goals because they can't decide what their goals are.

However, if you've learned how to make decisions, you will have little trouble planning for your future. The first step is often the hardest, and you've already taken that step.

You need to do some more research to determine what steps you must take to reach your goal. Then sit down with paper and pencil, and write a step-by-step, detailed plan of action. You must also dedicate yourself to carefully checking your progress over the next weeks, months, and years so that you can make changes in your plan when they become necessary.

Does this sound like a lot of work? It is, but you can do it. Think positively. You've already taken that first and most difficult step in any plan— you've made a decision. You know what you want out of life. Now it's time to figure out how you'll reach your goal.

Chapter Summary

- Having a plan of action can save you time, money, and effort.
- A plan organizes your activities.
- Knowing what the educational requirements are for your chosen career is an important part of planning.
- Career research should be an ongoing process, even after you're established in a career. It helps you remain aware of opportunities and protect yourself from trends that may work against your long-term goals.
- You need to plan time for personal duties, part- or full-time work, and for recreation, too.
- Knowing your goals will help you stay focused on what you want to accomplish. Having goals is an important part of the planning process.
- Short-term and long-term goals are equally important. With a plan, it is easier to stay on track for both.

Reviewing Vocabulary and Concepts

Write the numbers 1–12 on a separate sheet of paper. After each number, write the letter of the answer that best completes the following statements.

1. A person who puts things off is called a _____ .
   a. smart person
   b. busy person
   c. lazy person
   d. procrastinator
2. A plan forces you to sort things out in order of _____ .
   a. importance
   b. what you want to do most
   c. unimportance
   d. what's more inexpensive
3. The tests you take to discover whether you have learned the things that are needed for a high school diploma are called _____ .
   a. vocational tests
   b. S.A.T. tests
   c. G.E.D. tests
   d. scholarship tests
4. The _____ sometimes offer a chance to learn a skill.
   a. school counselors
   b. armed services
   c. mistakes you make
   d. television comedy shows
5. Colleges and universities have programs for different career areas that take an average of _____ years.
   a. 2   c. 6
   b. 4   d. 8
6. Technical-vocational centers and junior or community colleges offer two-year programs in which you can earn a(n) _____ .
   a. lot of money
   b. associate degree
   c. a master's degree
   d. minimum wage
7. Career research should be part of your plans for _____ .
   a. a year or so
   b. five years
   c. twenty years
   d. the rest of your working life
8. Some professions require that you _____ your own equipment.
   a. get rid of   c. provide
   b. make   d. sell
9. A careful career plan makes it possible for you to _____ while you learn.
   a. work two jobs
   b. sleep a lot
   c. have a lot of fun
   d. earn money

10. Someone who learns on the job is
    _____ .
    a. a procrastinator
    b. an apprentice
    c. a poor planner
    d. not educated
11. The reasons for doing something, or
    the things you want, are _____ .
    a. goals   c. mistakes
    b. frivolous   d. outcomes
12. Goals should be _____ .
    a. too high   c. discouraging
    b. realistic   d. expensive

Thinking Critically About Career Skills

Write your answers to the following
questions on a separate sheet of paper.

1. Do you think it is important for people to plan time for rest and recreation? Why?
2. Why is setting a "due date" for
   goals important? Why should goals
   be realistic?

Building Basic Skills

1. **Organization**   Write a detailed
   career plan. Include dates and be
   specific.

2. **Mathematics**   Calculate the income
   from two different summer jobs.
   Suppose that you have two job offers. Job A would give you valuable
   experience in your chosen career
   area, but you would receive low pay
   ($3.50 per hour, 40 hours per week,
   for 12 weeks). Job B would not help
   you reach your career goal, but it
   pays extremely well ($7 per hour,
   40 hours per week, for 10 weeks).
   You have decided that you will take
   Job B if you can make at least
   $1,000 more than you could earn at
   Job A. Which job would you take?

Applying Career Skills

1. Visit one of the vocational schools,
   private schools, or colleges in your
   area. Find out the subjects in which
   that school specializes. Research
   other qualities the school has to
   offer besides academic courses. Report your findings to the class in a
   three-minute oral report.
2. Speak to your school's guidance
   counselor about your career decision. Discuss the courses you can
   take to help you reach your goal.
   Make a list of those courses.

EMPLOYMENT SKILLS

115

PART TWO

FINDING A JOB

OBJECTIVES

In this chapter you will learn about
- finding job openings
- organizing your job search
- organizing information about yourself
- arranging for references

Wouldn't it be fantastic if you could touch a key and get a computer printout of all the job openings for which you are qualified? Unfortunately, a job search isn't quite that easy. Finding the job you want, rather than just any job, takes lots of hard work and effort.

Although often frustrating and difficult, your job search can also be exciting and rewarding. When you look for a job, you learn a lot more about the world of work. You also learn more about yourself.

Don't start your job search until you know what you want to do. Too many people look for just any job and end up with jobs they don't like. The first step in any job search is knowing what job you want.

If you know what job you want, you can begin your search. A good place to start is with this chapter. You will learn how to gather job leads and organize your search. You will be on your way to finding the job that's right for you.

Gathering Leads

A large part of a job search is detective work. Detectives have to look for clues to solve their cases. When you look for a job, you have to develop some of the same skills. You have to sniff out clues and put them together for a complete picture of the job you want.

You can find out about job openings in several ways. Those discussed in this chapter include talking to people, using newspaper ads, and going to employment agencies.

Talking to People

A simple way to find out about available jobs is to talk with your friends and relatives. Ask them if they know of any jobs. If they don't, ask them to ask their friends. News travels fast. So use it to your advantage.

Make a list of all the people you know who might be aware of a job for you. Write down the names of friends who have just been hired. They might have turned down another job that would be just right for you.

Add to your list the names of friends' parents who are working. People already working for a company often hear about job openings before the openings are made public. Each working person you know is like a doorway into that company.

Some young people feel it is unfair to use inside help to get jobs. This is true only if you are the wrong person for the job.

You would be the wrong person for the job if you couldn't do the work, or if you were dishonest about your skills. If you are not qualified for a job and a friend helps you to get that job, you risk making both you and your friend look bad. Otherwise, using inside help is one of the best ways to find a job. Many of today's job holders heard about their jobs by word of mouth—by simply talking to people.

Talking with other people is a simple and often effective means of finding out about available jobs. Do many people find jobs this way?

Using Newspapers

The newspaper can help you learn about jobs available in your area. Libraries have copies of newspapers if you do not get one of your own.

In the newspaper is a section of ads called the classifieds. *The **classifieds** list many different kinds of advertisements for such things as items for rent or sale.* Most important, the classifieds list job openings.

Different newspapers may organize the classified section in different ways. A paper such as the *Denver Post* may use

You can use the classified ads in the newspaper to find out whether or not there are any jobs available in your chosen career area. If you do not get a newspaper at home, where can you find a copy to check out the classifieds?

one way and the *New York Times* may use another way. At the beginning of most classified sections is a directory or some other guide. This directory tells how the information is listed.

Usually each type of ad has a number. The "help wanted" ads, for example, may have the number 2400. To find these ads, you would look in the classified section for the number 2400. A sample ad is shown on the next page. Notice the number 2400 and the title "Help Wanted."

Some newspapers in larger cities also divide the job list by geographic areas. A newspaper in Chicago might list the jobs by suburbs such as Evanston, Skokie, or Cicero. Other large city newspapers may use abbreviations such as NE (northeast) or NW (northwest), which tell you in what part of the city the job is located. Almost all newspapers divide the list by type of job, such as clerical, sales, or teaching.

The next step is to learn the meaning of the words used in a job ad. Sometimes ads in the classified section are hard to understand because they include abbreviations and special words. For example:

CONCRETE lab tech.
HS, exp. pref. Salary nego.,
exc. fringe. EOE M/F,
Mobile Premix Concrete Co., Inc.,
I590 W. 12th Ave.

Can you read and understand this ad? The abbreviations used are as follows:

lab = laboratory
tech = technician
HS = high school; this means a high school education is needed
exp = experience
pref = preferred
nego = negotiable; this means the firm is willing to talk things over
exc = excellent
fringe = fringe benefits; this means insurance, vacation, and other benefits
EOE M/F = equal opportunity employer male/female; this means the firm will hire a person of any race, ethnic group, religion, or sex

This is how the same ad would read if the abbreviations were not used:

CONCRETE laboratory technician.
High school education needed, experience preferred.
Salary negotiable, excellent fringe benefits. Equal
opportunity employer, male/female.
Mobile Premix Concrete, Incorporated,
1590 West 12th Avenue

Most newspapers use the abbreviations on page 120. Learning these abbreviations will make it easier for you to read the help-wanted ads. Throughout this book you have seen sample ads as part of the Opportunity Knocks information. You should note these ads do not use abbreviations.

Don't be too scared by the experience or education required in an ad. Most companies write ads for the ideal employee. They know that most people do not have all of the qualities described in the ad.

What does this mean to you? If you come very close to what they ask for in the job ad, apply. You may come closer to meeting the description than anyone else and get the job.

Be aware of the ways in which certain words are used. Some words are hard to define. Ads sometimes have words such as *bright, personable,* and *mature*. These words have different meanings to different people. If a job ad reads, "Company needs a mature truck driver," does "mature" refer to the person's age? Does it mean a person who is responsible? If you are responsible, apply for the job.

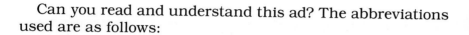

2400	Help Wanted

Detention Specialist
Career Opportunities

Min. age 19, Salary: $1,317/mo. (Shift Position). Closing date: January 12. Testing will consist of interview, psychological and mental ability tests, polygraph, and oral board. Psychological and mental ability tests will be conducted on January 15 at 1:30 p.m. at the Adams County Fair Grounds. Apply to the Adams County Sheriff's Dept., 1831 E. Bridge St., Brighton, CO 80601. EOE.

This is a typical help-wanted ad. What is the purpose of the number 2400 at the top of the ad?

Terms Used in Newspaper Ads

Abbreviation	Meaning
Adv'mt (also, ad)	Advertisement
DOE	Depends on experience; the work you've done before will affect the salary they offer
EOE	Equal opportunity employer; any person may apply for the job
Exc (also, ex.)	Excellent
Exp	Experience
K	Thousand; used with numbers to give salary; $10K means $10,000
Nego	Negotiable; you can bargain with them
PR	Public relations; communicating with the public, usually by means of TV, radio, or newspapers
Refs	References; people who can give information about you or your work
WPM	Words per minute; usually refers to typing or shorthand speeds
Apprentice	Someone who will be trained in a skill or trade
Benefits (also, ben.)	Insurance, vacations, etc., in addition to salary
Bonus	Money or gift in addition to the regular salary
Commission (also comm.)	Payment for selling something based on how much the customer paid for it and how many you sold
Minimum wage (also min. wage)	The least amount of money employers can legally pay a worker
Paid vacations or holidays	The company will pay for your time off
P.O.	Post Office; given with a number so you know where to mail your letter answering the ad
Promotable or advance from within	You will have a chance to move up to better jobs later on
Union	You must join an organization that bargains with the company for wages, benefits, etc., for its members; you must pay a fee

This chart lists many terms that are commonly used in newspaper ads. Why is it important to understand all parts of an ad?

Using Employment Agencies

An **employment agency** *is an organization that helps people find jobs.* Some employers don't like to advertise job openings in a newspaper. Instead they ask an employment agency to find someone for them. The people who need jobs go to the employment agency. Then the agency tries to match the people to the jobs on their list.

There are two types of employment agencies. One type is a private employment agency. The other is a public or state employment agency. Private agencies sometimes advertise in the newspaper. The state employment agency does not advertise jobs very often. Instead, you usually have to contact the agency to find out about the jobs.

Private Employment Agencies.   Private employment agencies charge a fee for matching people with jobs. *The* **fee** *is a certain amount of money or a percentage of your salary.*

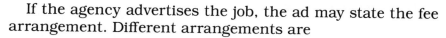

If the agency advertises the job, the ad may state the fee arrangement. Different arrangements are

- **Fee paid.** The employer pays the fee. You do not pay anything.
- **Half fee paid.** You pay half of the fee, and the employer pays half.
- **Applicant paid,** or just **fee.** You must pay all of the fee.
- **Fee refunded.** You pay the fee, but it is given back to you at a later time. This usually means the employer pays the agency later on.

If you ask a private employment agency to find you a job for a fee, you will have to sign a contract. The contract says the agency will find you a job. When you accept the job, the agency charges its fee. If you do not accept any of the jobs, you will not owe them any money.

Before you sign a contract, be sure you understand everything it says. The contract is a legal paper. Your signature means you will carry out the conditions of the contract. If you do not, the employment agency can take you to court.

An employment agency is an organization that helps people find jobs. What are the two types of employment agencies?

The contract will state

- **Who pays the fee.** This part describes the arrangement for payment of the fee.
- **The amount of the fee.** The fee charged is usually based on the job's salary. The higher the salary, the higher the fee. If you get a job that pays $800 a month, the fee will be higher than for a job that pays $600. The fee is usually equal to one or more months' salary.
- **How the fee will be paid.** Must it be paid all at one time or in parts? For example, the contract may say you must pay $37 by the fifth day of each month for eight months.
- **How much you will have to pay even if you don't stay with the company for long.** The amount owed is determined by how long you work for the company.
- **How much time you have to decide whether to take the job.** If you take the job within the time given, you must pay the agency its fee.

Again, a word of caution: Do not sign a contract unless you understand what it says. Be sure you know the fee arrangement. If you are not sure, ask for a copy to take home. Read it carefully. Have someone whose judgment you respect read it, too.

Also be aware that agencies only advertise the most appealing jobs. Those jobs may be taken right away. You might also find that these jobs are not quite as desirable as they sound in an ad.

Public or State Employment Agencies.   The public or state employment agency provides free service. All you must do is register with the agency. That is, you will have to

It is important to study contracts with employment agencies very carefully before you sign. You might want to ask your parents for advice. Why is understanding these contracts so important?

fill out a form. The form asks you your name and other personal information. It asks for your skills and interests.

A counselor at the agency will tell you about available jobs. The state employment agency, however, does not always arrange an interview for you. You may have to contact the companies yourself.

There are special agencies to talk to if you are interested in working for the government. Among these agencies are the city Civil Service Commissions, state Civil Service Centers, and federal Job Information Centers. Check the telephone book for addresses and phone numbers. Agencies are usually listed under "Government" and grouped by type: city, county, state, or United States government. Your librarian can help you find out about government agencies and how to locate the phone numbers in the telephone book.

On Your Own

You can also find a job by yourself if you know the type of job you want. The Yellow Pages of the phone book list companies. Businesses are listed by the goods they make or sell or the kinds of services they offer.

When you look for a job on your own, you do not know if the businesses you contact need new employees. You may have to contact a large number of companies before you find one that has openings. Be patient. This approach can be the most time-consuming of all. The suggestions given under "Should You Call or Write" in the next chapter may help make it easier for you.

In most newspaper classified sections there is a group of ads called "Situations Wanted" or "Jobs Wanted." These ads are placed by people like you who are looking for certain jobs. They hope employers will read the ads and give them a call. Sometimes these ads work, and you might want to try one. Keep in mind, however, that they cost you money. Most papers charge by the word or by the line.

CAREER Q&A

COMMUNITY RESOURCES

Q: How can I use my community to learn more about careers?

A: Talk to people in career areas that interest you. They may be able to recommend other people you can contact.

REVIEW YOUR WORK

1. How can talking to people you know be helpful in finding a job?
2. How would you go about finding a job through the newspaper?
3. What is the difference between private and public employment agencies?

Organize Your Job Search

A key to a successful job search is organization. Take it step by step. The time you spend now will be well worth it later on. If you are organized, your job search will go more smoothly. In the long run, you will save time and effort.

Job Lead Cards

You will talk to many people in your job search. It is easy to forget to whom you talked and what they said. Instead of saving scraps of paper or trying to remember names, set up a system for remembering.

Start by making a list of people who can help you find out about job openings. Add jobs listed in the classified ads. Add the names of the companies you've contacted.

Next, the names on this list need to be organized. A simple way is to use 3″ × 5″ cards or uniform slips of paper. Write each name from your list on a card. Each card should contain the following:

- person's name
- job title or type of work
- company and department
- address
- telephone number
- space for additional information

Job lead cards like this one help to organize your job search. Who should you make out job lead cards for?

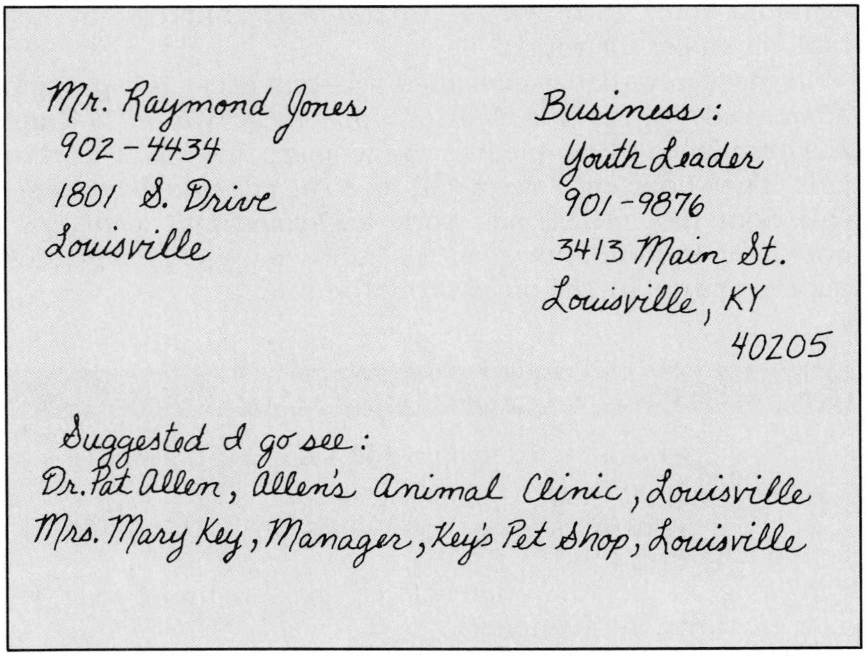

Mr. Raymond Jones
902 – 4434
1801 S. Drive
Louisville

Business:
Youth Leader
901 – 9876
3413 Main St.
Louisville, KY
40205

Suggested I go see:
Dr. Pat Allen, Allen's Animal Clinic, Louisville
Mrs. Mary Key, Manager, Key's Pet Shop, Louisville

Assume you want a job helping a veterinarian. You have called Mr. Jones, who is head of your youth group. He has given you the names of some people to call. The card for Mr. Jones might look like the one shown on page 124.

As you can tell from Mr. Jones' card, he has given you the names of two other people to call. One is Dr. Pat Allen, a local veterinarian. The other person is Mrs. May Key, an office manager for another veterinarian.

Make a card for Dr. Pat Allen and one for Mrs. Mary Key. Follow up with phone calls to Dr. Allen and Mrs. Key. After you have talked to these people, use the card for making notes about important information.

Keep your cards together and in order. If someone you have talked to calls you with a job, read that person's card and you will remember the person and the important facts.

Finding Information About Employers

You will want to know as much as possible about the employers to whom you apply for jobs. There are two important reasons for this.

First, you want the employer to like you. You know how flattered you are when someone takes the time to find out about you. People in business feel the same way. They'll be impressed that you took the time to find out more about their company.

Another important reason to learn about employers is that you want to be happy and successful where you work. You want to know what type of situation you will be working in. As you learn more about employers, you will like some businesses better than others. Then you can match what's important to you with what you learn.

What kind of facts might you want to find out about a business? That depends on the business, but here are some questions to get you started.

You should keep your job lead cards handy when you talk to potential employers. Why is this important?

- What kinds of goods or services are offered?
- Is the company growing and expanding?
- How large is the business, both in employees and profits?
- Do employees have a chance to move up in the company?
- Does the company have a good reputation with its employees as well as its customers?
- What type of employees does the company employ?
- What type of jobs does the company offer to employees?
- What benefits, such as additional training at company expense, insurance programs, or recreation and food facilities, does the company offer employees?

Finding a Job

It's usually not hard to find a job. You can open your local newspaper to the "Help Wanted" section almost any night of the week, call a few telephone numbers, and before you know it, you'll have a job. Of course the job may not pay much, and it may be boring, but you'll have found a job quickly without too much trouble.

Finding THE job, however—the job you really want—may not be quick or easy. Unless you are very lucky, you will probably have to work hard and plan your job search to find the job you want.

Looking for a job is something that most people do only a few times in their life. They don't do it because they want to. There are millions of people out of work, and there are always more people looking for jobs than there are jobs available. There is a lot of competition for jobs—especially for the best jobs. Job hunting can be discouraging and frustrating.

Reading this and knowing that you've never looked for a job before, you are probably wondering how you will ever find a good job—one that will pay well or help you gain some valuable experience. Don't worry. **THINK POSITIVELY.** If you really want that job, you'll find it.

You see, the key to finding a job is the same key to being successful once you have a job or a career. The key is hard work. If you work hard at finding a job, you'll find it. If you want that job enough to put in the time and effort, you will eventually find it.

Where do you start? You'll learn where to look and how to organize your job search in this chapter. Follow these suggestions. Make job lead cards. Contact as many people as possible, and don't quit until you find the right job.

Don't hesitate to ask for leads. Almost everyone will be eager to help you. Your parents, guardians, and older friends who are working will be on the lookout at their places of work. They will talk to people they know. You will call employers and ask them for leads. It will soon seem as though many people in your community are trying to find you a job.

Over and over you might hear, "No, we don't have any openings right now." Don't let those answers get you down. Just keep looking. Think positively. The job for you is out there somewhere. You'll find it.

If you have some information about a company, you can use it when you talk to people in that company. You can mention something about what you learned. For example, you might say, "I talked to a few people who do business with your store. They all liked the way the store was organized. They also liked the attention salespeople paid to them when they shopped." The people will know you are interested in the company and that you are adult enough to do some checking on your own.

There are several ways to gather information about a business.

- If you know any employees of the business, ask them about it.
- Talk to people who do business with the store or company. Ask them why they trade there. What do they like? What makes this business different from others?
- Call the business to see if there is a company magazine or annual report you can read.
- Call the Better Business Bureau in your area. Ask if they've had any bad reports about the company.
- Go to see the business if you can. This is easy to do if it is a store, and you can even look at a factory from the outside. How large does the business look? How busy does it seem to be? Are buildings in good repair? Are they clean? Finding information will take a little time and effort, but it will be worth it.

Gather Your Facts

The top salespeople are the ones who know the product they are selling inside and out. They know the strong and weak points of the product and can tell others about it.

Looking for a job means selling yourself. *You* are the product! The more facts you know about yourself, the better job of selling you will be able to do.

When you talk to employers, they will want to know about your education, skills, and interests, and about any jobs you've held. If you don't have accurate information or if you fumble around, you'll make a poor impression.

You'll also need your personal facts to complete application forms. You may also need a resume. Application forms and resumes are discussed in the next chapter.

Your personal information is needed each time you look for a job during your lifetime. If you organize your facts now, you can simply add to them as you get more experience.

OPPORTUNITY

KNOCKS

ADMINISTRATIVE ASSISTANT

Strong secretarial and administrative skills are always in demand for jobs like this.

ADMINISTRATIVE ASSISTANT

Would you like to work for a top marketing executive? Do you have excellent secretarial skills? Are you a self-starter? One of the country's leading real estate development firms wants you! Your administrative and word processing skills may be your ticket to success! Call for immediate appt.

Which do you think would be more important for someone applying for this job: strong secretarial skills or knowledge of the real estate business?

> *Personal Information*
>
> William L. Levine
> 3070 Rice Street
> Bridgeport, CT 06430
> (214) 555-3037
> Social Security number: 000-00-0000
> Age 18
> Birthdate: June 19, 19—
> Height: 6'1"   Weight: 180 pounds

You will need to have your personal information handy when you apply for jobs. How can preparing your information in advance help make your job search more successful?

Take out several pieces of blank paper. These are your work sheets. On the top of each sheet write one of these headings

- Personal Information
- Education
- Work Experience
- Activities and Interests
- Special Skills
- References

As you read through this chapter, fill out your work sheets. You do not have to show these sheets to anyone else now. Later, however, you will have to share the information with employers. The information you give may help them decide if you are the person they want to hire. Therefore, it is important to be accurate and complete.

Personal Information.   Employers need background information about you to get a better picture of who you are. They also need to know where you live in order to reach you. On your sheet, write this information

- full name
- address and zip code
- social security number
- place of birth, including name of city and state
- general health
- parents' or guardians' names, phone numbers, and work addresses
- name of person and phone number to contact in case of emergency

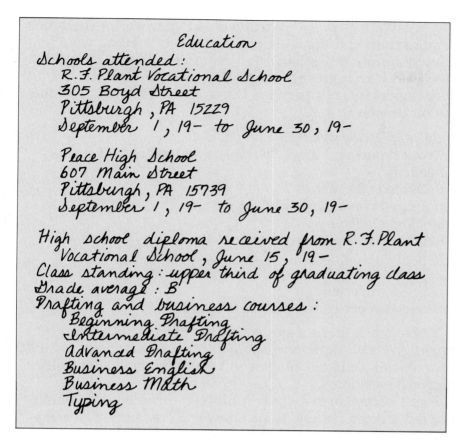

Education

Schools attended:
  R. F. Plant Vocational School
  305 Boyd Street
  Pittsburgh, PA 15229
  September 1, 19— to June 30, 19—

  Peace High School
  607 Main Street
  Pittsburgh, PA 15739
  September 1, 19— to June 30, 19—

High school diploma received from R. F. Plant
  Vocational School, June 15, 19—
Class standing: upper third of graduating class
Grade average: B
Drafting and business courses:
  Beginning Drafting
  Intermediate Drafting
  Advanced Drafting
  Business English
  Business Math
  Typing

Employers may also want to know about your educational background. Which courses should you list on your education work sheet?

Education.   Employers will want to know about any school classes you have taken which would help you on the job. They may ask you about your grades. They may also want to know about any special awards you have received, such as those for perfect attendance, good grades, or shop projects.

Mary Wong is looking for a job in drafting. What might interest an employer? Mary's educational background is listed above. On her work sheet Mary listed these things

- names, addresses, and dates of attendance for her high schools and vocational schools (list in order, beginning with the most recent one)
- diplomas or certificates she has earned
- rank according to grades in her graduating class (list only if you are in the upper quarter or third of your class)
- grade average (list only if As and Bs or 90s and 80s)
- school honors
- courses she has taken which are helpful for jobs she is interested in
- on-the-job training or other special training she has had

Work Experience.   Writing about your work experience is more than making a list of your jobs. It's telling what you have done on those jobs. For example, Mike worked as a stock clerk in a grocery store. The job title may not sound very important, but perhaps the work is. This is what Mike did on the job

- counted stock weekly
- wrote reports on stock to tell the manager what was needed
- unloaded shipments
- prepared fresh fruits and vegetables for display
- stocked shelves
- helped with yearly inventory
- helped customers find what they needed
- kept the store clean
- bagged groceries
- carried groceries to customers' cars

Every stock clerk's job is a little different. One employer might give a clerk more responsibility than another. Listing your duties tells an employer what you, not some other person, have done.

Don't forget to list your volunteer experiences—things you did but did not ask to be paid for. For example, you may have been a volunteer worker at a youth club. As a volunteer you may have helped organize activities, answer the phone, or put up displays. Maybe you volunteered to manage the basketball team. What did you do as manager?

This teen's job title is produce clerk. Why is it important for him to list the duties he performed as a produce clerk?

WORK EXPERIENCES

TOTAL VALUE GROCERY STORE
3051 SPRUCE STREET
SAN FRANCISCO, CA 94901
(415) 555-1616

STORE MANAGER -- MS. EDITH JONES
DATES OF EMPLOYMENT -- JUNE 15, 19— TO AUGUST 31, 19—

JOB AND DUTIES
    STOCK CLERK
            ·COUNTED STOCK WEEKLY
            · WROTE REPORTS ON STOCK TO TELL MANAGER WHAT WAS NEEDED
            · UNLOADED SHIPMENTS
            · PREPARED FRESH FRUITS AND VEGETABLES FOR DISPLAY
            · STOCKED SHELVES
            · HELPED WITH YEARLY INVENTORY
            · HELPED CUSTOMERS FIND WHAT THEY NEEDED
            · KEPT STORE CLEAN
            · BAGGED GROCERIES
            · CARRIED GROCERIES TO CUSTOMERS' CARS

SKILLS LEARNED
            · HOW TO TALK TO CUSTOMERS
            · HOW TO WORK WITH OTHERS
            · HOW TO TAKE AN INVENTORY
            · HOW TO WRITE WEEKLY REPORTS
            · HOW TO GIVE DIRECTIONS TO OTHERS

PAY
    STARTED AT $XX AN HOUR; AFTER 6 MONTHS WAS GIVEN A RAISE
    TO $XX AN HOUR

LIKED ABOUT JOB
            · MET NEW PEOPLE
            · LEARNED ABOUT HOW A BUSINESS OPERATES

REASONS FOR LEAVING
            · WANTED HIGHER PAY
            · NEEDED MORE FLEXIBLE WORK HOURS
            · WANTED MORE RESPONSIBILITIES

Making a list of your skills will help you present yourself in the best possible way for each employer. When listing work experiences, should you only list paid positions?

The more facts you can list, the more you'll remember to tell an employer about. Your list of experiences should include

- name, address, and phone number of each business or organization you worked for
- dates you began and left each job
- your job title and duties
- skills you learned on the job
- progress made on the job, such as pay increases, bonuses (extra pay), or moving on to higher jobs
- pay earned
- special assignments or awards
- what you liked and disliked about the experience
- your reason for leaving

The way Mike organized his work experiences is shown in the example above.

Activities and Interests.   Employers can learn more about you if they know what you do for fun or what you're interested in. An employer may even have interests like yours, and then you will have something to talk about. Some items to include on your work sheet are

- school clubs and/or teams you belonged to
- committees you served on
- offices held and special jobs done
- hobbies and leisure time activities you enjoy, such as basketball, fixing cars, sewing

Your interests and abilities can often be helpful in getting a job. Why do you think employers might be interested in your activities and interests?

> Wayne O'Connor
> Activities and Interests
>
> School activities:
> - Member of track team for 19- and 19- seasons
> - Member of drafting club; treasurer since 19-
> - On ticket committee for senior prom
>
> Hobbies:
> - Working with wood -- making cabinets, toys for kids
> - Stamp collecting
> - Photography -- our local paper used two of my photos of the Homecoming football game this year
> - Running -- Placed fifth in city marathon last year
> - Playing computer video games

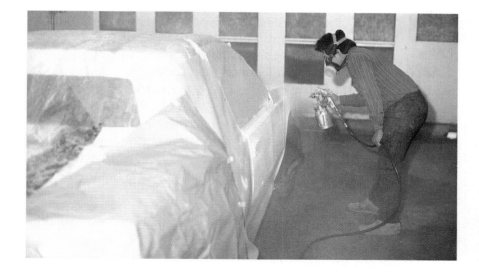

The ability to use power tools is a skill that should also be listed. Can you name some other special skills you might want to list?

Special Skills.   You have already made a list of your skills for Chapter 2. Add this list to the information you are gathering now about yourself. If you can speak a language other than English, operate a machine, or use some tools well, this is the time to list it. Possible skills would include

- drawing and painting
- math ability
- use of carpentry tools
- ability to speak Spanish
- ability to operate a cash register
- ability to use a computer

References.   When you apply for a job, most employers will ask you for your references. *Your* **references** *are people who know you and who know the kind of work you do or the kind of person you are.* Some of the people who might be your references include

- former or present employers
- former or present teachers
- people who worked with you on volunteer jobs
- sponsors of organizations you belong to
- reliable people in your city or community

It is best not to use the names of relatives as references. Employers usually feel that relatives might want to tell only the best things about you. People not related to you may be better able to see your weak as well as your strong points.

Always ask people first if you can use them as references. Ask, too, if they can give you a good recommendation. If they can't, then ask someone else.

DID YOU KNOW?

NOT JUST FOR FUN

Students who get involved with school clubs, sports, or leadership groups develop an edge when it comes to working with people. Mention your school activities when you go for an interview because it lets the employer know you have had successful experiences even if your grades aren't tops.

CASE STUDY Ramon asked for a recommendation this way:

"Ms. Bass, I'm going to apply for a job at Pete's Pet Shop. If I get the job, I'll be working there after school and on Saturdays. I was wondering if I could use you as a reference."

Ms. Bass replied, "Why Ramon, I'd be happy to let you do that. I was pleased with your work for me at the sandwich shop last summer. I'm only sorry that we don't need more help now so you could work for me while you're in school."

"I'm sorry, too. I really liked working here. So I can count on a good recommendation from you?"

"By all means, Ramon."

"Thanks a lot. I really want this job. It means a lot to me."

Thinking About the Case Study

1. In choosing Ms. Bass as a reference, did Ramon make a good choice? Why?

Asking people to be references is easy, and it helps them remember you. When you take the time to see them personally, they may speak even more highly of you.

Having at least three references is best. Be sure to write down information about each person. Include the person's name, job title, address, and phone number. Check to be sure the name and address are spelled right. An example of the way to list a reference is

Ms. Sue Bass, Manager
Sandwiches Unlimited, Inc.
1500 Pine Street
New York City, New York 10461
(212) 455-3044

REVIEW YOUR WORK

1. What information should go on job lead cards?
2. Why is it important to find out information about employers? What information would be helpful?
3. Why is it important to write down information about yourself before looking for a job? What information do you need to organize?

Building Your Future

One day there is an empty lot on the corner, the next day there is a fence around the lot and the whole area is teeming with workers in hard hats. Soon, where once there was an empty lot, stands a building.

Many people find themselves fascinated by the work that goes into creating and building a structure big enough to house a family or a business. If you feel this way, maybe you should explore a career in the construction industry. You will find that there are jobs in the construction industry for every skill.

Whenever a building is built, someone must design and create the look of the building. This is the job of the architect. Architects blend the beauty of the art world with the hard facts of engineering to produce a structure that is both pleasing to the eye and structurally sound. Becoming an architect requires a great deal of training and education. Especially needed are strong backgrounds in mathematics and mechanical drawing.

Architects, however, are not the only ones involved in the process of building new structures. Heavy equipment operators are needed to dig out the earth for the foundation. Cement mixers are needed to haul in and pour the cement.

Contractors and workers from many different fields are also involved in putting up a structure. Electrical contractors and workers are needed to wire the structure and see that the electrical needs are met. Plumbers handle the pipes for bathroom, kitchen, and all other plumbing fixtures and needs.

Framers build the general frame of the structure. Drywall installers and other finishers build the interior walls

and ceilings. Carpet layers, painters, and roofers also help to finish the structure. Throughout the construction, building inspectors check to be sure that the building meets all legal guidelines for safety and soundness.

Once the building is completed, real estate workers go to work to see that it is occupied as soon as possible.

As you can see, there are many workers involved with the building of most structures. This means that there is also a need for support workers, such as secretaries and payroll clerks for the construction companies.

If you would like to turn your fascination with the construction process into a career, see your guidance counselor. He or she can help you make sure that you take all the right courses so that you can build your career on a firm foundation.

Chapter Summary

- Gathering leads for finding a job is an investigative process. Three ways to job hunt are talking to people, using newspaper classified ads, and going to employment agencies.
- The section of the newspaper that advertises employment openings is called the classifieds.
- An employment agency is an organization that helps people find work. There are two kinds of agencies: private and public or state.
- You can find a job by contacting companies on your own.
- Always try to find out as much as you can about a business before you go for an interview.
- Remember, when you go for an interview, you should have all your information ready and organized.
- References are important. Before listing someone as a reference, you should talk to him or her.

Reviewing Vocabulary and Concepts

Write the numbers 1–13 on a separate sheet of paper. After each number, write the letter of the answer that best completes the following statements.

1. Gathering leads for jobs can be compared to _____ .
   a. being a detective
   b. climbing Mt. Everest
   c. working in a factory
   d. mopping a floor
2. In the newspaper, there is a section of ads called _____ .
   a. display ads
   b. church listings
   c. real estate ads
   d. the classifieds
3. These ads use a lot of abbreviations to _____ .
   a. make reading difficult
   b. save space
   c. be mysterious
   d. make them more interesting
4. There are two kinds of employment agencies: private employment agencies and _____ employment agencies.
   a. business
   b. factory
   c. public or state
   d. part-time
5. If you sign up with a private employment agency, be sure to read and understand _____ before signing.
   a. the contract   c. the work order
   b. your resume   d. the address
6. Your librarian can help you find out about _____ agencies.
   a. part-time   c. publishing
   b. temporary   d. government
7. Another place to locate types of businesses you might want to work for is _____ .
   a. bulletin boards at markets
   b. phone book Yellow Pages
   c. church directory
   d. club directories
8. The key to a successful job search is _____ .
   a. getting angry
   b. organization
   c. talking about it all the time
   d. taking a long vacation
9. A 3 × 5 card on which you list a person's name, job title, company, address, phone number, and additional information is _____ .
   a. a job lead card
   b. an interview record
   c. a waste of time
   d. a resume

10. There are two reasons to find out about companies you'll be interviewing with. One is because you want the employer to like you; the other is because _____ .
    a. you will want to be happy where you work
    b. you'll know when to take a vacation
    c. you will know how to dress
    d. you'll know how much they pay

11. Employers need personal background information about you because they _____ .
    a. are nosey
    b. don't trust you
    c. want to complicate things
    d. want a better picture of who you are

12. A fee is a _____ or a percentage of your salary.
    a. certain amount of money
    b. tax
    c. contract
    d. refund

13. _____ are people you know and who know the kind of work you do.
    a. Friends   c. Counselors
    b. Parents   d. References

Thinking Critically About Career Skills

Write your answers to the following questions on a separate sheet of paper.

1. There are millions of people looking for work each day, and there are more people than there are jobs. What does this mean to you as a job seeker?

2. Put yourself in an interviewer's place. What kind of person would you like to be talking to? What would you like this person to know about your company? What would you like to know about this person? List at least five questions you would want answered by a person you're interviewing.

Building Basic Skills

1. **Writing** Speak with a job counselor or someone who works for a private or public employment agency about how their agency helps people find jobs. Write a report that summarizes your findings.

2. **Mathematics** Calculate the employment agency fee if the agency gets you a job at $16,000 a year, and you sign a contract agreeing to pay 15 percent of your salary for your first year of employment.

Applying Career Skills

1. Make a list of at least three people that you could use as references for a job interview. Talk with these people to make sure they would give you a good reference. Save your list for later use.

2. Make a list of abbreviations found in the classified ad section that you do not know. Find out what the abbreviations stand for. Report your findings to the class.

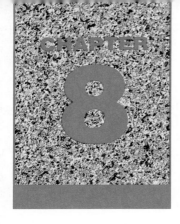

CHAPTER 8

APPLYING FOR A JOB

Applying for a job is not always easy. Experienced people and first-time job seekers all feel somewhat nervous. If you feel unsure of what to do, you are not alone.

Getting a job is important. You'll want to do your best, so that you are the person who is hired.

In this chapter you will learn how to contact employers and give them information about yourself. You will also learn how to prepare for and handle a job interview. By reading this chapter you will increase your chances of being successful in your job search.

Should You Call or Write?

There are three ways to contact an employer about a job. You may telephone, write, or stop in without an appointment. Which method works best for you will depend on each situation.

Telephone Calls

The telephone call is the most common way to talk to employers about a job. When you telephone, you want employers to form in their minds the best possible picture of you. You can lose a job opportunity by making a bad impression on the telephone. Here are some things to remember when you use the phone.

- Think about what you want to say before you call.
- Give your name.
- If possible, know the name of the person you want to speak with before you call.
- Identify the job you are calling about.
- Know your schedule so you can make an appointment without hesitating. Write dates, times, and addresses on your job lead card.
- Have your information sheets handy so you can answer questions.
- Be prepared to point out your qualifications for the job.

The telephone call is the most common way to contact employers about a job. What steps can you take before calling to help you make the best possible impression during the call?

- Speak clearly and loudly enough to be heard and at a medium speed.
- Don't have gum or food in your mouth.
- Keep loud noises out of the background. Turn off the radio, TV, or stereo and try to find a spot where you're alone.
- Keep the mouthpiece of the phone near your mouth and not under your chin or close to your cheek.
- Choose a sensible time. Many businesses close by 5 p.m., so do not call at 10 minutes to 5 or during the lunch hour. From 9 to ll and 2 to 4 are good times.
- Try to smile while you are talking. When you are smiling, your voice sounds more relaxed and happy. You can imagine you are smiling at the person to whom you are speaking. Does that seem silly? If you think it does, try it. If you can, record your voice when you are smiling and when you aren't. You will hear the difference.

Writing a Letter

Employers often ask to be contacted by letter. In many cases they do this to find out which applicants can write good, clear English. In other cases, writing a letter is necessary because the job is out of town. In each of these situations, how well you write your letter will determine whether or not you are given an interview.

Your letter may give all the necessary information, as does the sample on the next page. Your letter might introduce your resume, which should be attached. (Resumes are discussed on page 145.)

Going to your first job interview can be a very stressful but exciting event. Why do you think job interviews can be stressful?

In the first paragraph of your letter, identify the job you are writing about. Mention how you found out about the job. Was it through a newspaper ad or did an employee with the business tell you about the job?

The next paragraph should talk about your abilities. Tell why you are a good person for that particular job. If you do *not* send a resume, you should briefly describe your school record and your work experience. If you *do* send a resume, you should mention that the resume is enclosed.

The final paragraph should contain two items. It should include a request for an appointment at the employer's convenience. It should also state information about when and how you can be reached.

Remember, your application letter will represent you to the employer. Is it better to type or use longhand in preparing your letter?

1111 Latham Avenue
Cheyenne, Wyoming 98760
May 17, 19— —

Mr. Porter Eliot, Manager
MacDonald Oil Company
890 George Street
Cheyenne, Wyoming 98760

Dear Mr. Eliot:

On June 6, I will graduate from Cheyenne High School after three years as a business student. I would like to apply for the assistant secretarial position you advertised in the Cheyenne Journal on May 16.

During my business training I have taken the following courses:

Typing I and II	Shorthand I and II
Business Math	Business Machines
Bookkeeping I and II	Business English

After my last skill tests, my typing speed was 75 words per minute with two errors, and my shorthand speed was 100 words per minute. I was in the upper fourth of both my typing and shorthand classes. I was also a member of Junior Achievement, and I wrote a column about job opportunities in Cheyenne for our school paper.

Since 19-- I have worked after school for Perkin's Grocery in Cheyenne as a checker. During the summer of 19-- I was a receptionist for Ace Trucking Company, also in Cheyenne. While there, I operated an IBM Memory Typewriter, the Xerox 1500 copier, and a call director with fifteen lines.

I'd be happy to meet with you for an interview. You may reach me at the above address or by phone at 555-1697 after 4 p.m.

Yours truly,

Linda Ibbetson

Linda Ibbetson

Use the following checklist to help you with your letter.

- Is the letter neat, preferably typed on good 8 ½″ × 11″ paper?
- Is it short, no more than four or five paragraphs?
- Does it mention the job for which you are applying?
- Does it sound interesting?
- Does it refer to your resume (if enclosed)?
- Did you sign your name in ink?
- Does the letter look balanced on the paper?

Stopping By

Just to stop by and apply for a job without calling first is usually not a good idea. People might think you don't care how busy they are. They might also think you are not very serious about wanting a job since you haven't called ahead to make an appointment.

Of course, there are exceptions. For some jobs, such as factory work, appointments are not usually necessary. The job ad may tell you just to stop in, or you may be passing by and wish to make an appointment later.

If, for some good reason, it is necessary for you to go in without an appointment, be sure to apologize and explain your reasons.

Just to stop by and apply for a job without an appointment is usually not a good idea. Why do you think it is acceptable in this case?

Application Forms

For almost all jobs, you will be given an application form to fill out. *The* **application form** *asks for information about you, your education, and your work experience.*

A sample application form is shown on the next page. Application forms vary from company to company. Some forms are long; others are short. The questions on each form are different.

Application forms may look simple to fill out, but it is easy to make a mistake. Take time to study the form before you write in the information.

The easiest way to be prepared for filling out an application form is to carry a summary of your information with you. You needn't carry all of your work sheets, but dates, addresses, phone numbers, and correct spellings of names are especially important. That information can be written on small index cards or in a small notebook. Keep these facts with you and you will be less likely to forget them or make mistakes.

People will form an impression about you based on the way you fill out the application form. You cannot be too neat or careful when filling out an application form. The following guidelines will help you keep from making a mistake.

- **Read the entire application form before you write any answers.** Notice how much space you have for each answer to prevent running out of room or cramming in information. Think about your answers before you write them, and make sure you put the information on the correct lines.
- **Read the instructions.** Does the form tell you to print, write, or type the information? Find out if your last name comes first or your first name.
- **Be neat.** By planning how you are going to answer each item, you won't make a mistake. Planning helps you avoid erasing or crossing through answers. If you make many mistakes, ask for another form. Some people ask for two forms right at the beginning. They use one as a rough copy. The second form is the finished and accurate one that they turn in.
- **Give all the information requested.** Some questions may not apply to you. For example, the form may ask for military service, and you have probably not served in the military. Still, you should not leave this question blank.
- **Answer questions that don't apply to you in one of two ways.** You can write *NA* in the blank. NA means "not

APPLICATION FOR EMPLOYMENT

Name_____   _____
        Last   First   Middle   Social Security Number   Date

Address_____ Home Telephone Number_____

City_____ State_____ Zip Code_____ Period of Residence_____

Previous Address_____   _____
          Street   City   State   Zip Code   Period of Residence

Position Applying For_____ When Available_____ Salary Expected_____

Have you previously applied for work with us? ( ) Yes   ( ) No   If yes, when _____

Referred By (Name)_____

Is there anything that would prevent you from performing the duties of the position for which you are applying? ( ) Yes   ( ) No
If yes, explain_____

Are you currently under the care of a doctor? ( ) Yes   ( ) No   If yes, describe in full_____

Have you ever been convicted of a felony? ( ) Yes   ( ) No   If yes, describe in full_____

Do you have a Driver's License? ( ) Yes   ( ) No   If yes, give number and state issued_____

Person to notify in case of emergency_____ Relationship_____ Phone_____

EDUCATIONAL DATA

SCHOOL	NAME	CITY & STATE	MONTH & YEAR FROM	TO	DEGREE OR GRADE LEVEL COMPLETED	AREA OF SPECIALTY
Grade						
High						
College University						
Graduate School						
Trade, Business or Other						
Special Skills (List)				Typing Speed WPM		Shorthand Speed WPM

RECORD OF PREVIOUS EMPLOYMENT

(Detailed explanation may be attached to indicate any special employment experience)

PAST EMPLOYERS Company Name, Address, Phone Number	Department(s) Worked	Supervisor(s) Name	Position(s) Held	Employed From	To	Rate Of Pay	Reason For Leaving

You may contact all of the above listed employers except _____

For Applicant's additional comments or information not covered by the Form, such as; career, interests, plans, objectives, etc. _____

This Company complies with Title VII of the Civil Rights Act of 1964 (as amended), Executive Order 11246, Sec. 402 of the Vietnam Era Veteran's Readjustment Assistance Act of 1974 and Sec. 503 of the Rehabilitation Act of 1973 (as amended).

This Application will be retained in our active files for one (1) year only. If you wish to submit another application after this period of time, please feel free to do so.

I agree to abide by all the rules of the Company and will obey the orders and instructions of my supervisor. I will use and wear all safety appliances furnished me by the Company and will be careful in my work and not expose myself or other workers to unnecessary dangers.

In the event of my employment, I understand that a physical examination may be required to be passed.

It is understood that false statements on this application may result in my dismissal.

Signature of Applicant _____ Date _____

applicable." The other way is to draw a short line through the blank. Either method means you have read the question and it does not apply to you. If you don't use one of the two ways, the employer may think you avoided answering the question, or that you were careless and did not see it.

- **Know the kind of work you want.** If the application asks what kind of job you want, write a specific job title. For example, instead of writing "something secretarial," write "a secretary, a clerk-typist, or a receptionist." By all means, avoid writing "any job." The person reading the application may think you're desperate or that you'll change jobs soon.

- **Double-check the completed form.** Make sure you have responded to every item. Check for spelling. If you are not sure of the spelling, ask to use a dictionary or spelling aid or use another word—one that you can spell. Make sure you sign the form on the line asking for your signature. The form usually asks for the day's date. Be sure it is the correct date.

The Resume

For your first jobs, you will probably be asked to fill out an application while you are in the company's office. Sometimes, though, you may apply for a job out of town, or later on you may have to write to ask for an appointment.

In these cases you may have to give information about yourself in the form of a resume. *A* **resume** *is a summary of all the important information about you.* It will show your personality and give you a chance to point out your best qualities.

You will want to type your resume very neatly on good paper. Your goal will be to write your resume in such a way that the employer will want to hire you.

Look at William's resume on the next page. At the top, it states the type of job William wants. Next it points out things William has done which help to make him the right person for the job. School is listed next, then work experience. Finally, any activities or interests related to the job are given. Some people also list references at the bottom of their resume.

Remember, your resume represents you. It may even have to speak for you to someone who has never met you or talked to you! Be sure it is done neatly and that there are no

CAREER Q&A

TYPECAST AS A WINNER!

Q: If I don't type, can I send in a handwritten resume?
A: Handwritten resumes can really leave the wrong impression. It is always best to type your resume, even if you have to pay to have it done. Remember, your resume is an important part of the impression you make with employers!

A resume gives your important background information so employers can quickly find out what they need to know about you. How should your resume be prepared?

William Dean

336 Chestnut Street
New Orleans, Louisiana 70068
(504) 555-9900

OBJECTIVE: Would like a job working with cars. Goal is to become supervisor of an auto service center someday.

QUALIFICATIONS: Have had two semesters of auto mechanics at school.
Am interested in old cars, and my uncle and I compete in the car rodeo every month.
One of four finalists chosen for the Small Engine Fair.

EDUCATION: Uptown High School senior. Will graduate in June. Enrolled in vocational program.
Related courses: Auto Mechanics I and II
                              Small Engine Repair I

WORK EXPERIENCE: 19XX to 19XX—Attendant at filling station that has six islands.
19XX to 19XX—salesperson for small parts department at Benton Auto Parts Company.
Have also had part-time jobs, such as cleaning yards and repairing lawn mowers after school.

ACTIVITIES
AND INTERESTS: Member of Uptown High School Industrial Arts Club, 19XX-19XX.
Member of Electronics Club, Uptown Youth Center, and Auto Rodeo Club.

---

misspelled words. Make several photocopies and keep them on hand. Save your typed original in case you need to make more copies.

REVIEW YOUR WORK

1. What should you remember when calling an employer about a job for the first time?
2. What information should be included in a letter asking about a job? What other points should you keep in mind when writing the letter?
3. What do you need to remember when filling out application forms?
4. When might you use a resume? What information should you include in your resume?

The Interview

When going on job interviews, remember that you want a job. Also keep in mind that the company needs someone to fill a position. An interview is a two-way street. The people interviewing you are as eager to make a happy match as you are.

A job **interview** *is a get-acquainted meeting between the job seeker and the employer.* In this section you'll read about interviewing . . . how to get ready for it, what goes on, and what you should do afterward. When you go to your first interview, you will know what to expect. You'll also stand a good chance of being successful if you follow the suggestions given.

Before the Interview

What you do before the interview is as important as what you do during the interview. One thing you can do is to worry a lot. "Maybe this person won't like me." "I'm not sure this is the right outfit to wear." "I have the worst time talking to strangers. I won't be able to think of a thing to say."

Don't let yourself think such thoughts or you'll talk yourself into failure. Most people who fear the worst find their concerns never come to pass.

Think positively. Remember the good impressions you made on people in the past. Remember the times you went into new situations and handled them well. Keep these thoughts in your mind.

A job interview is a get-acquainted meeting between the job seeker and the employer. What do the interviewer and the interviewee have in common?

How can you get your interview off to a good start before it even begins? Go through a practice interview. Give some thought to your grooming and dress. If you pay attention to details *before* your interview, you'll be more relaxed during the interview.

The Practice Interview.

If you can, arrange with a friend to do a practice interview. Act it out. If possible, ask a friend who has already been on an interview and knows what one is like. Going through a practice interview helps you know what to expect. It also helps you find out if you're prepared.

If you can't arrange a practice interview, make an appointment for an interview for a job that would *not* be your first or second choice. This way you can have a real interview. You can find out what to expect and get rid of some of your nervousness. You'll be more sure of yourself when an important interview comes along. Who knows? The "practice" job may even be better than you first thought, and you may want to go after it!

Don't forget what you learned in Chapter 7 about ways to gather information about employers and work it into the interview. Practice this, too.

Grooming and Dress.

Be sure you're well-groomed. Well-groomed people are clean and neatly dressed.

Why is good grooming important? If you get the job you will be a representative of the company. Employers generally hire people who dress and behave about the same way they do. Being well-groomed is also one of the ways you show others you have pride in yourself.

Poorly groomed people often lose out before they get started. Employers take one look and eliminate these people, regardless of their skills and abilities.

How can you tell whether or not you're well-groomed? Being clean is very important. Start or finish the day with a shower or bath. Take one even if you don't think you need it. When people are nervous, they are more likely to perspire. You are not as aware of your body odors as other people are. Deodorant and perfume do not cover up body odor.

Clean, short- to medium-length fingernails are best. When you shake hands with people, your nails will be one of the things they notice. Dirty or long, clawlike nails are a "turn off" to others. If you wear polish on your nails, be sure it is not chipped. Stick to the average range of colors and avoid extremes.

You should always be clean and neatly dressed for an interview. Why do you think this is important?

The length and style of your hair are also important. Your hair should look businesslike. Extreme or very trendy hairstyles could keep you from getting a job. You may be as good a worker as others with a more conservative style and never have a chance to prove it. People sometimes judge others with flashy hairstyles more harshly. It's not fair to judge others this way, but it's done.

If you have an unusual or ornate hairstyle, think about making it simpler so it won't hurt your chances of getting a job. After you get the job, you may be able to let your hair grow again. By that time you will have shown you can do a good job. Others may be more willing to accept your "new look." At the very least, be sure your hair is clean and brushed.

Dress conservatively. *Conservative* dress means "middle-of-the-road" dress. Avoid extremes. For example, if you are looking for a job in a factory or repair shop, clean work clothes or a shirt and jeans would be appropriate dress. For an office job, a shirt, tie, and jacket would be best for a male. For a female, a skirt and blouse or a businesslike dress are good choices. Avoid shoes with very high heels, fancy sandals, loud colors, sexy styles, gaudy jewelry, heavy makeup, and heavy perfume.

Check to be sure that your clothes are clean and pressed. Spots and dirt can take away even from the appearance of new and costly outfits.

If you wear sunglasses, take them off before you enter the office. Do not wear them on the top of your head. Employers will want to look you in the eye when they talk to you.

During the Interview

Both job seekers and employers use the interview to look at each other carefully. Employers want to be sure they have the right person for the job. They want someone with the right skills who will "fit in."

Job seekers, too, must be sure they make the right choice. During your search, you may have more than one job offer. If you find out as much as you can about each company during the interview, it will be easier to make that right choice.

For a beginning job, an interview may last anywhere from a few minutes to half an hour. For more advanced jobs, it may last much longer.

Compare the opening minutes of the following interviews an employer, Mr. Chang, has with two job applicants.

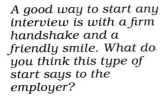

A good way to start any interview is with a firm handshake and a friendly smile. What do you think this type of start says to the employer?

CASE STUDY   Mr. Chang: "How do you do, John. I'm Mr. Chang."

John: "Uh, hi."

Mr. Chang: "Sit down and let's talk. Tell me a little something about yourself."

John: "There's not much to tell."

Mr. Chang: "Let me ask you a question then. What makes you think you can do this job?"

John: "Why not? I want some kind of work."

Mr. Chang: "Well, I've enjoyed meeting you, John. We'll be in touch."

John: "Sure."

Thinking About the Case Study

1. If you were Mr. Chang, how would you feel about hiring John?
2. What types of problems did you notice John having during the interview?

Here is the second interview.

CASE STUDY   Mr. Chang: "Sita, it's nice to see you. I'm Mr. Chang."

Sita: "I've been looking forward to meeting you, Mr. Chang."

Mr. Chang: "Sit down and let's talk a bit. Tell me a little about yourself."

Sita: "Let's see. I'm finishing high school now, and my grades are pretty good. I worked while I was in school. This year, my senior year, I'm working up to 20 hours a week. I was given more responsibility and a pay raise just last month. Right now I'm looking for a full-time job where I can show what I can do."

Mr. Chang: "What makes you think you can do this job?"

Sita: "When I learned about the opening, I talked to people who do the same kind of work. I asked them what it was like. I'm pretty sure I can do it. For one thing, I have a lot of the same responsibilities in my part-time job."

Thinking About the Case Study

1. If you were Mr. Chang, how would you feel about hiring Sita?

Every business handles interviews differently. If the business is a small one, the owner will probably talk with you. In larger companies, interviews are usually done by the supervisor of the job or someone from the personnel department. *The* **personnel department** *consists of people who handle matters such as hiring new employees and arranging for employee benefits.* The people who work in personnel departments speak for the employer.

When you apply for a job, you will speak to someone in the personnel department, with your possible supervisor, or with both. It is best, of course, if you can talk with the boss of the job you're applying for. Then you will both have a chance to get to know one another and find out whether or not you would work well together.

Nonverbal Behavior.   Not all the information exchanged during an interview is spoken. Much information is communicated through nonverbal behavior. **Nonverbal behavior** *is what a person* does *rather than what he or she says.* For example, an interviewer with a messy desk, who can't find your resume, is saying something nonverbally about the way she or he conducts business.

There are two types of nonverbal behavior that you should be aware of during an interview. One is body language; the other is attitude.

Body language *refers to the messages people deliver through their mannerisms.* The *way* a person walks, sits, stands, or speaks conveys a message. You know that when people laugh it usually means they are happy or amused. When you are relaxed, do you drum your fingers on the table? Probably not, because drumming fingers usually means someone is nervous.

What does body language have to do with interviews? Your body language can make either a good or a poor impression on the interviewer. Following are some suggestions for positive use of body language.

- Offer to shake hands with the interviewer. People like others who give them a firm handshake and who look them in the eyes.
- Sit down only when the interviewer invites you to.
- Sit up straight in the chair without slouching and slumping. People with good posture look self-confident and alert. Slouchers look as if they can't wait to climb back into bed.

It's natural to be a little nervous. You have probably seen people swinging their legs, playing with their hair, cracking

Your nonverbal behavior tells others a lot about you. Which person do you think is making the best impression?

their knuckles, or tugging at their clothes. These are nervous habits, and people doing these things look unsure of themselves. These habits can take away from what you're saying during an interview. The interviewer will probably focus on the nervous habit rather than on you.

Take a deep breath and try to relax as much as possible. You will find that most interviewers try to make the meeting as pleasant and comfortable as they can. This, in turn, will help you to relax.

Attitude *is the way you think and feel about certain topics or life in general.* Your attitude causes you to act in certain ways. Your attitude affects your performance. For example, people who enjoy school usually earn better grades than those who have a bad attitude about school.

Your attitude can affect your chances of being hired for a job. It can show up in an interview. In fact, interviewers will make a point of finding out what kind of attitude you have.

Following is a conversation Gene had with Ms. James when he was being interviewed for a job. What type of attitude does Gene seem to have?

Ms. James: "Gene, tell me a little about school . . . how well you did and what you liked about it."

Gene: "School was school. I didn't think it was all that great. The teachers were okay, I guess. I didn't like the homework, and sometimes classes were boring. I'd rather be busy doing something than listening to someone talk."

Ms. James could easily tell that Gene didn't have a very good attitude about school. She was concerned that Gene's bad attitude would carry over to the job as well. If Gene did have a good attitude, he didn't show it during the interview.

An employer is looking for a person who has a good attitude. Such people help make the company successful. These people are also easier to work with. Even if you do not feel absolutely great about something, try to find something good to say. Who knows? You may find more good things than you thought were there.

In Chapter 9 you will learn more about how to build a good attitude.

REVIEW YOUR WORK

1. Name four steps you can take before the interview that will help you get off to a good start.
2. How can your nonverbal behavior help you during an interview? How can your nonverbal behavior hurt you?
3. Why is your attitude important during an interview?

What You'll Talk About.   During most interviews the following subjects are discussed:

- what the job involves
- the type of worker the company believes it needs to do the job
- the type of work that interests you and that you enjoy
- the type of worker you have been in the past
- salary or wages
- hours and other working conditions

Be ready to answer questions the interviewer may ask you. Thinking about answers ahead of time helps you feel more confident. Every interviewer asks different questions. There are, however, some general questions which are often asked. Here are a few.

- Why do you want to work for this company?
- Why should we hire you?
- What other work have you done? What have you learned from it?
- What did you like most and least about school?
- What was your greatest accomplishment or success in school?

An interview is also a time for you to ask questions of the interviewer. You should prepare these questions in advance. What types of questions might you ask?

- What did you like most and least about the jobs you have had?
- What would you like to be doing five years from now?
- Did you miss a lot of work or school because of illness?
- What sort of pay are you looking for?
- Why did you leave your last job?
- What are your strengths? your weaknesses?
- Are you willing to work extra hours? How many?
- When can you start work?

Most of these questions are general, and you probably know the answers. However, if you are asked something you do not know, don't be afraid to admit you don't know it. People can usually tell when you're not telling the truth, and they trust you more if you are honest with them.

Remember to use the interview for your own questions. The interview is your opportunity to get to know something about the company and the people who work there. The more you can find out about the company during the interview, the greater your chances of making the right job choice.

The interviewer may ask what questions you have. Think of some of the things you want to know. You might ask

- What would a person in this job do each day? What would my responsibilities be?
- Can you tell me a little more about the products you make?

- What services do you offer customers?
- What kind of training do you give employees?
- How do you evaluate or judge employees' work?
- How do you work out people's schedules?
- Will I have to join a labor union?

Ask a few other questions before you ask about the pay. Money is important. It is also important, however, to show that other things mean as much to you as money.

Additional Interview Tips.   Following is a list of what you should and shouldn't do during an interview. Remember, however, that every interview is different. Very few "rules" apply to every interview.

Read these suggestions over and think about them. Use them when you think they will help you, but don't worry about whether you are always doing the "right" thing. Remember, it's important to relax and use your own common sense.

- **Arrive about five or ten minutes early.** In this way you won't be rushed, out of breath, and nervous. You will give the impression that you are a dependable and well-organized person. Businesses have schedules to meet and they expect employees to get to work on time. If you come to an interview late, people naturally assume you will be late for work, too.

Being on time for appointments shows you are dependable. How can you be sure to be on time?

- **Go to your appointment alone.** Don't bring friends or relatives with you. It's natural to be nervous, but bringing a crowd along won't help you. Employers look for people who can stand on their own feet.

- **Have your information and papers with you.** By all means take your information card (page 143) and your resume if you have one (page 145). You may also need a driver's license or other records, depending on the job.

- **Be sure you know the name or names of the people with whom you are going to talk.** Also, be sure that you pronounce the names correctly. Names are very personal. People do not like to have their names pronounced incorrectly.

- **Limit yourself to no more than two interviews in a day.** If you go on too many interviews in one day, you'll end up looking like you just finished a race. You'll feel rushed and won't be at your best.

- **Avoid naming a salary or wage, if you can.** It is difficult, especially for a beginner, to know the amount of money to ask for. If your guess is too low, you might not get what others get for the same work. If your guess is too high, the interviewer may think you expect too much or that you won't be happy with the job.

   The safest method is to ask the interviewer the pay range for the job. Then you can name a figure within that range. Another method would be to say, "I'm willing to negotiate (discuss and bargain) salary (or wages) with you. If you can tell me what you're willing to pay, I'm sure we can work something out."

- **Don't eat or chew gum.** If you want to chew gum or eat candy, do it before or after the appointment.

- **Speak up and talk clearly.** Pronounce your words carefully. Don't use slang words.

- **Avoid doing all the talking; don't interrupt the interviewer.** An interview is a two-way conversation. When one person does all the talking, the other person doesn't have a chance to say much.

- **Guard what you say about former employers.** Granted, there are bosses who are unfair and hard to work for. Nevertheless, be careful about running someone down. You will sound like a complainer and make a poor impression.

   If you left your last job because you were treated unfairly and you have to tell the interviewer, try to be fair yourself. Rather than say, "Mr. Jones never gave me a chance," say something like, "I guess Mr. Jones and I got off on the wrong foot." Or you might say, "I would

Legal Profession

Perry Mason never lost a case. Ben Matlock always figured out who the real villain was before the jury returned its verdict. The men and women of L.A. Law may have lost once or twice but at least they always looked great.

The legal profession has long been a favorite for television and the movies. There is excitement in our process of justice. The jobs of lawyer or judge seem so glamorous and thrilling. Because of this appeal, many people choose a career in law.

Unfortunately, there is more to becoming a lawyer than just desire. Lawyers have to attend three years of law school after they have graduated from college. Law school is tough, and many students quit before graduation. More students find that after law school they can't pass the Bar exam that is required for lawyers. Becoming a judge is even more difficult, since only the best lawyers are chosen for this job.

If this sounds too tough for you, don't be discouraged. If you are interested in the legal system, there are plenty of jobs other than those of judge or lawyer.

Strong secretarial skills could land you an interesting and high-paying job as a legal secretary. A legal secretary plays a vital role by providing administrative and clerical help to busy lawyers. Another job that is interesting and pays well is that of the paralegal. Paralegals help out lawyers by handling some of the more routine or time-consuming chores related to the legal profession.

If you would like to work a little closer to the courtroom, you might want to look into a career as a court clerk, court reporter, or bailiff. A court clerk han-

dles all the paperwork that relates to the court. A court reporter uses a special machine to keep track of everything that is said and done while the court is in session. A bailiff provides needed security services for the court including managing and guarding all prisoners and evidence.

Other jobs related to the legal profession include file clerk and journalist.

If you are interested in a career in the legal world, see your guidance counselor and begin to plan your career today. Whether you become a lawyer or a court reporter, you can make your interest in our legal system pay off for you in an exciting and rewarding career.

rather work under different conditions." You can let others know the situation was not right without sounding mean or angry.

- **Sell yourself.** When you go on an interview, you are selling yourself as a future employee of the company. One of the qualities that impresses interviewers is enthusiasm. **Enthusiasm** *is eagerness and interest.* People who have enthusiasm take an active interest in what's going on around them. One way to show your enthusiasm is to let people know you're interested in the business. You could say, "At this company employees have a chance to move up on the job. I think that's great! I want to work where I can move ahead."

    Because you are just beginning your work life, you probably won't have a lot of job experience. In this case you must sell yourself by stressing personal qualities and the skills you learned in other ways.

    You can say, "I'm a good worker. My grades in school were good. In my part-time jobs I've gotten pay increases. I've always been willing to pitch in and help." It is important to take advantage of the chance to tell about yourself. If you don't, the employer may not find out about your strong points.

- **Be honest.** If you were fired from your last job or made a mistake you have to tell about, don't try to cover it up with a lie. Show that you are a person who takes responsibility for your actions. Show that you can learn from your past mistakes. What counts is the way you handle your mistakes.

- **Thank the interviewer when the interview is over.** Say you enjoyed meeting him or her. If you are still interested in the job, tell the interviewer so.

    By the end of the interview, you may or may not know whether you have the job. If nothing is said, you may ask, "When can I expect to find out your decision?"

After the Interview

If you learn during the interview that you can start the job, or you have to return for tests or another interview, write down the date, time, and place. Show you are a businesslike person. You will also have a reminder about what you need to do next.

Remember—even if you don't get the job, each interview you have is a good learning experience. After the interview is over, ask yourself some questions about how the interview went.

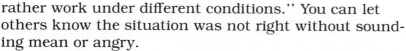

OPPORTUNITY

KNOCKS

MEDIA TRAINEE

Entry-level jobs are important steps on the way to your goals. An interest in advertising might lead you to a position such as this.

MEDIA TRAINEE

Great advertising agency likes to hire bright, bubbly career-minded people. At entry level you'll assist with charts, graphs, tables, correspondence, and phones. Promotable spot. Good typing skills and office experience helpful.

Does a person in this job have an opportunity to move up within this company?

The interviewer may tell you when you can expect to hear from him or her regarding the job. What can you do if you have received no word by that time?

- What kind of person did the interviewer seem to be looking for?
- How well did you sell yourself?
- Did you talk too little or too much?
- How can you improve your interview skills?

   Answering these questions can help you increase your chances of succeeding on your next interview. For example, if you didn't seem to have the skills needed, next time stress that you learn quickly and that you want to develop new skills. It would also help to look back at your past experiences again to see how they could help you. You may have overlooked some skills or qualities you have that are important for the job you want.

   If people spent a lot of time talking to you and showing you around the company, it's a good idea to write them a follow-up note. Thank them for their time and interest in you. Say you hope they will give you a chance to show what a good worker you are.

If you want a particular job and do not get it, of course you will be disappointed. Did you know that most people are turned down several times before they get a job?

If you are turned down for a job, ask the person whether he or she knows of another company that needs people. You may get a good lead on another job.

You could also ask why you did not get the job. It may be that you did not have the experience or skills needed. On the other hand, you may have lacked some of the qualities they want in their employees. If they are willing to tell you the reasons, it will help you do better at the next interview.

The interviewer may have told you that he or she would contact you within a certain time. If you don't receive a call by the end of that time, telephone to see whether or not a decision has been made. If the decision still hasn't been made, your call will serve as a reminder. If someone else got the job, you will at least know you need to keep looking. Thank the person for having taken the time to talk to you.

How Employers Make a Choice

Naturally, an employer will not hire you unless you already have or can learn the skills for the job. However, other things can make a difference as to whether or not you are chosen.

Why People Are Hired

It is probably safe to say that a person having the following three qualities will be seriously considered for the job. If more than one applicant has them, other things become equally important. However, if you are lacking in even one of them, your chances for getting the job decrease.

1. **Pleasing Personality.** All employers want to hire friendly, happy people. They *don't* want to hire people who seem to be bored and unhappy most of the time. This is especially true when employers are hiring workers who will come in contact with customers. During the interview the employer will pay close attention to your personality. He or she will be looking for someone who will get along with co-workers and the company's customers. Do you have a "winning" personality? You don't have to talk a lot to show you have a pleasant personality. If you think you could improve, Chapter 11 has some suggestions for developing a more positive attitude.

DID YOU KNOW?

THE DUKE

Before he began his lengthy career as a movie great, John Wayne was a Fox Studio prop man. A director called him aside when he noticed Wayne loading furniture into a truck.

2. **Good Appearance.** First impressions are very important, and the employer's first impression of you often depends on your appearance. You've already read about the importance of being well-groomed and well-dressed. Do not underestimate the importance of this quality. If the applicants are equal in every way, the employer will probably hire the best-dressed, best-groomed person. Remember, best-dressed does not mean the most expensively dressed.

3. **Ability to Communicate.** During the interview, the employer will pay close attention to the way you speak. The ability to communicate is very important in the working world. Employers know their businesses will operate more smoothly and more efficiently if their workers can speak and write clear, correct English. Chapter 11 has suggestions for improving your communication skills.

Most employers are looking for people who have enthusiasm. How can you show enthusiasm during a job interview?

Your personality can be very important in helping you land a good job. What type of personality are employers looking for?

Why People Aren't Hired

According to recent studies, these are the five top reasons why people aren't hired:

1. Personal appearance is unclean or sloppy, or clothing is not right for the job.
2. Thinks he or she knows it all.
3. Can't communicate clearly—hard to understand.
4. Seems to have no direction or plan for life or work.
5. Doesn't care—lacks enthusiasm.

Compare this list to the one giving reasons why people *are* hired. How are they alike? Do you sound more like the people who are hired, or those who aren't?

Before You Accept

You have already spent a lot of time planning your career. The jobs you applied for should have been those that fit into your career plan.

What will you do, however, if you receive two offers for jobs that you think you would like? What if you are offered a job close to what you want, but you think maybe you should look a little further? The following are some factors to consider before you accept a position.

- **Responsibility.** You know how much responsibility you want. However, what if the job offers more, and you're not sure whether or not you can handle it? Don't be afraid to give it a try. The employers would not offer you the job unless they thought you could do it. You will be given time to learn.
- **Hours.** Some jobs demand more time than other jobs. How many hours a day do you want to work? Will this job provide you with enough hours to earn the amount of money you need? Will you be called upon to work more hours than you feel you should?
- **Health.** Any health problems you might have should have been considered in your career plan. You must also consider that the job itself may raise health questions. For example, do other workers smoke a lot? Will you be expected to lift heavy objects?
- **Location.** How will you get to and from work? If you have your own car, will heavy traffic be a problem? How long will the drive take? How much will gas and car upkeep cost? Is parking provided by the company? If so, is the parking free, or do you have to pay? What other ways could you get to work? Is there a car pool you can join?

    Larger towns have bus, subway, or train systems. You need to know the schedules and where to catch a ride. How much does it cost? How long will it take?

    To be realistic, you should subtract your travel costs from your salary. You should add travel time to the hours spent on the job. If time and money are important to you, a job close to home may be better than one far away.

You will need to look at the job location and how you will get to and from work. Why should you consider this prior to making a decision about taking a job?

Applying for a Job

If you are like most people, you will start to get nervous the moment an employer says, ''Yes, we do have an opening.'' The more you want that particular job, the more nervous you will be. By the time you actually walk into the interviewer's office, you may be so nervous you'll have forgotten some important information.

Almost everyone who applies for a job feels this way. There are so many ways that you can ''mess up'' when applying for a job. You can make a mistake on the application form and end up smearing ink all over. You can misspell a word or two on your resume. Worst of all, if you get an interview, you can fail to think of anything intelligent to say. With all of these opportunities to ruin your chances, they'll surely hire someone else. Right?

Wrong! Everyone else feels the same way, and everyone else will have just as many chances to ''mess up.'' Don't be so hard on yourself. You aren't the only person out there who gets nervous and makes mistakes. We all do.

THINK POSITIVELY. You are an intelligent, hard-working, sincere person, aren't you? You can do a good job for the employer, can't you? You want the job and will put 100-percent effort into it, won't you? Then you have every reason to expect that you will make a good impression on the employer and that you'll be hired.

Don't be discouraged if you aren't hired for every job. It may be that several people with more experience and

training applied for the job. Don't think that you did something wrong. Trust your own opinion. You'll know after the interview what sort of impression you made.

Remember—almost everyone is nervous when meeting people for the first time. Chances are the interviewer will also be nervous. This is only natural. Concentrate on what the interviewer is saying and what you are saying, and your nervousness will diminish.

Don't try to be something you're not. Don't try to impress the interviewer. Just be yourself. The interviewer wants to hire someone he or she likes, and the interviewer will like you if you are honest and sincere. So think positively. You can be honest and sincere, can't you?

- **Co-workers.** The people you work with can make a job pleasant or unpleasant. You will be happiest if you work with people with whom you're comfortable. Did you like the people you met during your interview? Did you seem to "fit in?"

- **Pay.** When comparing pay, consider such points as how often you will receive raises; whether or not benefits, such as a longer vacation, help make up for lower pay; and whether or not you will have to buy uniforms. Will a low starting pay grow quickly if your work is good?

- **Help with education.** Companies may help pay education expenses if the courses will help you on the job. You may even be given time off during working hours to go to class.

- **Insurance benefits.** Types of insurance plans include health, life, and dental. Each company offers different insurance benefits. Some companies pay part of the costs; others pay all.

  Health care costs are expensive, so think about the insurance plans you can get. Many large companies have group insurance coverage or a health maintenance organization (HMO) plan.

  Group insurance pays all or a percentage of medical expenses for doctor's fees, tests, and hospital costs. A number of services may not be covered. With group insurance, you choose your own doctors.

  HMO is prepaid, or paid in advance, health care. It covers almost all medical, hospital, and drug costs. Dental costs are usually not included. You can select only from the doctors in the HMO group. Usually, all HMO services are located in the same building.

- **Company rules.** Some people work better in a more relaxed place. They like to put their feet up while they fill out a report. They don't like to wear suits of "good" clothes, and they work better in jeans. Other people prefer to work where things are done "by the book."

  Before you take a job, you should learn what the company expects of you and whether or not it has any rules about dress and other matters. Are you willing to work in a place with lots of rules? Would you be happy in a place with no rules? Think about it before you accept a job.

- **Relocating.** What is the chance you will be transferred? You might look forward to a move to a new area, or you may want to stay where you are now living. If you refuse to move, there is always a chance that you may not advance on the job as quickly as you might like.

Before you take a job, you should learn what the company expects of you and whether or not it has any rules about dress and other matters. When might you ask about company rules?

REVIEW YOUR WORK

1. Identify four topics that will probably be discussed during an interview. Name four questions an interviewer might ask you.
2. Name six things you can do during the interview to help make it successful.
3. What questions can you ask yourself after the interview is over?
4. Name the five reasons why a person may not be hired.
5. Name four things you should consider before accepting a job offer.

Chapter Summary

- The telephone call is the most common way to contact employers about a job.
- A letter to an employer should be neatly typed on good paper and written in clear, correct English.
- Stopping by a work site without an appointment to apply for a job is usually not a good idea.
- Almost all jobs require you to fill out an application form.
- A resume is a summary of all the important information about you. Your resume should be neatly typed on good paper.
- An interview is a get-acquainted meeting between the job-seeker and the employer.
- A pleasing personality, good appearance, and the ability to communicate are three qualities that employers look for in new employees.

Reviewing Vocabulary and Concepts

Write the numbers 1–10 on a separate sheet of paper. After each number, write the letter of the answer that best completes the following statements or answers the following questions.

1. Which of the following is not one of three ways to talk to an employer about a job?
   a. write a letter
   b. telephone
   c. fill out an application form
   d. stop by without an appointment
2. When telephoning an employer, you can make your voice sound more relaxed and happy by _____ .
   a. thinking pleasant thoughts
   b. smiling while talking
   c. standing
   d. listening to music
3. A good letter of application form is *not* _____ .
   a. neat
   b. signed in ink
   c. typed
   d. more than one page long
4. Stopping by to apply for a job without an appointment is _____ .
   a. usually not a good idea
   b. the best way to see an employer
   c. never done
   d. a way to prove you are serious about the job
5. Application forms are _____ .
   a. not required for most jobs
   b. required for almost all jobs
   c. best completed in pencil
   d. never required
6. When completing an application form, you should _____ .
   a. answer all questions
   b. try to write as quickly as possible
   c. not worry about the type of job
   d. never print
7. A typed summary of all the important information about you is your _____ .
   a. application form
   b. job lead card
   c. references
   d. resume
8. For males, a good grooming and dress choice for an interview situation is _____ .
   a. very long hair
   b. dirty or spotted clothing
   c. conservative clothing
   d. none of the above

9. For females, a good grooming and dress choice for an interview situation is _____ .
   a. a very fancy hairstyle
   b. shoes with very high heels
   c. conservative clothing
   d. none of the above
10. Who should ask questions during an interview?
   a. the interviewer only
   b. both the job-seeker and the interviewer
   c. the job-seeker only
   d. neither the job-seeker nor the interviewer

Thinking Critically About Career Skills

Write your answers to the following on a separate sheet of paper.
1. Why are good communication skills so important to most employers? What steps can you take to improve your communication skills?

2. When looking for a job, is it more important to make a good impression during an interview than it is to be neat and accurate?

Building Basic Skills

1. **Writing** Write a job application letter to an employer.

2. **Mathematics** Calculate the amount of time you should allow for getting to an interview. Suppose you want to arrive five minutes early for a 2:00 p.m. interview. The normal driving time to the area where you will be interviewed is 20 minutes. You need to make a stop on the way that will take 15 minutes. You think you should allow 15 minutes to find the office and park your car. You also believe you should allow 10 extra minutes for the possibility of heavy traffic. What time should you leave for your interview?

Applying Career Skills

1. Look through the classified advertisements section of a local newspaper to find at least ten jobs that you think you might enjoy. How many of these jobs request interested people to telephone? How many ask for a resume?
2. Visit a place of business, such as a clothing store or a restaurant. Take note of how the employees are groomed and dressed. Make a list of how you would dress and look for an interview at such a business.

ON THE JOB: WHAT YOU CAN EXPECT

KEY TERMS

entry-level position
downtime
wages
piecework
salary
commission
overtime
initiative
probationary period
cost-of-living increase
merit increase

OBJECTIVES

In this chapter you will learn about

- the qualities and kinds of performance employers expect from their employees
- the considerations you can expect from your employer
- the different categories of work hours
- the different methods of paying employees

Congratulations! You have just accepted an offer for a job that you really wanted. All your hard work and effort have paid off. You are now ready to start to work.

Whether you are still in school or you have graduated, your first job will probably be an entry-level position. *An* **entry-level position** *is a job at the beginning level.*

Some other positions at higher levels may look more glamorous, powerful, and interesting. Try to remember it is the way you do your job that brings importance to the job and recognition to you. Treating your job as an important one and handling it that way can give you satisfaction and recognition.

During your first days and weeks on the job, you will learn a great deal about the working world. If you are not sure what to expect when you start work, this chapter will prepare you. You will read about the standard methods used to calculate your pay. You will learn about the basic levels of performance that most employers expect from all their employees. You will also find out how employers evaluate their workers. After completing this chapter, you will know what you need to do to be successful on the job.

Making the Change

If you don't already know, you will soon learn that the working world is very different from school life. If you go to school and work part-time, you will need to adjust to the differences almost every day. The following hints will help you make the change from student to worker more easily.

- **Work faster.** One of the biggest differences between school and work is the pace. There's an old saying: "Time is money." Most employers want to get as much work as possible done each day. They will usually expect you to work faster than your teachers have at school.
- **Don't expect a lot of praise.** In school, your teachers make a special effort to tell you when you are doing good work. They do this to build your confidence and to encourage you to learn even more. Many bosses, however, do not have time to praise all their workers. Even when they notice that you've done outstanding work, they may not say anything. So don't be disappointed if you fail to get the pat on the back that you think you deserve.
- **Be prepared to work without interruption.** Work days are longer than school days, and there aren't as many vacations. In fact, you may not get any vacation at all. Part-time workers and beginning workers usually must work several months before earning a vacation.
- **Learn to tell the difference between what "ought" to be and what is.** In almost all schools, everyone is treated fairly. The schools are governed by public laws that all teachers, principals, and students must obey. In the working world, each employer makes many of his or her own rules. You will not always agree with these rules. You must learn, however, to do things the way your employer wants them done or find another job.
- **Be responsible for yourself.** In school, teachers remind you when your work is due. If you have a hard time, they

You will be expected to work faster on a job than at school. Why do employers want fast workers?

may give you a chance to do the work over. If you are absent, they will let you make up your assignments. On the job, however, if you are absent, you will not always get reminders. You may not get a second chance. You must be responsible for yourself and your work.

- **Try to make life easier for your boss.** In school your teachers try to support you. They try to help you to learn as much as possible in the easiest and fastest ways they know. In the working world, however, you are the helper rather than the person being helped. Your job is to help your employer's business succeed. The more you can do to help, the more valuable you become to your employer.

Your Work Hours and Pay

Just as you must use schedules to get through the school day, you will need to learn how time is kept in the working world. This section will make you familiar with the common terms and procedures involved in keeping track of work time. This will be extremely important to you since your pay will usually be determined by your work time.

Work Time

The average work week is eight hours per day, five days per week, Monday through Friday. Not all employees work a normal calendar week, however. Many employees work part-time. Some full-time employees must work weekends or during hours other than eight a.m. to five p.m.

Employers and workers need to keep track of what they do with their time, as well as the number of hours they work. Following are some common ways of identifying work time.

Downtime.   Workers can't do their jobs when their machinery breaks down or there is a power failure. *Any time during which workers can't work, for whatever reason, is called* **downtime.** Workers are expected to find out if there is other work they can do to keep busy. Downtime is considered work time by some companies, and workers are paid even if they can't work.

Break Times.   Is a rest break or lunch break considered work time? Some companies think so. They think that employees work harder when they have breaks, so they pay the workers for the time they are on breaks. Other companies, however, do not consider the breaks as work time and do not pay for them. Make sure you know your employer's policy regarding breaks.

There are not as many breaks during work as there are at school. Do you think this will be a difficult adjustment?

Sick Time. Most companies pay employees even when they are sick and can't work. Many companies do not, however, provide sick pay until employees have worked for the company for a certain period of time. Most companies pay for only a limited number of sick days.

Learning Time. Some jobs allow workers to attend classes during regular working hours. Your boss may want you to take such a class. If so, you will be paid while taking the class. If you decide to take a class on your own after working hours, you will not be paid. However, the company may be willing to pay for books and the cost of taking the class.

How You Are Paid

The money you earn is called *wages, salary, or commission.* **Wages** *usually refers to pay figured by the hour or by the piece.* If your wages are $3 per hour and you work two hours, you earn $6. Obviously, with hourly wages, the more hours you work, the more money you make.

If you are paid by the piece, your payment method is called piecework. **Piecework** *means that you receive a set amount of money for each piece completed.* Piecework is common in factories.

If you are making bottlecaps at 2¢ each, and you make 200 in an hour, your wages for those caps will be $4 an hour. If you are tired or lazy the next hour, and make only 50 bottlecaps, your wage for that hour would be $1.

A **salary** *is a set amount of money for a certain period of time.* Salaries are usually figured by the year. The payments are then divided evenly and paid to you each month, or every two weeks. For example, a worker earning a salary of $12,000 a year would be paid $1,000 a month or $500 every two weeks. Most workers who earn a salary receive the same amount of pay regardless of the number of hours they work. Their pay is not figured by the hour.

Some workers are paid a commission. *A* **commission** *is a percentage of the money you bring in for the company.* For example, suppose you are selling cleaning supplies door to door at a 10 percent commission. You will get $1 for every $10 worth of products you sell.

Most beginning salespeople receive a salary plus a commission. As they learn how to sell their products, more of their pay is based on commissions and less on salary.

The average work week is eight hours per day, five days per week. Why is it important for each employee to keep track of his or her work time?

Overtime *is work beyond the regular hours.* Overtime pay is usually one and one-half times the regular pay, and it usually starts after 40 hours. A part-time worker is usually paid at the regular rate for any extra hours until a total of 40 hours is reached. Then overtime pay begins.

For example, Ted does maintenance work at a hospital. He earns $6 an hour. Last week he worked 44 hours, or 4 hours overtime. He received $240 for the first 40 hours and $36 for the overtime.

Instead of overtime pay, some companies give an equal amount of time off. If you worked 46 hours one week, you would not get extra pay, but you would only have to work 31 hours the next week. You would be off one and one-half times the hours you put in (6 hours plus 3 hours). You will learn more about calculating your pay in Chapter 16.

REVIEW YOUR WORK

1. Name three things you can do to make the change from school to work easier.
2. What is an average work week?
3. Explain the difference between salary and wages.

Opportunities in the Armed Services

I want to work for a big company!

If this statement expresses your feelings, you might want to consider a career with the largest single employer in the United States—the United States armed services. Together, the Army, Navy, Air Force, Marine Corps, and Coast Guard employ more people than any other employer in the country.

The armed services have jobs in virtually every desirable field from audiovisual technician to zoning expert. Unlike most other employers, the armed services are willing to train you. Serving in the armed services can make you eligible for financial aid to help cover the cost of a college education.

Of course, there are a couple of catches. First, if you enlist in the armed services, you have to be willing to commit yourself to staying with them and obeying their rules for a set period of time. Most first-time enlistments require at least a two-year commitment. Second, along with an enlistment in the armed services comes the increased possibility that you will be asked to fight for your country or spend time in a dangerous part of the world.

Looking at just a few of the jobs available in the armed services might help to give you a better idea of all the different types of opportunities that exist. If you have an aptitude for mechanical work and a high school diploma, you can spend your time in the armed services learning how to be a helicopter mechanic. An interest in food services could lead to a job in the camp mess, where you will learn how to prepare meals for 5 people to 500 people.

If you have an interest in police work, you could become a military policeman (M.P.). Training as an M.P. can open the door to a career in civilian law enforcement. If your interests run toward communications, the armed services provide training for every type of job from radio repair and radar technician to training as a radio announcer or as a newspaper reporter.

For those that want to work with their hands, the military has many construction jobs. You might find yourself working with everything from a hammer and nails to heavy equipment, such as earthmovers and sea cranes. There is also paperwork in the armed services, as in every other business. Skilled office workers are always needed to help process and complete this important paperwork. The armed services offer training in every aspect of office technology from word processing to accounting.

Do any of these jobs sound interesting to you? If so, ask your guidance counselor for more information regarding a career in the armed services. Who knows? You might find that you are tailor made for a life in uniform.

Expectations

Your relationship with your employer or supervisor will play a big part in determining your success on the job. This relationship works two ways. Your employer will expect certain things from you; you can expect certain things from your employer. The better job you do of meeting each other's expectations, the happier everyone will be.

What Your Employer Will Expect

Your first days on the job will be important ones. You will want to make a good impression, and your employer will want to find out what kind of worker you are.

You'll probably make some mistakes at first, but don't worry—everyone makes mistakes. Don't try to do everything at once. You will have plenty of time to make a good impression over the weeks and months ahead. Just take your time and listen to what you're told.

Don't be afraid to ask questions. Your employer will *not* expect you to know everything right away. In fact, he or she will be impressed with your concern for doing your job right.

What *will* your employer expect from you? Most employers expect at least the following things from all their employees.

A Full Day's Work.   Some workers spend a lot of their time talking to their friends. Others may sneak in late or quit working early. If your employer is paying you for eight hours of work, then you are expected to give eight hours of work in return. Doesn't that seem fair?

Consider this example. Company X has 50 workers. Each worker earns $6 per hour and is allowed two 15-minute breaks. These breaks cost the company a total of $150 every day. If each worker takes another 5 minutes at each break, the extra time costs the company $50 more every day. That's $250 each week. If you were the owner of the company, would you want workers to take more than the 15-minute break?

Many workers do *not* give a full day's work for a full day's pay. Some of your co-workers will probably arrive late, "goof off" during work hours, and take extra long breaks. If you value your job and you expect your employer to treat you fairly, work at least the number of hours for which you are being paid. Many of the most successful people work even more hours.

DID YOU KNOW?

CLOCK WATCHERS

When Thomas Edison opened his first small factory, he had only one clock on the wall. The employees kept their eyes on the clock, eager for quitting time at the end of the day. Edison then placed dozens of clocks, all set at different times, around the room. The workers soon realized the clocks were inaccurate, so they stopped watching and got on with their work.

Employers look for workers that are willing to learn new skills. Why do you think some people avoid learning new skills?

Initiative.   **Initiative** *is the quality of doing what needs to be done without being told.* People with initiative do not wait to be told what to do. They look for work that needs to be done.

For example, suppose your boss gives you an assignment and then leaves for the day. You have four hours left on your shift, but you finish the assigned task in three hours. What would you do? Would you "kill time" until your shift was over? Would you look for something that needed to be done?

Willingness To Learn.   New skills and experiences can be fun and exciting. They help you grow. Are you willing to grow, or are you afraid to show that you don't know everything? At the very least, employers will expect you to learn the skills you need to perform your duties properly.

Friendliness and Cooperation.   Most jobs simply can't be done unless people get along with one another. This means that friendliness and cooperation are extremely important for a business to be successful. Is doing something for someone else a big "pain in the neck" for you? Are you often grouchy? If so, your employer may look for someone more willing to cooperate and get along with others.

Dependability.   A dependable person is one who comes to work every day and who does what he or she is asked to do. Being dependable means that people can depend on you and that you won't let them down. It means you follow directions. If you don't understand the directions given, ask questions that will make them clearer.

What You Can Expect

Of course, you will expect many things from your employers. Some employers will make you happier than others. However, you have a right to the following:

- **Fair treatment.** By law, employers cannot discriminate (make decisions) against you because of your sex, race, religious beliefs, age, or physical condition.
- **Your pay.** You can expect to be paid regularly and on time.
- **A safe place to work.** Under the Occupational Safety and Health Act, an employer is required by law to make your place of work safe.
- **On-the-job training.** Some companies are not as careful about training new workers as they should be. You may have to watch another worker or follow your supervisor's lead until you learn what is needed. Most employers will see that someone is there to help you learn.

Employers are required by law to provide employees with a safe place to work. How can employees help to keep their workplace safe?

Employers expect a full day's work from each employee. Does this mean that employees are not allowed to have any fun on the job?

- **A review of your work.** Most companies review all employees once or twice a year. Those who have done well may be rewarded with pay raises. Those who have not done well may be warned. You will read more about work evaluations below.
- **Honesty.** Just as your employers will expect honesty from you, you may expect it from them.

Evaluations

You are evaluated when you apply for a job. The employer or manager looks you over to see if you are right for the job. The employer looks at how you dress, talk, and act. The employer also asks other people—your references—about you. If your evaluation is fine, you'll get the job.

Evaluation starts again when you report to work. A new job requires training, and evaluation goes on during your training. *The training period is also known as a* **probationary period.** It may last as long as six months.

The probationary period lets your employer look at such things as:

- how fast you learn each task
- how well you complete each task
- how well you listen
- how well you follow directions
- your appearance
- how patient you are while learning
- how well you get along with other people
- whether you practice safety habits

At the end of the probationary period, both you and your boss should have an idea of how well you do the job. If you do a poor job, your supervisor may decide that a change is necessary. In this event, if you are lucky, the supervisor may put you in a different job—one that better matches your abilities. Every job is not for every worker. Sometimes it's hard to tell how you will work out in a position until you are actually on the job. If you are not so lucky, you may have to look for a job elsewhere.

Some employers will not tell you how well you are doing until it's time for your evaluation. Others will give you help and evaluate you informally as the days and weeks move along.

An evaluation isn't something to fear. Ask yourself, "Have I been doing a good job? Have I worked to the best of my ability?" If so, you have nothing to worry about. Your efforts will show up in a good evaluation. The evaluation will give you a chance to look back and see how you have grown and progressed.

CAREER Q&A

DUE CREDIT

Q: If I feel I have done a better job than my boss gives me credit for, what can I do?

A: Keep a record of the work you do very well and the jobs you do that are beyond those expected of you. The next time your boss talks to you about how you are doing on the job, you will have a record of your accomplishments to show him or her.

CASE STUDY

Ms. Hayakawa is the type of employer who lets her workers know how they are doing on the job. She is in charge of the toy department for a large department store. She has ten salespeople working for her. Every few hours Ms. Hayakawa takes a walk through the toy section to see how her salespeople are doing. She checks to see if they are busy. She notices if they help customers right away or let them wait. Her salespeople need to know about the toys they're selling. They must be pleasant to the customers. Ms. Hayakawa tells her salespeople what they can do to improve. She also discusses the good things they do. Not all employers are as helpful.

Thinking About the Case Study

1. If you worked for Ms. Hayakawa, do you think you would know what type of evaluation to expect?

```
┌─────────────────────────────────────────────────────────────┐
│                    Evaluation Form                          │
│   Employee Name _____ Date _____    │
├─────────────────────────────────────────────────────────────┤
│                                                             │
│   Unsatisfactory: employee seldom meets minimum standards   │
│   Satisfactory: employee always meets minimum standards     │
│   Excellent: employee usually does more than the minimum    │
│                                                             │
│                     ───────────────────                     │
│                                                             │
│                  Unsatisfactory   Satisfactory   Excellent  │
│   1. Reliable          ☐              ☐             ☐        │
│   2. Reports to work   ☐              ☐             ☐        │
│      on time                                                │
│   3. Personal appearance ☐            ☐             ☐        │
│   4. Follows directions  ☐            ☐             ☐        │
│   5. Finishes work       ☐            ☐             ☐        │
│      on time                                                │
│   6. Cooperative         ☐            ☐             ☐        │
│   7. Gets along with     ☐            ☐             ☐        │
│      other employees                                        │
│   8. Quality of work     ☐            ☐             ☐        │
│   Comments _____       │
│   _____       │
└─────────────────────────────────────────────────────────────┘
```

Written evaluations should help you understand what you have done well and the areas where you can improve. What do the signatures on a written evaluation form mean?

Written Evaluations

Some employers use written evaluations to evaluate their employees. This is almost always true in larger companies. The written evaluation may look something like the form on this page.

The supervisor or employer fills out the form and signs it. Most employers show the form to their workers. The employer and employee discuss the information on the form. Then the worker signs the form.

The signatures on the evaluation form are a type of protection for both parties. The signatures mean that the employer and employee both understand what was written on the evaluation. It is a way to prevent misunderstandings.

At this point, it would be a good idea to think about the areas in which you want to improve. You could help yourself a great deal if you took the time to think about and write down a few goals you want to work toward. Share them with your boss. In this way, you will be seen as a person who wants to grow on the job.

Following are stories of two workers. Using the form below as a guide, how would you evaluate each worker?

- Al has just been hired as head food line attendant at Snaps Fast Food Emporium. He must open the restaurant, turn on the lights, and start the grills. He is the one who must make the coffee. He has half an hour to do this before the others report to work.

  Each morning Al has been 15 minutes late. He gets the restaurant unlocked and the lights turned on, but the grill isn't hot and the coffee isn't ready. Al has a friendly personality, but the other workers are upset with him. They are running late because of Al. The customers grumble about the slow service.

- Peggy has been working at the Sunshine Nursing Home for a month. She is in charge of the recreation program for the residents. She was trained by the former recreation director, but she didn't follow his suggestions. Her boss warned her, and Peggy has been doing better. However, now she seems angry at the boss and blames co-workers for pointing out what she was doing.

Informal Evaluations

Some companies, usually smaller ones with fewer employees, use an informal evaluation. Supervisors make pay and promotion decisions without using formal, written guidelines. They may take an employee aside and informally talk about how the work is going.

Some employers prefer to informally evaluate employees. Which type of evaluation—formal or informal—do you think you would prefer?

In many companies, supervisors evaluate worker performance on a regular basis. How are evaluations handled at your school?

Sometimes people think silence means approval. Silence, however, does not help you improve on the job. After all, you'll want recognition for any improvement you have made.

If you don't get any information about how you are doing on your job, ask for it. You might start off by saying, "Mr. Williams, I've been working here for three months. I'm interested in knowing how I'm doing. I'm sure your ideas would help me a lot." Saying this or something similar shows you are interested in doing a good job.

Pay Raises

Whether or not you earn a pay raise at work depends on several things. Good workers are usually rewarded. Additionally, people who do more than what is expected have the best chance of earning raises. How well are you doing your work?

How much responsibility do you have? If you are given added responsibility, your pay may also be increased. If your responsibilities include a promotion, a pay raise is almost always given.

Every company has a set of wage or salary guidelines it follows. Find out what the guidelines are so you will know where you stand.

A pay raise is always good news! What are the two types of pay increases a worker may get?

Most companies review your work on a regular basis, usually every six months or every year. After your review, there are two types of pay or salary increases you may get: cost-of-living increases and merit increases.

Cost-of-Living Increases

A **cost-of-living increase** *is a raise given to help workers keep up with rising prices and costs.* It is usually given to all employees. Such raises usually amount to about five percent of your current salary or wages. A cost-of-living increase normally has little to do with how well you did your job.

Merit Increases

A **merit increase** *is given because the employee has done the work well.* Merit increases are usually larger than cost-of-living increases. Even if they are small, the best thing about merit increases is that they show the company is happy with your work. Workers who are doing poor work do not receive merit increases.

REVIEW YOUR WORK

1. Name three things employers expect from workers.
2. Name three things you have a right to expect from an employer.
3. What is a probationary period?
4. Name four things an employer will be evaluating during your training.
5. What is the difference between a merit increase and a cost-of-living increase?

On the Job: What You Can Expect

Those first few days, or weeks, on a new job can seem like they will last forever. You may feel like the least skilled person alive.

It will seem as though everyone else knows so much. They'll know how to do things you have no idea how to do. They'll move quickly and smoothly, seeming to accomplish so much so fast. They'll do it once and do it right. You'll have to do everything over and over—and still it may not be right.

The boss will tell them quickly, or maybe just nod in a certain way, and they'll be off to do the job he wants done. You'll stand there listening while the boss explains in great detail how to do a simple task. Five minutes later, you'll have forgotten everything you were told and will need to go back and ask again. You may go home at the end of the day feeling as though you accomplished little.

If this is how you feel the first few days in a new job, cheer up! Everyone goes through a difficult learning period when they first start a new job. **THINK POSITIVELY.** You will make it through this time, and you will become a valuable employee. You will soon be looking back on those first days and laughing at how inexperienced you were.

Too many of us are unrealistic. We expect to step right in and do all the work just as fast and efficiently as people who have done the job for years.

You *will* learn to do the job as well as anyone else, but it will take time. Be patient.

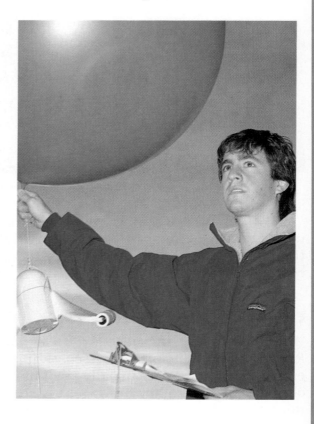

Employers do not expect you to know how to do your job on the first day, or even for the first few weeks. All they ask is that you pay attention, follow orders, and try your best.

Don't be afraid to say, "I don't know." Don't be afraid to ask questions. Employers can't train you unless they know where you need help. They don't want workers who are know-it-alls; they would much rather have workers who are willing to learn.

You will ask questions, won't you? You will try your best? If so, think positively and you'll become the skilled and valuable employee you know you can be!

Chapter Summary

- The working world is very different from going to school. At work, you will have to keep up a faster pace and work longer days.
- All new employees go through a learning period that is demanding for both the employee and the boss.
- Wages refer to pay figured by the hour or the piece.
- Piecework means you are paid a certain amount for each piece you finish.
- Salary is a set amount of money for a certain period of time.
- Commission is a percentage of the money you bring into the company.
- Overtime pay is usually one and one-half times the regular pay.
- Your work relationships with your boss and co-workers play a big part in job success.
- Your employer will expect a full day's work, initiative, willingness to learn, friendliness, and dependability.
- You can expect your pay, safety, training, regular evaluations, honesty, and fair treatment with regard to race, sex, religion.
- A job evaluation lets you know how well you're doing on the job and where you need improvement.

Reviewing Vocabulary and Concepts

A. On a separate sheet of paper, write the numbers 1–10. After each number write the term from the word bank that best completes each statement.

Word Bank

overtime
piecework
probationary period
commission
merit increase
downtime
initiative
wages
salary
cost-of-living increase

1. A _____ is given to reward an employee who does exceptionally well.
2. _____ is a period of time during which employees can't work.
3. When you work 45 hours in one week, you are working five hours _____ .
4. If you see something that needs to be done and you go ahead and do it, you are showing _____ .
5. _____ is a term used for jobs in which a certain amount of money is paid for each piece of work completed.
6. A period of several months during which a new employee learns a job is a _____ .
7. _____ usually refers to pay figured by the hour or by the piece.
8. A _____ is a percentage of the money that you bring in for the company.
9. A pay increase known as _____ helps you keep up with rising prices.
10. A _____ is a set amount of money paid for working a certain amount of time.

B. Write the numbers 11–15 on a separate sheet of paper. After each number, write the letter of the answer that best completes the statement.

11. Work days are _____ than school days.
    a. longer
    b. shorter
    c. harder
    d. more fun
12. In the working world, your job is to _____ your employer's business success.
    a. ignore
    b. praise
    c. overlook
    d. help
13. There are two kinds of employee evaluations; one is informal, the other is _____ .
    a. oral
    b. formal
    c. written
    d. poor
14. Many companies provide _____ for employees who are sick and can't work.
    a. a doctor
    b. sick pay
    c. counseling
    d. medicine
15. Some companies have found that _____ help employees to work better.
    a. breaks
    b. suggestions
    c. reprimands
    d. commissions

Thinking Critically About Career Skills

1. Some employers are considering going to a four-day work week. This means that the employees will work ten hours a day for four days, to maintain the 40-hour-a-week schedule. Would you be in favor of that? Why or why not?
2. Other businesses have decided to allow their employees to be on flex-time. This means they can choose to work whatever hours they want, as long as they fulfill the 40-hour a week schedule. What advantages to flex-time can you name? Would you like being able to do this?

Building Basic Skills

1. **Mathematics**   Calculate your new salary if you are making $13,500 a year and are given a five percent merit increase.
2. **Mathematics**   Calculate the cost of 50 employees who are slow in coming back from morning and afternoon breaks every day. If it is costing your company $250 extra per week (as in the example given on page 177), how much would that be in a year? in five years?
3. **Research**   Use newspaper and magazine articles to find out how flex-time helps big cities with their transportation problems. You might want to read about how it was used in Los Angeles, California, during the 1984 Olympics. Write a one-page report that summarizes your findings.

Applying Career Skills

1. Look at problem 2 under Building Basic Skills. If you were the owner of a company suffering these losses due to employees that abused their break times, what would you do to change the situation?
2. With a partner, act out a job evaluation. Take turns being the boss and the employee. Use the text as a guide for some of the things you will be talking about during your evaluation meeting.

HUMAN RELATIONSHIPS ON THE JOB

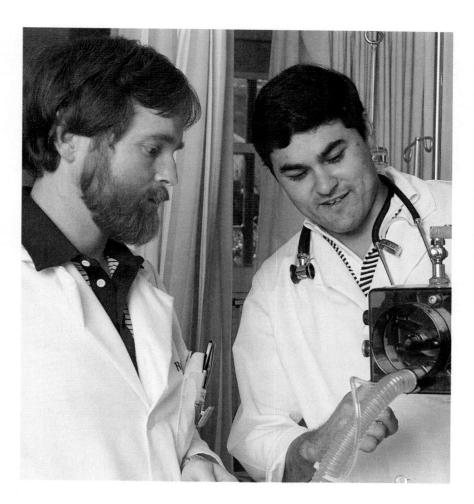

CHAPTER 10

KEY TERMS

emotions
objectively
compromise
destructive criticism
constructive criticism
defensive
stress

OBJECTIVES

In this chapter you will learn about
- the steps in problem solving
- how to get along with others on the job
- how to be happier with yourself on the job

People who are successful in their jobs will tell you it takes hard work. In addition to doing their jobs well, they make an effort to get along with others. They keep a sense of humor and try to look at the good side of things.

Most problems on the job stem from your relationships with others. People can annoy you by making negative remarks such as, "Try not to make a mess of this." Sometimes people lose their temper or blame you for problems even when it's not your fault.

Although you will probably enjoy most of the time you spend working, you will also face some challenges when dealing with people on the job. No one is perfect. By solving the problems you face, you can learn from them and make your relationships at work more pleasant.

In this chapter we will talk about some of the human problems you might face on the job and how you can handle them. You'll also find tips that will help you get off on the right foot with co-workers.

Problem Solving on the Job

No matter who you are, you will have problems from time to time. The way you go about handling these problems will show how mature or wise you are.

Some problems are more difficult to handle than others because emotions are involved. **Emotions** *are feelings.* When you get angry, for example, it's hard to see ways to solve the problem. It helps to look at problems objectively. *Viewing a problem* **objectively** *means seeing it without emotion.* Try to look at the problem as an outsider would.

Take the time to think about the problem. Below are some steps you can follow to handle problems more objectively. You may notice they are similar to the decision-making steps you read about in Chapter 5.

1. **Face the problem.** Some people don't want to admit that a problem exists. Sometimes the real problem may be hard to recognize. This is especially true if the problem is complex.
2. **Stretch your thinking.** Come up with as many solutions as possible. There may be several ways to handle it. Try to consider what the results might be if you followed each solution.
3. **Pick a solution.** Select the solution that seems to be the best. Keep in mind the results you think the solution will have.
4. **Try out the solution to see how it works.** Has it solved the problem? Has the problem become worse? Be sure you have given the solution a fair chance of working. If it doesn't work out, try another solution.

There may be times, however, when nothing you do seems to help solve the problem. You will have to accept that fact. You may not like this situation, but remember you did your best.

REVIEW YOUR WORK

1. Why are problems between people often difficult to handle?
2. What are the four steps in problem solving?

Getting Along with People

You already have a lot of experience in getting along with people. You have probably discovered that some people are easier to be with than others.

Unpleasant people can make your work surroundings uncomfortable and unpleasant. Then you are less likely to do a good job. You certainly won't enjoy your work.

It's to your advantage to do everything you can to keep good relationships with co-workers and customers. The end results of being pleasant are certainly worth the thought and care you put into these relationships.

Losing your temper is not a way to keep good relationships. Why do you think it is especially important to keep good relationships with co-workers and customers?

Working together is an important part of many jobs. Can you name one important guideline for getting along with others?

Building Relationships

It's impossible to get along with everyone all the time. There will be people you don't like. Not everyone will like you. Relationships with customers and co-workers, however, are easier to maintain if you keep the following points in mind.

Treat Others Considerately.   Treat people as you would like to be treated. When you've had a bad day, you may not be at your best. You may be cranky or even a little short with people. You want people to understand and overlook your bad days. Your co-workers have bad days, too. Don't expect them to be in a good humor all of the time.

If a large part of your job consists of dealing with customers, you have an added responsibility. You are representing your company. You are expected to be friendly and helpful. This may not always be easy when a customer is cross and seems to find fault with everything.

Being short-tempered and rude with unpleasant customers does not help the situation. The customer may be wrong and may handle the situation poorly. If you do the same, the situation will become worse. Be thoughtful and considerate. You may find that you can make the customer smile. Even if you don't, the customer will have a hard time finding fault with you. What is more important, you will be happy with your own behavior.

Understand the Other Side.   Try to understand the other person's side. Another way to say this is to be open-minded. As you look around, you'll see that many people are under pressure in their jobs. Deadlines have to be met. Sometimes there is too much work to do and too few people to do it. This can be true for both your co-workers and your employer.

Employers are responsible for everyone who works for them. There is a lot riding on the decisions your employer makes . . . profits, employees' jobs, competition, and customer relations. Employers have to look at a bigger picture than does each employee. What seems very important to you may not be that important to your employer, and vice-versa.

Before you react, try to think of the position the other person is in. You may see things differently. As a result of thinking about other people, your reaction will probably be a more effective one.

Look at Your Own Behavior.   Make sure you are not the person at fault. Sometimes your behavior can hurt or offend others. Try to be aware of how you appear to someone else.

For example, Meg and Jane were in charge of publicity for the school dance because they always had clever ideas. Meg thought of several posters and announcements they could make. However, when Meg and Jane held their first planning meeting, Jane did all the talking. She never asked about Meg's ideas. Meg didn't like Jane's take-charge attitude.

When the next school dance came around, Meg did not want to serve on the publicity committee with Jane. Jane couldn't understand why. After all, the publicity they had done for the first dance was successful. Jane will not be able to understand Meg's feelings until she looks at her own behavior.

Speak Carefully.   Think of the way others will feel when they hear what you have to say. Compare Sylvia's comments with Beth's. Which would you rather have said to you?

Sylvia: "Your writing is too messy. How did you ever get through school? I can't understand a word you've written. How do you expect me to do my own work right?"

Beth: "I'm having a hard time reading your writing. Maybe my eyes aren't too good. Could you help me out by writing more clearly? Then I won't make any mistakes."

By "blaming" her own eyes, Beth tried to protect the other person's feelings. At the same time, she was truthful about

It is important to continually look at your own behavior to be certain that you are not at fault. What should you consider when looking at your own behavior?

what needed to be done. The other person didn't have to guess about what was on her mind. She was clear about the effects of the messy writing.

Sometimes people aren't aware that what they're doing is causing a problem. Once they know there is a problem, they need a chance to straighten it out. By asking the other person for help, Beth gave that person a feeling of doing something useful instead of just correcting a bad habit.

Learn to Compromise.   You cannot have your own way all of the time. When people don't agree, sometimes the best thing to do is to compromise. *To* **compromise** *means that both people give up something in order to come to an agreement.*

It takes more than one person to compromise. Both people must have the chance to state how they feel about the problem. Both must know how much they are willing to give. Both must be willing to change. It is not a compromise when one person makes all of the changes.

CASE STUDY Veronica and Mark worked at the bowling alley. Their boss asked Veronica to work the following Saturday. Veronica asked Mark if he would work instead. Mark wasn't happy about it, but Veronica said, "This is special. A close friend is getting married. I really would like to go to the wedding."

Mark said, "Let's compromise. I'm scheduled to work Sunday, but some friends are coming to visit me. It would be nice to have the time to spend with them. I'll work on Saturday for you if you'll work for me Sunday."

"That's fine. I have some plans, but I can change them. Sure, I'll work for you. Thanks."

Thinking About the Case Study

1. What did Veronica give up in this example of a compromise? What did Mark give up?
2. Are all compromises this easy?

Other Tips.   Here are some additional ideas for developing good relationships with others.

- **Let other people know you're interested in them.** Listen when they talk. If you know someone loves cats, share a story about a cat. If you eat lunch with some co-workers, tell them you had a good time. If you know someone had a big event planned, such as a party, ask how things went. They will appreciate your interest.
- **Smile.** Smiling shows warmth. People like being around others who look happy to see them.
- **Make others feel important.** Everyone wants to feel important. Haven't you felt good when someone asked your opinion and really listened to what you said? Weren't you flattered when a person pointed out something that you did well?
- **Show a sense of humor.** People like being around those who can laugh at themselves. When everything seems to go wrong, that's often the best time to laugh. Of course, humor can be misused. When you make fun of others, you are misusing humor. People are sensitive about the way they look, talk, and act. When you make jokes, be sure they are jokes everyone will find funny.
- **Try to avoid fights.** People often say things during arguments that they later wish they hadn't said. When your feelings are hurt, it takes a while to get over it.

Good relationships on the job can make work more enjoyable for everyone. What is one tip for building good relationships on the job that is easy to follow?

Of course, there are times when you have to disagree. However, you don't have to turn it into a fight. You can show respect for the other person if you say, "I understand your point, but I can't agree with you."

- **Help others.** If you finish your work early, maybe you can help someone else. You'll be making a friend. It's hard to dislike someone who helps when you need it.
- **Avoid gossip.** Sometimes people gossip because they want to hurt another person. Passing "the news" along might make them feel important. Unfortunately, gossip can hurt people or cause trouble.

Some people think they can get in good with others if they tell all they know about everyone else. These people may be popular for a while, but it probably won't last long. People will wonder what the gossiper is saying behind their own backs.

Also, you may be in a position of trust at work. You may know information about your boss, customers, or co-workers. If you share that information, you will no longer be trusted.

The "Wait and See" Period

Some people want to be liked right away. They hurry to make friends so they won't be alone. Sometimes this is a mistake. It takes a while to make good friends.

You have probably been through testing periods before. You will go through them each time you begin a new job. You will be unsure of the new job and the new people you meet. The people you meet will also be unsure about you. Both of you must go through a "wait and see" period.

After a while you will begin to feel comfortable with one another. It may be a week, or it may be several weeks. It's important to remember that people already working for the company have certain ways of getting along. It may take a while for you to fit into the group.

Conversational Skills.
Developing good conversational skills can help ease you through the wait and see period. You may have noticed that some people seem to be naturals when it comes to making conversation. They always seem to say the right thing at the right time. Others seem to have difficulty thinking of what to say. They may be uncomfortable when they first meet new people.

Are you good at making conversation? You can sharpen your skills very easily. Think of conversation as having the following three levels.

New workers must often wait through a testing period before other workers will begin to feel comfortable with them. What is this period called?

Human Relationships on the Job

No matter where you go in the world, you will find all kinds of people. Some will never stop talking; others will hardly say a word. Some will brag and boast about how wonderful they are; others will be timid and feel sorry for themselves. Some will be honest and sincere; others will be dishonest and hypocritical.

You will probably like most of the people you meet. Some you will like a lot. However, there will probably be others whom you would just as soon avoid.

When you're on your own time— after school, after work, weekends— you can spend your time with whomever you want. Work is a different matter. Unless you own your own business, you won't be able to choose the people you work with. You'll have to work with the people who are there, on the job, whether you like them or not.

To make matters worse, work often creates problems between people. People disagree about the best way to do a job. They disagree about who is supposed to do a certain job. Deadlines and countless other pressures on the job can make everyone tense and irritable. Work sometimes makes even the most pleasant people difficult to get along with.

With all of these potential problems, you should still **THINK POSITIVELY** about working with people. The good relationships will far outweigh the bad. Additionally, with a positive attitude, you will be able to keep the problems to a minimum.

You will meet lots of interesting people at work, and you will make many new friends. Working with people is probably the easiest and fastest way to get to know people. If you are the quiet, shy type who has difficulty making small talk, you'll find work an especially good way to begin new relationships.

You will encounter a few people who will want to boss you around, or who will want you to do all the work. If you follow the guidelines in this chapter, however, you will be able to handle these kinds of problems. If serious problems develop, talk to your parents, guardians, or trusted friends. Be honest and sincere, and work at doing the best job you can. Keep thinking positively. If you do these things, you will make many friends on the job and your people problems will be few.

- **Small talk** is about everyday things such as the weather, a book, or what you did yesterday.
- **Idea talk** is about your opinions or what interests you. It's what you think about something. For example, you may have an idea about how to get more people to go to school games, or you may have an idea about how to celebrate co-workers' birthdays.
- **Feeling talk** is how you feel about something. You may say, "I get angry when people throw cans out of car windows."

During working hours there will be a lot of idea talk. You'll be asking questions, giving information, making requests, and solving problems.

At first you may feel a little uncomfortable talking to the same people before and after work and at lunch. Depend on small talk at those times. Small talk is an important part of everyday conversation. It's an icebreaker.

Talk about what's happening next weekend or what you saw on TV. Your hobbies or others' hobbies are also good topics. Later, as you get to know others, you will feel more comfortable sharing your personal ideas and feelings.

Another way to get conversations going is to ask about the other person. Peter did this when he was talking to Sharon: "Sharon, I've noticed you read sports magazines. What sports are you interested in?" In this way Peter let Sharon know he wanted to get to know her better.

If you don't talk to people, they may think you don't care, that you do not like them, or that you are "stuck-up." However, you may be lucky to be around people who are friendly. They may start most of the conversations. At other times, it will be up to you to get the conversation going.

CAREER Q&A

TOO SHY?

Q: What can I do if I am shy and really have a hard time starting a conversation?
A: Look around for a person who has shown an interest in you. Try asking a question about something that really interests you.

Looking and Listening.   Looking and listening can help you in your new job. In most businesses there are ways certain things are done. People may all wear the same type of clothing. They may all go out to lunch every day. By looking at what others do, you can learn the company style. Here are some of the things you might want to observe:

- the way people dress
- the time everyone begins to work
- when people stop working
- what others do at break time
- how often people talk to each other socially during work hours
- what personal things people keep at their work stations, such as pictures or plants

- whether people eat lunch together
- if people do things together outside of work

What other things do you think you want to observe?

In some ways, you will want to be like the others. In other ways, you may not want to be like them. Let's look at one or two examples.

Suppose people at work dress very casually. The women wear mostly pants or skirts with blouses or T-shirts. The men wear jeans and T-shirts. If you got all dressed up and wore a jacket and tie or a fancy dress, you would stand out. You would look different. Your co-workers might think you feel you are too good for them.

On the other hand, suppose people begin work 15 or 20 minutes later than starting time, take long breaks, and quit work early. What do you think you should do?

As a new employee, you know the boss will be watching you closely. Since you want to make a good impression, it may be best in this case to be a little different from the others. Be on time, but try not to draw too much attention to it. Your co-workers may feel you are trying to show them up. As a new employee, however, you can't afford to copy their habit.

You can learn a lot about how a company works by looking at things such as work habits and dress. How would you describe the way the people at this art studio dress?

As a new employee, the boss will be watching you closely. What should you do if everyone else takes longer breaks than they are allowed?

To remain friendly with co-workers, you might begin work in a less obvious way. For example, straighten papers on your desk, look through some work orders, or get your tools organized. You will be working, but others will probably not feel as uncomfortable.

REVIEW YOUR WORK

1. Why should you make an effort to get along with others at work? Give three reasons.
2. List six guidelines for good work relationships.
3. What are the three levels of conversation? Give an example of each.
4. What does it mean to compromise?

Getting Along with Yourself

You treat other people the way you treat yourself. If you respect and like yourself, you will probably feel the same way about co-workers, friends, and family.

For example, if you make a mistake and then punish yourself with such statements as "I'm really stupid . . . I *never* do anything right!" you are putting yourself down. If you do this, you will probably put others down when they make mistakes. If you say "I made a mistake but I *will* get it right the next time!" you are giving yourself a break. You understand that nobody is perfect. You will forgive others when they make mistakes.

How you feel about yourself will affect how you solve problems at work. It will be especially important to you in handling criticism, competition, and stress.

Handling Criticism

Listening to people tell you how to improve is not always easy. However, the way criticism is given often affects the way you accept it.

CASE STUDY   Mr. George said, "Mary Ellen, can't you ever do anything right? I told you I wanted these notices out by five o'clock today. They'll never be finished on time. If I want something done around here, I have to do it myself!"

Mary Ellen replied, "I'm sorry, but it's not my fault, Mr. George. This machine slows me up."

Thinking About the Case Study

1. Did Mr. George treat Mary Ellen with respect?
2. Do you think Mary Ellen will feel good about working hard for Mr. George?

Criticism is the opposite of praise. Mr. George's criticism of Mary Ellen is an example of destructive criticism. **Destructive criticism** *focuses on just the bad things and gives the person no help.* Criticism is destructive when

- it's said in an angry voice
- what is wrong is never clearly pointed out
- it is meant to hurt
- no suggestions for improvement are offered

Generally, criticism is given when people want you to improve what you are doing. What is the difference between destructive and constructive criticism?

Mr. George could have criticized differently and still told Mary Ellen he wasn't pleased with her work. He might have said: "Mary Ellen, it's almost five, and it doesn't look as if those notices will get out today. You could have worked faster if you had set up the machines differently. Let me show you what I mean."

In the second example, Mr. George is using constructive criticism. **Constructive criticism** *is designed to be helpful.* Criticism is constructive when

- it is said in a calm voice
- it centers on the problem and not the person
- hurtful remarks are not made
- suggestions for improvements are given

Generally, criticism is given when people want you to improve what you are doing. Anyone who is new to a job will have a lot to learn and must expect criticism.

Criticism is usually meant to be helpful, even though it may not sound that way when you hear it. You have no way of knowing how people will criticize you. You have to be prepared to accept both constructive and destructive criticism.

When Someone Criticizes You.   Criticism usually hurts no matter how it's delivered. It's hard to feel good when you are told you did something wrong. You can't control how others criticize you. You can, however, control how you react. You can react to criticism in a positive way or a negative, defensive way.

Being **defensive** *means not accepting responsibility for what you have done, or getting upset about a kind of criticism that is not important.* You are being defensive if you do the following.

* Admit the problem but blame other things or people. Mary Ellen did this when she told Mr. George the machine slowed her up.
* Admit the problem but try to get the person to feel sorry for you. "I couldn't do it because I have a headache."
* Get *too* mad at yourself and put yourself down. "I'm just not good enough. I'll never be able to do it right."
* Stay upset about criticism for hours no matter how small it might be or how kindly you were told.

The best way to avoid defensive behavior is to keep a positive attitude. Remember, you can and will do better next time. Making a mistake does not mean you're a total failure. It's not the end of the world. Here are some examples of positive responses:

"Yes, I have been careless about being on time. I'll try to do better."

"I'm sorry this happened. It won't happen again."

"I appreciate your telling me this. How can I do it better next time?"

People who respond to criticism in a positive way generally impress others. People who work at correcting weaknesses are the ones who move ahead in their jobs.

When You Criticize Others.   If someday you become a supervisor, you may have to correct or criticize others. Even if you don't become a supervisor, you may meet people who affect your work in a negative way. Either way, you will have to handle the task carefully. What would you do about the following?

* Steve is a nice guy with a good sense of humor. He keeps everybody laughing and makes working fun. However, he is always borrowing money for lunch or soft drinks. He seldom pays his debts. Today he asked you for $3.
* Kate can get work done faster than anyone else. She is good, too, and never makes a mistake. When she finishes

CAREER Q&A

WHEN YOU'RE RIGHT

Q: If I know I am right about something at work, should I state my opinion about it?

A: You should state your opinion, especially if an improvement can be made or if someone could be injured. Do it in a positive way. Repeating and insisting can become negative. Be sure your ideas are clearly understood. If you are right, chances are good people will find out.

The best way to avoid defensive behavior is to keep a positive attitude. What are some positive ways to respond to a supervisor who criticizes you about sloppy work?

early, however, she likes to come over and talk to you. So far you've managed to get your work done on time, but you've noticed your boss watching the two of you lately.
* Everybody likes Arthur and knows he needs the job. He used to be on time, but for the past month he's been late. You have been covering for him and doing more than your share of the work. You're getting tired of it.

The best way to criticize someone else is to think about how you'd like to be treated in the same situation.

* Do you like to be embarrassed?
* Do you like to be told there is something about you that other people do not like?
* Do you like to have your feelings hurt?
* Do you like to have everybody else know what you have done wrong?

People are far from perfect. *You* are not perfect. Let the other person know you understand that.

Talk to the other person alone. Don't bring up the subject in front of other workers. Discussing the problem in front of others makes the situation even more embarrassing.

We all like to think other people like everything about us. Chances are the other person will feel hurt when you bring up the problem. So choose your words and the way you talk about the problem carefully.

At work, you may have to criticize others. Why is it helpful to talk to the other person alone?

Ask the other person to help you understand why he or she is making the mistake. This allows the person to explain, and most people are willing to explain.

Competition

How do you feel about competition? Some people always want to come in first place. They don't like to settle for second place. These people would probably be happy working in a job for a company that encourages competition. Other people prefer jobs that have less pressure. They prefer to work at their own pace and not to be measured against someone else's performance.

Some jobs are more competitive than others. Some companies are more competitive than others, too. Some companies offer prizes to workers who turn out the most work or sell the most products. Competition usually increases the amount of work that gets done on the job.

Competition can sometimes help develop a team spirit. Competition makes a worker try a little harder. It can help you become a better worker because you set higher goals for yourself.

If you enjoy competition, you will enjoy working for a company that encourages it. However, competition can be harmful. It is not good if

- the quality of your work goes down
- you find yourself disliking people just because they won and you didn't
- losing makes you angry or upset
- winning becomes so important you forget about everything else
- you feel nervous or as though you are under too much pressure

Competition can be either positive or negative in its effects. Be sure the job and company you choose match your own feelings about competition.

Stress

Pressure on a job can come from competition, from trying to meet deadlines, or from a boss or co-workers who expect too much. Everyone needs to know how to cope with stress. **Stress** *is the effect that pressure often has on people.*

- Get plenty of exercise. Exercise allows your body to work off the nervousness and other side effects of stress.
- Get enough rest and the right kinds of food. Your body can't cope with trouble if you don't treat it right.
- Take things a day at a time. You don't have to do everything all at once. Work toward your goals a little bit each day. Solve your problems one step at a time. There's an old saying that seems to fit here: "Don't bite off more than you can chew."

How can you tell if you're under stress? Here are some common signs.

- You feel you can't reach goals set for you either by yourself or someone else.
- You have trouble persuading others to do what you want. You argue with other people.
- You feel someone else is forcing you to do something against your will, and you don't know what to do.
- You aren't proud of the work you do or don't feel you do it very well.
- You tire easily.
- You don't like the work itself.
- You don't get along with the people at work.

Exercise is a good way to deal with stress. What is one way not to deal with stress?

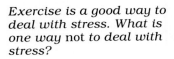

Not all stress is bad. Like sports, stress can be a form of exercise. It makes you try harder to change things. It gives you a challenge.

Unfortunately, too much stress for too long a time can cause illnesses such as ulcers. Stress can cause people to forget the good things about themselves. If you find yourself under a lot of stress, try some of the following.

- Talk about it with someone you trust. You don't have to work everything out all by yourself. No one is that strong all of the time.
- Don't use drugs or alcohol to help stress. People who have used these to help themselves through hard times will tell you that they only make matters worse. The sense of relief you might feel is only temporary. The stress will still be there when the effects of the drugs or alcohol wear off.
- Do something each day just for pleasure, such as playing the guitar, swimming, or reading a good book.

The best way to deal with stress is to learn about yourself. Know when you are nervous, grouchy, or cranky. Know your limits.

REVIEW YOUR WORK

1. What is the difference between constructive and destructive criticism? Give an example of each.
2. How does stress begin? What are some signs of stress?
3. Name four things you could do to handle a stressful time in your life.

Computer Careers

You drop a token into the slot. Suddenly, you're blasting away aliens, you're in the race of your life, or you're leaping turtles on your way to save a captured princess. This is the world of video games. It's exciting, colorful, and fun. Unfortunately, you're not likely to make much of a living by playing video games.

That does not mean this exciting, colorful, and fun world has to be completely cut out of your working life. If you love video games, you might also find that you love the world of computers. The world is becoming increasingly dependent on computers. That means a need for people who can program, operate, and maintain computers.

Computer programmers are people with strong math skills who can create ways to get the computer to do new jobs. A computer programmer is the one responsible for the functions of your favorite video game. Programmers create programs to entertain, to teach, and to handle complicated business and technical jobs. Most programmers have at least a college degree in computer science or math.

Computer operators feed computers the information they need to do a job. This process is called data input. As a computer operator, you would work with a computer and a program created by a programmer. Fast, efficient computer operators are always in demand.

Like everything mechanical, computers sometimes break down. When this happens, a computer technician is called in to get the computer or computer system up and running again. Many computer technicians spend a good part of their time traveling from one busi-

ness to another, helping to solve computer problems. Most computer technicians have at least a high school diploma and some vocational or technical training.

If you would like to mix your interest in computers with your strong people skills, you might want to look into a career in computer sales or customer support. As a computer salesperson, you will be expected to know how the computers work and what they can do so that you can hook a customer up with the right machine. Customer support workers help to keep existing customers happy by making sure that their computer system stays up to date.

If computers interest you, talk to your guidance counselor. He or she can help you turn today's hobby into tomorrow's career.

Chapter Summary

- One of the single most important skills for doing well in the working world is being able to get along with your co-workers.
- Emotions—yours and other people's—often make problems on the job more difficult to solve.
- The best rule to follow on the job as well as elsewhere is to treat others as you would like to be treated.
- There is always a "wait and see" period when people are new. It's better not to force yourself on others.
- Learning conversational skills can smooth the way to getting along with others.
- By looking and listening, you will become sensitive to "clues" that will help you fit in with the group.
- There are two kinds of criticism, one is destructive, the other is constructive. Listen to both constructive and destructive criticism, don't become defensive, and try to make the changes that are needed.
- Stress management is important in the working world.

Reviewing Vocabulary and Concepts

Write the numbers 1–13 on a separate sheet of paper. After each number, write the letter of the answer that best completes the following statements or answers the question.

1. _____ is another word for feelings.
   a. Nerves   c. Emotions
   b. Relationship   d. Psychology
2. If you are viewing something _____, you are viewing it without emotion.
   a. objectively
   b. at a distance
   c. without your glasses
   d. emotionally
3. It's _____ to get along with everyone all the time.
   a. easy
   b. impossible
   c. not a good idea
   d. necessary
4. Being short-tempered with an unpleasant customer or co-worker often makes the situation _____ .
   a. worse   c. go away
   b. better   d. continue
5. It's a good idea to look at your own _____ to see if you may have caused a problem without meaning to.
   a. clothing   c. work space
   b. hair   d. behavior
6. Compromise means _____ .
   a. both people give up something to reach an agreement
   b. one person gives in totally
   c. neither person gives in
   d. signing a contract
7. When you make fun of other people, you are _____ .
   a. being very entertaining
   b. misusing humor
   c. being the office grouch
   d. making yourself fit in
8. Three conversational levels are _____, idea talk, and feeling talk.
   a. speech making   c. small talk
   b. baby talk   d. rap talk
9. If you share information you shouldn't, you can no longer _____ .
   a. be trusted
   b. go out with the gang
   c. work with a group
   d. take breaks

10. The period of time it takes you before you feel comfortable with your new job, your new co-workers, and they with you, is known as the
_____ .
a. trial by fire
b. a test
c. wait-and-see period
d. probation

11. Someone who uses an angry voice and hurtful remarks when criticizing is giving _____ .
a. destructive criticism
b. constructive criticism
c. good advice
d. competition

12. Criticism is _____ when it is said in a calm voice, centers on the problem and not the person, gives helpful instead of hurtful remarks, and also gives suggestions for improvement.
a. destructive
b. uncalled for
c. good advice
d. constructive

13. When people are _____, they don't accept responsibility for what they have done.
a. lonely
b. unhappy
c. defensive
d. uninformed

Thinking Critically About Career Skills

Write your answers to the following questions on a separate sheet of paper.

1. Imagine that you work in a shoe store. One of your co-workers is sloppy in the way he handles making change for customers, and you need to speak with him. How could you tell your co-worker that he needs to be more attentive in a constructive manner?

2. What are some things you could do if a co-worker is "goofing around" a lot while you work steadily and you feel that nobody notices his behavior but you?

Building Basic Skills

1. **Mathematics** Calculate your rank in a company sales contest. Worker A has sold 35 products at $48 each, Worker B has sold 20 products at $48 each and 2 products at $99 each, Worker C has sold 15 products at $48 each and 10 products at $99 each. You have sold 17 products at $48 each and 6 at $99 each. List the totals for each salesperson in order from highest to lowest.

2. **Writing** Write an outline for a 500-word essay on the advantages and disadvantages of competition.

Applying Career Skills

Using the principles presented in this chapter, do the following activities.

1. Try making a new friend. This will give you practice in building new relationships. It can be a new student in your school, someone you've met on an after-school job, or a new church member. On a separate sheet of paper, write your new friend's name, age, and where you met him or her.

2. Choose a partner from this class and act out a problem-solving scene. Switch characters so you each have a chance to be on both sides of an issue. Make up several different situations. After a rehearsal, present the best one to the class.

BASIC SKILLS AND ATTITUDES FOR SUCCESS

Tim wanted to be an accountant. So when his English class was studying a unit on public speaking, Tim wasn't interested. He knew he was not going to be a public speaker, and he didn't try to learn.

Now Tim wishes he had paid more attention. His boss wants him to teach new employees about the way accounting is handled in his firm. Tim, however, feels uncomfortable in front of an audience. Tim's boss thinks Tim can be successful and has suggested he take a public speaking course. Tim thinks about the opportunity he missed in high school.

Like Tim, many people fail to take advantage of their opportunities because they are not prepared. They haven't developed the basic skills and attitudes that all workers need to be successful. You might say, "Why should I learn how to spell? I'm not going to be an English teacher." Knowing how to spell is an important part of a great number of jobs.

Employers are willing to teach you how to do the jobs they want done. They are not so willing to teach you the basic skills that you are supposed to learn in school. Additionally, employers usually don't have the patience or time to deal with problems caused by a worker with a poor attitude.

Developing basic communication and math skills and a positive attitude will be keys to your success in the working world. Most people who have progressed from assembly line workers or salespeople to become supervisors, managers, or company presidents have several things in common. They have positive attitudes, and they have developed strong basic skills.

What meaning does this have for you? You may change jobs any number of times during your work life. On each job, you will be tackling new problems and learning new routines. With all of these changes, you will need a positive attitude and basic skills on every job.

In this chapter you will learn about the basic communication and math skills that all employers want their workers to have. You will also learn about the great importance of having a positive work attitude. Now is the time to start improving your skills and attitude.

Communication Skills

Communication *is getting your message across to others.* At work you communicate with many people—your boss, co-workers, and customers. You need to make yourself understood. Every day you'll have to write messages and understand what you read, as well as listen and talk to people. You don't want to be embarrassed because you can't speak or write clearly. You'll want to be the best communicator you can be.

Speaking

Talking to people is an important part of everyone's work. Even a forest ranger or security guard has to report to someone that everything is okay. Information must be exchanged. Instructions must be given and received. How you speak may affect your work and that of others as well.

Your speaking, listening, reading, and writing skills will play a big part in your success in the working world. What are these skills called?

Perhaps you have heard someone who had a really good speaking voice. Did you pay attention? Did you want to know more about the person? Good speakers usually get attention. People take notice of them.

Clarity (being clear), tone, speed, loudness, and pronunciation are some of the differences between a good speaker and a poor speaker.

Being Clear.   Cluttered messages are like cluttered closets. Everything is mixed up. The ideas get lost. Getting your ideas across can depend on how clear and easy the message is to understand. There are several things you can do.

Use simple words. Save your fancy words for another time. Hard words make messages harder to understand. For example, why say, "Increased utility justified additional computer expenditures," when you can say, "We spent more money on computers in order to better use them"?

Make one point at a time. Avoid putting too many ideas in a sentence. Read the following statements. Notice that the second statement is much easier to follow than the first.

"In addition to being cost effective, the new plan should work well since it is easy to set up and takes people into account, as well as saving money for the company."

"The new plan should work well. First, it is easy to set up. Second, it takes people into account. Third, it will save money for the company."

Tone, Speed, and Loudness.   Vary your tone as you talk. Have you ever listened to yourself talk? What do you sound like? Does the tone of your voice go up and down?

People who speak in the same tone speak in a monotone. "Mono" means one, and monotone means one tone or level. People who speak in a monotone have a hard time holding others' attention. You can vary your tone the way a singer does with a song by adding low and high notes. Don't change your tone too much, however, or you won't sound natural.

It's best to speak at an even speed. If you speak too fast, people will miss what you are saying. If you speak too slowly, people will get bored. Somewhere in between is better.

Make sure you talk loudly enough, but not too loudly. Have you ever pulled back when someone used a loud voice? The reverse happens when someone speaks in a whisper. You bend toward the person and strain to hear. If listening is too much work, you may even give up entirely.

Pronunciation.

The way you say words is called **pronunciation.** People with lazy speech habits are hard to understand. Always try to pronounce words clearly.

Have you heard people say: "b'lee me," "plennee a time," "jemman," "ast," "worl" when they mean "believe me," "plenty of time," "gentlemen," "ask," "world"? Their close friends may understand them, but their friends may not be able to hire them for jobs. You must be sure everyone can understand what you have to say.

The sound of your voice can either help or hinder your efforts to communicate a message. Is there anything you can do to improve the sound of your voice?

You can improve the way you pronounce words. If you are having a hard time saying a word, ask a teacher to pronounce it for you. Listen to the way people who speak correctly say their words. Watching educational television shows can be a good way to hear correct pronunciation. Repeat the words several times after you hear them. Ask others to listen to you say the words correctly.

REVIEW YOUR WORK

1. What are the basic skills that you need to be successful on the job? Why are they important?
2. To be sure you are understood when you speak, what points should you keep in mind?

Listening

Most people have poor listening skills. They think about what they are going to say next, while the other person is still talking. What happens? They don't really hear what is said. Most people want to say the right things themselves, but how can they if they don't hear all of the conversation?

Good listening means that you hear and understand what someone says. Good listeners make fewer mistakes than poor listeners. Good listeners also make better impressions on others. You know how good you feel when someone wants to hear what you have to say.

There is much more to listening than just hearing what the speaker is saying. Are most people good listeners?

Some people think listening is just being quiet when someone talks. It's more than that. You can be a better listener. Here's how.

- **Pay attention.** This means stopping whatever you're doing while the person talks. Don't write. Don't doodle. Don't think about what you are going to do next week. Pretend the person speaking is the only other person in the world at that moment.
- **Don't interrupt.** Wait until the speaker has finished before you say anything. Smiling or nodding your head as you listen tells the speaker you understand him or her.
- **Ask the speaker to repeat the information if you don't understand.** Ask questions. Ask the speaker to give an example to make a point clearer.
- **Check what you hear.** Repeat in your own words what you think you heard. For example, you can ask, "Did I hear you say . . . ?" Then the other person can tell you if you did or did not hear correctly.

It doesn't take a lot of work to be a good listener. It does take practice.

Writing

Sometimes job ads ask you to write a letter in reply. How well you are able to write may decide whether or not you get an interview.

In business you often have to send out memos, letters, directions, and announcements. Good writing skills can help you get ahead on the job.

The best way to learn to write is to practice. Have a teacher or someone who writes well read what you have written. Ask for ideas about how to improve. You may even want to take a business English class.

Good writers follow these basic guidelines:

- **Consider the audience.** Direct your words to the people who will be reading what you write. One group of people may be able to understand one kind of message but not another. What causes this difference? There are many factors. However, most important are the experience and background of the readers. Keep in mind what they already know about your topic. Think about what additional information they may need in order to understand your message.
- **Outline what you are going to say.** Think about what you want to say. Then arrange the points you want to

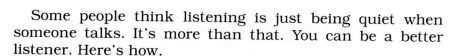

OPPORTUNITY

KNOCKS

MEDICAL SECRETARY

There are hundreds of different careers available to people with an interest in medicine. Your strong secretarial skills and medical interest could lead you to a career like this.

MEDICAL SECRETARY

Fast-paced downtown doctor's office looking for efficient medical secretary to help with front office work. Must be excellent typist, have neat appearance and be able to learn medical terms. Prior experience preferred but not required.

What type of jobs do you think this person would be asked to do?

Writing skills can help you succeed on the job and at school. What is the best way to learn to write?

make in order: first, second, third, and so on. Follow the outline when you write. Your writing will be clearer and better organized.

- **State the most important point first.** Then give the details—the what, how, or why. Then go on to the second most important point and give details, and so on.
- **Stick to the point.** As you write, be sure to follow your outline. If you write about ideas not in the outline, you have not thought things through carefully enough.
- **Be brief.** People have limited time. They appreciate getting the facts quickly.
- **Be clear.** Use simple words. Reread what you have written. Does it say what you want it to say?
- **Be accurate.** Are your facts straight? Are you saying what you mean?
- **Be correct.** Check spelling, grammar, and punctuation.
- **Be polite.** Things go more smoothly when people are considerate of one another.

Good writing can get your message across clearly and quickly. Your writing represents you when you are not present. It shows others how organized your thinking is.

Working with Animals

Her patient was a quiet one. Doctor Nguyen knew that she wasn't going to get much information from him. She was going to be on her own to find out the problem. Out of habit she reached out to feel his nose. She pulled her hand back and smiled. Whatever was wrong, she knew it wasn't too serious yet—Sparkey's nose was still moist and cool.

Doctor Nguyen is a veterinarian. Her patients are animals, and their owners depend on Doctor Nguyen. If you have a love for animals, perhaps you've considered a career as a veterinarian. Veterinarians combine their love of animals with exceptional skills in science and medicine. It is a tough job and one that is hard to get. Veterinarians must attend three to four years of veterinary school in addition to getting a bachelor of science degree from a college or university. There are only a few veterinary schools in America, and less than 10 percent of those who apply are accepted as students. Only the very best students ever make it as veterinarians.

You don't have to be a veterinarian, however, to work with animals. There are many jobs and careers available for people who wish to work with animals.

You might like a career as an animal control officer. Animal control officers protect people from stray or dangerous animals and protect animals from people. You could also help to protect wildlife by becoming a fish and game warden. This job is perfect for someone who wants to combine a love for animals and the outdoors with an interest in police or public safety work.

If you like animals and entertainment, you might look into a job as an animal trainer. Animal trainers need to be exceptionally loving and patient to turn our furred and feathered friends into tomorrow's stars.

If you would like to combine your aptitude for business with your love of animals, you might go into business for yourself as the owner of a pet store, an animal grooming facility, or a kennel operator.

There are many other jobs and careers available for people who love animals. To find out more, see your guidance counselor and start planning today. Remember, you need to make a career plan to see you through because it's a jungle out there.

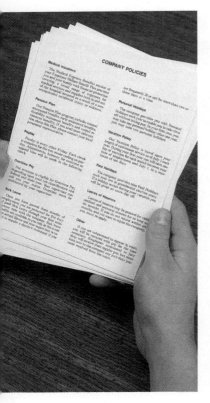

No matter what your job, you need to be a good reader to succeed in the working world. Can you name some ways to improve your reading skills?

Reading

At work you will need to read directions and memos. Depending on your job, you may have to read complaints, reports, newspapers, or books. It is very hard to get a job or to work your way up in a job if you can't read well.

If you are having trouble reading, do something about it now. Save yourself the embarrassment of not being able to read well when you are an adult. Find a class that will help you to learn to read. These classes may be offered in your school or in your neighborhood. Practice reading—books, magazines, anything that interests you.

Good readers use different styles for different types of reading. For example, if you have to remember what you are reading, read slowly. Detailed reports and instructions should be read slowly. If you need only to get the general idea of something, read more quickly.

Here are some ways to improve your reading skills.

- **Look over the material first.** Read the first paragraph, the headings, and the last paragraph. This will give you a general idea of what you'll be reading. Then go back and read all the material.

  For example, if you looked over, or surveyed, this section, "BASIC SKILLS AND ATTITUDES FOR SUCCESS," you would learn that it covers communication skills, such as speaking, listening, writing, and reading, as well as math skills and attitude.
- **Look for phrases.** Phrases are groups of words. If you read a sentence in phrases, it might look like this:

  In the box
you will find
all of the directions.

  Reading phrases speeds up your reading. Reading one word at a time holds you back.
- **Do not say the words out aloud.** Reading aloud keeps you from moving ahead.
- **Avoid rereading lines.** Rereading is a bad habit to get into. It slows you down. Even if you are having trouble with some sentences, keep on reading until you've finished a paragraph. By then you will get the general meaning. Then, if you have to, go back.
- **Recall what you read.** Right after reading a section of material, stop and tell yourself what you just read. It works! You will remember what you read for a longer time.

Many companies post safety messages on company bulletin boards. Why does this make reading skills especially important for workers?

- **Try to figure out the meaning of new words from the words around them.** Sometimes the other words will give you an idea of what the unknown word means. See if you can guess what "expedite" means in the next sentence. "Expedite the order because they need it as soon as possible." If you guessed that "expedite" means "speed up," you are right.
- **Wait to look up the meaning of a word.** Write it down and look it up later, so you do not break the flow of reading. Of course, sometimes nothing makes sense unless you know what a word means. Then you must look it up right away.
- **Write new words on cards.** Put down the meaning. Add a sentence using the word. Review the cards often. You have to use a word about 25 times before it becomes part of your vocabulary.

Can you think of other ways to help yourself become a better reader?

Mathematics Skills

Mathematics is one of the most important tools we use today. We live in the age of science. Almost all science depends in some way on math. Computers, space shuttles, even special effects in the movies, could not exist if it were not for math.

If math has been hard for you, you may not like it much. However, if you help yourself get better at it, you may like it a lot more. Either way, math is here to stay. It's best to try to like it.

You may think that machines can do all of your math for you. Unfortunately, this is not true. People use math every day to

- understand paychecks
- write bills
- understand contracts
- make change
- check the change they receive
- figure income tax
- weigh items
- measure things
- check inventories

Many jobs require special math skills. Can you name a job that requires no math skills?

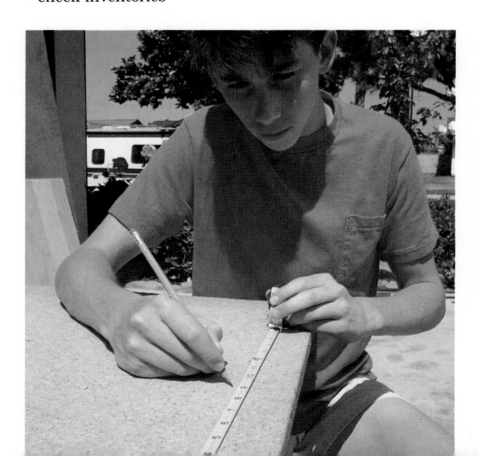

It's best to learn enough basic math to help you do your job without making mistakes. You may need math to help you see someone else's mistake . . . like the wrong amount on your paycheck!

Also, keep in mind that math develops good thinking habits. It helps you learn to put things in order, to take one step at a time.

If you want to improve your math skills, you might try the following suggestions. Even if you are good at math, you may find ways to increase your interest.

Strengthening your math skills now could be your key to the right job for you. Can you name some ways you can strengthen your math skills?

- Ask your math teacher for special help. Maybe all you need is practice. Maybe you became "stuck" at one point in learning about math. What you did not learn then affected all your work later on. For example, if you did not memorize your multiplication tables properly, you probably have trouble with long division, too. Your teacher may be able to help you get "unstuck," and the rest will take care of itself.

- Ask at your school or public library for books on improving math skills. Then use the books!

- Check your TV listings for public television programs on math skills. Don't be embarrassed if the programs are designed for children. You would not turn down a gift of a new stereo just because someone wrapped it in children's paper, would you?

- If your school allows you to use a calculator in math class, leave yours at home. Another method is to do the problems first by yourself, then check them with the calculator. The more you work with numbers, the easier it gets.

- Try the buddy system. If you have a friend who also has trouble with math, improve your skills together. For example, Joe designed three multiplication problems for Nirad each day, and Nirad designed three long-division problems for Joe. Each was given his problems in the morning and had all day to work them out. Then after school, the two friends checked each other's work. If they were unsure of answers, they asked a teacher. They made a game of it, and after two weeks the loser had to buy the winner's lunch!

A plan like this works even better if you and your friend have trouble in different areas. If you are good in English and your friend is good in math, you can trade your knowledge. If you can't find a close friend who is interested, ask someone else you know to be a tutor. Maybe you can work out a similar trade.

Basic Skills and Attitudes for Success

Throughout this book, and especially in this chapter, you've read about the importance of communication skills, math skills, and a positive attitude in the world of work. Are you getting the message? Do you believe what you're hearing?

If not, talk to employers. Ask them what they're looking for in employees. They'll tell you they want workers with good attitudes. They want workers who can communicate. They want workers who can solve problems and think for themselves, which often means solving math problems.

Employers feel they can teach you the skills you need to do the job they want done. They can't or don't have the time to teach you reading, writing, and arithmetic, or how to have a friendly, positive personality.

How do you stack up against the people your age as far as communication skills and math skills are concerned? What grades have you earned in English and math classes? Are you satisfied with your basic skills?

What about your general attitude toward life? Do you feel good about yourself? Do you get along well with most people? Do you approach most days with enthusiasm and happiness?

If you were unable to answer yes to all of these questions, don't waste your time worrying about it. Instead, start to work immediately to improve. **THINK POSITIVELY.** You can improve a great deal.

You are young and still in school. What better time and place to improve! You are surrounded by teachers and counselors who want to help you and who know how to help you. If you have the desire, the teachers in your school can help you do your best at communicating and solving math problems.

You can also improve your general attitude if it needs improving. There are lots of good suggestions in this chapter. If you can honestly judge your strengths and weaknesses and then make a firm decision to improve, you *can* improve. You can become the kind of employee all employers want to hire. More important, you can develop an attitude that will help make you successful and happy in all areas of your life.

- Play math games whenever you have a few minutes to spare. While you are waiting for a bus, say your multiplication tables from 2 to 12. You might also try writing them on a scrap of paper while you ride to school. If you are watching TV and a commercial comes on, try to guess what the product costs. Then figure the sales tax on it.
- Use another interest to help you build an interest in math. For example, if you like horses, make up math problems for yourself based on that. How long is a race track? How long is half of that? A third? Horses are measured in hands. How long is a hand? If a horse measures 16 hands, how tall is the horse in feet and inches?

   Do you like rock music? Did you know that music is based on math? A musical tone is made by vibration. If you stretch a string and then pluck it, the string produces a tone. The tone produced depends on how many times the string vibrates each second. If you make a string vibrate 256 times per second, you will produce the tone of C on the scale. If you cut the string in half, it vibrates twice as fast—512 times per second. The note it produces is still C, but it is higher on the scale. Maybe your math teacher will let you make a report to the class on math and music. If it's a good report, you may even get extra credit.

   Math doesn't have to be a problem for you. You can improve your math skills with a little effort and a little patience. At the same time, you will be improving your chances for an interesting and rewarding career. Below are several math problems for your review. If you cannot work them correctly, you may need special help.

- Suppose you need 10 feet of rope. You go to the hardware store to buy it. Rope is sold for $.25 a foot. It is also sold in packages of 15 feet for $3.00. If you wanted the best price per foot, which would you pick?
- You are paying your bill at the local fast-food restaurant. Your hamburger and shake come to $1.89, including tax. You give the cashier $2.00. How much change will you get back from the cashier?
- You found a sweater you want to buy in a mail-order catalog. The price is right. Originally it was $25.50, but is has been cut to $18.50. How much will you save? You decide to buy 2 sweaters. The state sales tax is 5%, and shipping and handling are $2.80. What is your total cost?

CAREER Q&A

FROM CLASSROOM TO JOB

Q: How do I know that what I learn at school will help me when I go to work?

A: Sometimes it's hard to see how a skill you learn in the classroom will directly help on the job. Look for ways to apply classroom learning to everyday life. Talk to your teachers and ask them for help in how to apply what you are learning to the world of work.

Attitude

Your **attitude** *is your general outlook on life.* It's the way you react to people and situations. Your attitude varies from day to day depending on your mood and how things are going. In general, however, you probably have either a positive or negative attitude.

If you want to be happy and successful in your work, you must have a positive attitude. Do you know what it means to have a positive attitude? *A* **positive attitude** *is a general way of looking at the world that makes life more enjoyable for you and everyone around you.* If you have a positive attitude, you make the best of a bad situation. You try to help yourself and others. You are usually happy and enthusiastic.

Employers want to hire workers with positive attitudes. They don't want workers who have negative attitudes. *A*

Your attitude is your general outlook on life. What is a positive attitude?

negative attitude *is a way of looking at the world and only seeing the bad side of things.* People with negative attitudes complain a lot and make other people unhappy. No one likes to work with people who have negative attitudes. Most of the people who lose their jobs lose them because of their poor attitude—not because they can't do the work.

Read the following conversation Sam and Diane are having about Mike, one of their friends. Judging from the conversation, they like and respect Mike. What qualities does Mike have that make him talked about?

CASE STUDY

"Have you heard about Mike?"
"No. Tell me. I'm ready to hear good news. It's been a really dull day."

"Well, Mike just made the All-State Basketball team . . . first team! I can't believe it. In junior high, the coach wouldn't even put him on the second-string team. He couldn't bounce a ball and walk down the court at the same time. Do you remember?"

"Yeah, I remember. I also remember the time he spent practicing. He really wanted to play basketball. He went out every day and shot baskets even when no one else believed in him. I couldn't figure him out."

"That's Mike. He doesn't let other people's ideas about him get him down. If yesterday was a bomb, that's all the more reason why today is going to be better. At least that's what Mike thinks."

"I know. Sometimes I wonder what makes him tick."

Thinking About the Case Study

1. Would you say Mike has a positive attitude or a negative attitude?
2. How did Mike's attitude affect his dream of playing basketball?

What *does* make Mike tick? Mike is probably not much different from a lot of people you know. Of course, they may not all spend hours practicing basketball shots, but they share the same outlook. They have a good attitude about themselves and about life. There's a slang expression, "Don't let the turkeys get you down." People with a good or positive attitude don't let the so-called turkeys get them down.

No one is happy all of the time, and sometimes there are very strong reasons for being unhappy. However, a positive attitude can help you get through a tough time. Likewise, a negative, or bad, attitude can make a tough time even worse.

You can complain to yourself, "Hey, this is a tough spot to be in." You can even place the blame on someone else. "I'm in trouble, and it's all my parents' fault." A better way is to say, "This isn't all bad. I'm doing okay at school. I'm busy in the electronics club. I have some good friends." If you have a good attitude, you look for good things in yourself and in others. When you look for good things, you help them happen.

Your attitude also affects how other people feel about you. Do you know anyone who seems to complain all the time or who never wants to do what the group is doing? Do you ever want to tell that person to shape up?

A positive attitude

- helps you stay alert
- helps you get things done
- creates a good impression on others
- inspires others to be positive
- makes you a pleasant person to be around

Think of the people you like to be around. They are probably people with a positive outlook. What can you learn from people with good attitudes? How are their attitudes shown in everyday events? How would you describe a person

Have you noticed that some people seem to be happy and cheerful most of the time, while other people seem unhappy and angry every day? Which type of person do you think employers want to hire?

POSITIVE ATTITUDE   NEGATIVE ATTITUDE

with a good attitude? Perhaps you would include the following items in your description. People with good attitudes

- are friendly to people they meet
- try to get along with others and make things work out
- know there isn't just one way to do something and can change when they must do something differently
- are willing to be the first to try something new
- believe in themselves and others
- are willing to work toward a goal
- are more likely to look at the bright side of things rather than the dark side.

Having a good attitude doesn't mean putting your head in the sand and refusing to see a real problem. It *does* mean you don't dwell on what's bad. You can see the problem, but you know that tomorrow is a new day with new opportunities.

How can you improve your attitude? Here are some suggestions from those who have succeeded in doing just that.

- Look at people who seem to have good attitudes. What do they do and say? How do they act? How do they go about solving problems?
- Look at your good points. Think about what you do well. Better yet, take out a piece of paper and list the things you like about yourself and the things you do well. As you add to the list, you'll see that you have a lot going for you. Your strengths will help you to make good things happen.

DID YOU KNOW?

SEND IN THE CLOWNS

Have you ever been called the class clown? Ringling Brothers Barnum and Bailey Circus conducts a clown training school in Florida. Approximately 30 clowns are selected from a class of 300. Those who graduate are offered a two-year contract starting at more than $200 per week.

People with positive attitudes are proud of their achievements. How can looking at your accomplishments help to improve your attitude?

People with positive attitudes can usually be found with smiles on their faces. Who do you think is generally happier, a person with a positive attitude or a person with a negative attitude?

- Start saying "I can" more often than "I can't."
- Work at improving one skill or interest at a time. Pick one you do only fairly well. How can you do it better?
- Spend time around people who have good attitudes and who make you feel good. Their qualities and outlook will rub off on you. Avoid people who are negative or who put you down.
- Give yourself a break. Don't be too hard on yourself. Even successful people have failures. Everyone strikes out sometimes. People who succeed, however, learn from their mistakes. If they can't figure it out themselves, they ask for help. They don't give up. People who have confidence believe they will make it the next time.

REVIEW YOUR WORK

1. How does having a good or poor attitude affect a person?
2. What are some characteristics of people with good attitudes?
3. How can people improve their attitudes?
4. Why do people sometimes miss out on good opportunities? How can you take advantage of your good opportunities now?

Chapter Summary

- Developing basic communication skills, math skills, and a positive attitude are keys to success in the working world.
- Good communication skills are a must on the job.
- Listening is also a communication skill. Good listening is more than just being quiet when someone else speaks.
- Writing is another communication skill. Good writers consider the audience, outline what they are going to say, state the most important point first, and stick to the point.
- Reading is a communication skill as well.
- Mathematics is an important tool in today's workplace. It's best to know enough basic math to help you do your job without making mistakes or to help you recognize someone else's mistake.
- Your attitude or general outlook on life affects how happy and successful you are in the workplace.

Reviewing Vocabulary and Concepts

Write the numbers 1–12 on a separate sheet of paper. After each number, write the letter of the answer that best completes the statement or answers the question.

1. In most workplaces, people have to _____ .
   a. work hard
   b. punch a time clock
   c. communicate
   d. listen a lot

2. _____ is considered one of the basic communication skills.
   a. Speaking
   b. Watching TV
   c. Smiling
   d. Eye contact

3. It's a good idea to use simple language so your message will be _____ .
   a. ignored
   b. admired
   c. okayed by your boss
   d. clear

4. People with lazy speech habits are said to have _____ .
   a. poor pronunciation
   b. a lot of friends
   c. little education
   d. a speech impediment

5. There is more to _____ than just being quiet.
   a. communication
   b. talking
   c. listening
   d. making a good impression

6. Some employers want you to answer their job ads with a letter because they want to _____ .
   a. make things difficult
   b. see if you have writing skills
   c. see if you're serious about wanting the job
   d. avoid meeting you in person

7. Your writing will be better organized if you _____ .
   a. use small words
   b. always use a typewriter
   c. try to be humorous
   d. outline what you plan to say

8. It is _____ to get a job or work your way up in a job if you can't read well.
   a. easy   c. hard
   b. very easy   d. impossible

9. Reading aloud _____ .
   a. helps you learn to read
   b. slows your reading down
   c. speeds your reading up
   d. gets everyone's attention
10. _____ is one of the most important tools we use today.
   a. A calculator
   b. A hammer
   c. Math
   d. Telephone
11. Music is based on _____ .
   a. vibration
   b. math
   c. language
   d. reading
12. If you have a(n) _____ you make life more enjoyable for yourself and for everyone around you.
   a. job
   b. a car
   c. negative attitude
   d. positive attitude

Thinking Critically About Career Skills

1. Do you think people can tell how educated you are by the way you talk? How do you feel about people who don't speak clearly? Explain your answers.
2. If you can use a calculator, do you still need to worry about having good math skills? Explain your answer.

Building Basic Skills

1. **Writing**   Write a 400-word newspaper or magazine article about building a positive attitude. Include advice helpful to people your age.
2. **Mathematics**   Calculate the costs of several calculators. Calculator A, which normally sells for $69.99, is marked 20 percent off; Calculator B, which normally sells for $79.95, is marked 40 percent off; Calculator C, which normally sells for $99.50, is marked 50 percent off. If the calculators are of equal quality, which would you buy?

Applying Career Skills

1. On a separate sheet of paper, make a list of three jobs you might enjoy. For each job list as many tasks as you can think of that are a part of doing that job. Beside each task write a *C* if the task requires communication skills, an *M* if the task requires math skills, and an *N* if the task requires neither math nor communication skills. Remember that reading and speaking are both communication skills.
2. With a partner, make a list of activities that people can do to help improve their attitude. Using photographs cut from magazines, put together a poster that shows people enjoying these activities. Label your poster ''Positively Happy.''

MAKING PROGRESS TOWARD YOUR GOALS

KEY TERMS

promotion
networking
giving notice
letter of resignation
fired
laid off
severance pay
unemployment
  compensation

OBJECTIVES

In this chapter you will
  learn about
- how you can grow on
  the job
- more responsibility—
  whether or not you
  want it and how to
  get it
- changing jobs and
  companies
- what to do if you lose
  a job
- reevaluating your
  career goals

After you have been on the job for a while, take a look at
your career plan. How are you doing? Where are you on your
career path? Are things going pretty much as you expected?
Have your goals changed at all?

In this chapter you will read about some things you can do
to avoid setbacks and to make progress toward your ultimate
career goal. You will learn how to grow and advance in your
present job. You will learn how to change jobs and what to do
if you lose a job. You will also learn about the importance of
re-evaluating your goals so that you can adjust to personal
and economic changes.

Growing on the Job

You will probably hold more than one job during your career. Some of those will be jobs along the way to the job you want most.

You should look for ways to get the most from every job, no matter how low it is on your career ladder. Try to think of each job you do as the most important position in the company. Challenge yourself to do it the best way you can. At least once each week ask yourself, "How can I do myself a favor this week? What new skill can I develop? What new knowledge can I acquire?"

There are many things you can do to learn more and develop new skills. Following are some suggestions about ways you can grow on the job.

- **Do your present job as well as you can.** There is no substitute for taking care of your regular duties. Some people are so eager to get ahead that they spend all their time on "extras." Meanwhile, the work they are already responsible for is left undone or poorly done. Others may devote lots of effort to the parts of the job they like and no effort to the parts they don't like. Do your assigned work to the best of your ability. That's your first task. Everything else comes second.

One important way to grow on the job is to do your present job as well as you can. Why do you think this is so important?

- **Volunteer to do more.** When your regular duties are finished, ask your boss if there is something else you can do. Be willing to pitch in and lend a hand. Both your boss and co-workers will remember how helpful you were.
- **Look for opportunities to learn on the job.** There will be certain tasks you will want to learn because they fit in with your career plan. At the same time, you can never guess how something that doesn't appear in your plan might help as well. Never turn down a chance to learn. Instead, *look* for opportunities to learn new skills.

CASE STUDY   Lisa was a member of the typing pool. Her job goal was to become an executive secretary.

One day her supervisor asked for typists to learn to use a new word processor the company had recently bought. Some of the typists refused. They felt they'd be stuck with more work than the others. Lisa had always wanted to learn how to use a word processor. This was her chance. She easily mastered it, and her workload was no heavier than before. One day when a secretarial job opened up in the company, Lisa was considered for it because of her new skill.

Thinking About the Case Study

1. How did looking for opportunities to learn on the job help Lisa?

- **Get more education or training.** Take advantage of every opportunity to further your education. The more education and training you have, the more career choices you will have. Usually the people with the most education and training also make the most money. Remember the educational sources discussed in Chapter 6? They include adult high school, on-the-job training, vocational-technical schools, private schools, colleges and junior colleges, and the armed services.

Ask at the company's personnel office what training is available through the company. Will the company help pay for classes you take elsewhere? Find out what courses you need to qualify for a better job.
- **Be willing to try new things.** You may have a favorite way of doing something. You feel comfortable with it and

see no reason to change. However, that doesn't mean you shouldn't try a new way just to see how it works. You never know—you may like it better. It may also give you an idea for a third way that is even more terrific than the other two. Being open to new things is necessary if you are going to grow.

More Responsibility

As you grow on the job, gradually you will be given more responsibility. You may even be given a promotion. *A* **promotion** *means getting a job higher in rank than the one you already have.* For example, you might be promoted from clerk-typist to secretary, from secretary to administrative assistant, or from a salesperson to supervisor of sales.

Do You Want More Responsibility?

Before you accept more responsibility, ask yourself if you really want it. For example, a promotion may mean that you will have to spend more hours on the job. If you have lots of homework to do, you may not have time to handle the added work. Like everything else about your work life, a promotion must fit in with your career plan.

As you grow on the job, you might be given a promotion. What is a promotion?

Something else to consider is whether you are ready for more responsibility. For example, if you must supervise others, will you be able to correct those who need it? Some people find it hard to criticize others. Will you be able to take the extra pressure that more responsibility creates?

A promotion may also require that you move to a new place. It may be for a short period of time while you are being trained, or it may be permanent. It may mean you will have to live away from family and friends. Will you be willing to go?

Just because you may not be ready for more responsibility right now doesn't mean you won't be ready later. You must take an honest look at yourself and at your goals. If you feel that more responsibility is right for you at this time, then give it a try.

How To Get More Responsibility

Perhaps you've decided you *do* want more responsibility. To learn if you're showing employers you're ready for it, ask yourself these questions.

- Have I learned all I can about my present job?
- Do I finish what I start?
- Is the quality of my work above that of other workers?
- Do I usually do my work without mistakes?
- Must someone keep telling me what to do?
- Have I been with the company long enough to have proved myself?

You will probably not be given more responsibility until you have learned to handle the work you already have.

Once you are sure you're doing your present job well, look for ways to help other people do their jobs *before* you're asked. This proves to your employer that you can handle more work and responsibility.

There are many ways to prove you can take on more responsibilities. Some ways are

- helping other workers
- working late when there is a need
- coming to work early when necessary
- finding things that need doing but that no one has asked you to do

If you are willing to do more than your share, it increases your chances for a promotion. Remember this when your boss asks you to do something extra. If you can, volunteer to do the extra work without being asked.

If you want a promotion, you may have to prove to your employer that you are ready to take on more responsibility. How can you do this?

As you read in Chapter 9, you need initiative to move ahead in your career. Sometimes it takes a lot of initiative to get ahead on the job. Initiative helps you become successful. Don't wait around hoping good things will happen. *Make* them happen.

REVIEW YOUR WORK

1. Name three ways you can grow on the job.
2. Name two reasons why you might *not* want more responsibility.
3. Define initiative.

Changing Jobs and Companies

As much as you might like your first job, the chances are very good that you won't keep it forever. In fact, people change jobs on the average of six times during their lifetime. There are a lot of reasons for the changes people make. Sometimes people leave jobs because the job isn't as good or as interesting as they thought it would be. Others may want to move ahead faster than they are doing now. They may want to learn and use new skills. Still others may want more responsibility or more money.

There is also a good chance that the job you have will change. Very few jobs stay the same. Your job may be combined with another one or be done away with completely. The working world is always changing, and you'll have to keep up with it.

When you think about a job change, you'll need to think about your career goals. Select each new job as carefully as you did the first one. As you know, thinking ahead and planning are the keys to getting where you want to go.

Looking for the New Job

When you look for a new job, use the same methods discussed in Chapters 7 and 8. It's usually a good idea to look within your present company for the job you want. You may also want to try networking.

Networking.   *Using people you know to learn about opportunities is called* **networking.** When you are part of a network, you receive information from some people and pass information along to others. Everyone you know in the work world, not just friends or family, should be a part of your network.

Networking is especially helpful when you are looking for a different job. The more contacts you have in different companies, the more doors that can be opened to you. You can find out about job openings before they are advertised. You can get the names of the right people to call.

The chances are very good that you won't keep your first job throughout your entire career. What should you consider when you think about changing jobs?

Networking is also helpful within a company. If you want to be transferred to a different department, get to know the workers there. They can let you know what's going on. They may also mention your name to supervisors.

Keep in mind that when you are part of a network, you, too, must share information. If you know that John is leaving and Susan is looking for a job, pass the word about the opening to Susan. The more help you give, the more you will receive.

DID YOU KNOW?

POSTAL WORKERS

Cats have been officially hired by the British Post Office for more than a century. In the mid 1800s, mice had invaded the postal sorting rooms to the point where the mail was chewed to bits. Cats were brought in and actually received a weekly salary for catching the mice. Today, cats are still on the payroll at three different post offices in London.

Transfer Within the Company.   Does your present company offer the kind of job you're looking for? If so, you may want to transfer rather than go to a new company. When you transfer, you stay with the company but change your job. There are several advantages to this.

- If you have a good work record, the company will be more willing to give you the job than someone they don't know.
- You won't lose benefits during the change.
- You know what to expect from your present company.
- A new company may present new problems.
- The longer you work for a certain company, the better it looks on your work record.

Being Fair to Your Present Employer.   Keeping your present job while looking for a new one somewhere else is not easy. You will need to be careful about how you act in your present job. It is important that you continue to do good work. Your present employer is still paying you, and he or she deserves your best efforts. Also, keep in mind that you don't have the new job yet. You don't want to lose your present job or leave with a poor record.

It's best not to tell anyone at your present company that you are looking for another job. Also, you have to be careful about taking time off. Do not call in sick just to get a day off. If your present employer finds out, you may receive a poor recommendation.

There are other ways to find time for interviews. If you have a long lunch hour, you may be able to schedule the interview during lunch. Another possibility is to trade work hours with someone else. Perhaps you could take a few hours off on one day and make them up another day.

If you have worked on the job long enough, you may be able to use some of your vacation time to look for another job. There is also the chance that you can go for an interview after working hours. Other employers certainly understand

Calling in sick just to enjoy a day off after you have given notice is an example of not being fair to your present employer. Why is it important to be fair to your present employer?

that you want to continue to do a good job where you are now working. Explain this to them. They may agree to meet with you after working hours.

The person interviewing you will probably want to obtain a recommendation from your current employer. If your employer doesn't know you are looking for another job, it could be difficult for you. Tell the interviewer that you know a recommendation is important, but that your employer does not know you are looking for a new job. The interviewer may suggest how to handle the problem.

Leaving the Old Job

When you take a new job, you want to start off on the right foot. When you leave a job, it's just as important to do it right.

Staying Friendly.   Try to stay on good terms with your present employer. A poor relationship between you and your employer can cause problems for you even if you move on to a new company.

Working in Nature

Many young people hear the words *job* or *career*, and they immediately see themselves tucked away behind some desk or counter and spending all day indoors away from nature.

If you have a love for nature, you might be relieved to know that there are hundreds of careers available to you.

At the top of the list are the natural scientists. Scientists such as *zoologists* (who study animals) or *botanists* (who study plants) do fascinating and important work that helps us to know more about our world and take better care of it. These scientists have college degrees in their fields and spend a great deal of their time conducting research and reporting their findings.

If your interests are a little less scientific, you might enjoy being a forest ranger or game warden. These people help to protect both people and animals and to keep the peace in our state or national parks and wilderness areas.

If your love of nature centers around plants and flowers, you might look into working in, managing, or owning a nursery. Here you could combine your love of nature and your retail skills into an interesting and rewarding career.

Perhaps you are interested in a career that keeps you in touch with outdoor recreational activities, such as swimming or skiing. In this case you might enjoy working as a lifeguard or as a member of the ski patrol. Since both of these are seasonal jobs, you might also need to find a temporary job for times when the beaches or ski resorts are not open.

As you can see, there are many careers waiting for nature lovers. However, if you think you might enjoy one of these jobs, you need to start your career climb *indoors*—in your guidance counselor's office, learning more about what is available.

CASE STUDY   Aaron was leaving his job in the parts department of Acme Motors. He was glad to be able to get away. Everything was getting to him. There was no chance to move up to a better job, and Mr. Sellers, his boss, always gave him a hard time. Aaron took a new job at Space Age Motors. During his last week at Acme, Aaron's conversations with co-workers sounded like this:

"You've got to be dumb to keep on working in this sweat shop. I wouldn't stay here if they paid me a million dollars. Who wants to look at old sour-face Sellers every day? He's never had a good thing to say about anyone. In fact, he's got to be the grouchiest person I have ever met.

"What you need to do is get a great job like I did. They know how to treat people over there. I'm not kidding. I'm going to make almost twice as much as you're making here, and I won't have to work as hard. You can't beat it. I've got the best deal in town. When are you going to wise up and get out of here?"

Thinking About the Case Study

1. If Aaron somehow lost his new job, do you think Mr. Sellers would be willing to rehire him?

Mr. Sellers may be the worst boss alive. The people remaining on the job, however, don't want to hear it. They may enjoy working there, or they may not have a choice. People don't want to hear others run down the place where they work. Even if they don't like their jobs, they don't want to be reminded about it.

When you're leaving a job, it's better not to talk about your new job unless someone asks you. If people ask you why you're leaving, be positive. If you can't be positive, it's best not to comment.

Tell your boss and the people you worked with that you were glad to have had the chance to get to know them. Try to leave with good feelings. Then, if you need a recommendation for another job later on, you'll stand a better chance of getting one.

Giving Notice.   It is important that you give notice. **Giving notice** *is telling your employer you will be leaving.*

The usual notice is two weeks. The reason for giving notice is to give your employer time to find a replacement. If your

A BAD RECOMMENDATION

Q: What can I do if I know my employer is going to give me a bad recommendation when I leave my job?
A: Continue to be pleasant and do the best job you can. Avoid making the situation worse by being late for work and showing a poor attitude. Try to look back at the way you handled your job. What were the problems? How could you have handled them differently?

Making Progress Toward Your Goals

Your first few jobs in the working world will probably be *entry-level* jobs. These are the lowest-paying jobs, usually the most routine jobs, and often the jobs few other people want to do. You'll be taking lots of orders, and you probably won't have many opportunities to be creative, make your own decisions, or make a lot of money.

If you've set your goals high—as you should—there will be many steps between your first entry-level job and your ultimate career goal. You will have to wait a long time and do lots of hard work to reach your final job.

Few people start at the top. Almost all successful people "pay their dues." You, too, may need to work long hours at dull, routine jobs to gain the experience, skills, and knowledge you will need later.

If your entry-level job seems dull and boring, don't be discouraged. **THINK POSITIVELY.** That job is probably a necessary step to a better job. You can probably learn much more than you think if you just give the job a chance.

Think about your job as the most important job in the company. Do your job to the best of your ability. Whether you are sacking groceries or negotiating contracts, doing quality work will make you feel good. You can achieve a great deal of satisfaction from any job if you know you are doing it as well as it can be done.

When you have a chance, notice the work that's being done around you. Look for opportunities to learn

new skills. Ask your boss and other workers to explain why certain jobs are necessary and why certain actions are taken. Imagine yourself doing the various jobs. Could you do that job? Would you enjoy it?

Be patient! If you work hard and learn, you'll get your chance. At times it will seem as if you're standing still, making no progress. It may seem as if no one has noticed you and your skills and abilities. Be patient, be alert, and be ready. You'll move up the ladder one step at a time. If you work hard and think positively, you will eventually get to where you want to go.

```
                                    1516 W. Lake
                                    Billings, Iowa 62741
                                    September 12, 19--

Mr. Sam Einisman
Better Mortgage Co.
1112 North Street
Huxley, Iowa

Dear Mr. Einisman:

      This letter is to officially inform you that my last day of work
will be September 28, 19-- . I am leaving to take a position with the
First Trust and Savings Bank. I believe this position will give me an
opportunity to develop new skills.
      I have learned a lot in my job at Better Mortgage. I'm glad to
have had the chance to work with you.

                                    Sincerely,

                                    Mark Kelly
                                    Mark Kelly
```

You may need to turn in a letter of resignation when you leave a company. What information is included in a letter of resignation?

position is hard to fill, you may want to give a little more notice, if you can.

In some places of business, you're also expected to turn in a letter of resignation. *A* **letter of resignation** *is a written statement of your intention to leave the company.* Your letter should briefly state when and why you are leaving. It's important to be positive. An example of a letter of resignation is shown above.

When you turn in your resignation, ask if there is anything special you need to do before leaving. You may need to complete some forms to be kept on file.

When you leave a job, there is always a chance you'll want to keep in touch with some of the people who work there. You may have made some good friends. Leaving a job does not mean you need to leave your friends.

REVIEW YOUR WORK

1. What is networking?
2. What does giving notice mean?
3. Why is it important to be pleasant and polite when you resign from a job?
4. What is a letter of resignation?

Losing Your Job

No one plans on losing their job, but it happens. Some workers can't seem to learn the necessary tasks, or they don't do them well enough. These workers may be fired. *Being* **fired** *means a worker loses a job because he or she was at fault.*

If the company doesn't have enough work for everyone, or if the company is short of money, workers may be laid off. *Being* **laid off** *means that losing the job was not the worker's fault.* New workers are often the ones laid off first.

Workers who are laid off may receive severance pay. **Severance pay** *is a cash amount given by the company to help make up for losing the job.* Payment is usually based on the length of service. For example, an employee might receive one week's pay for every year worked.

Many companies who lay people off try to rehire them as soon as they can. This depends on why the layoff was necessary. It can take a long time for a laid-off worker to be called back to work. Many are never called back.

If you have been working for at least several months and are laid off, you may be able to receive unemployment compensation. **Unemployment compensation** *is money paid to you from a fund that employers pay into.* If you think you are eligible for unemployment compensation, contact your state employment service. Most states require that you be ready and able to work and that you spend time each week looking for a new job.

If you are fired, you must think about the reasons and try not to let it happen again. Everyone makes mistakes, but only people who learn from their mistakes keep from repeating them. Don't blame someone else, even if someone else played a part in it. Think about what *you* could have done differently.

If you were laid off, try to remember it was not your fault. Many companies find layoffs necessary. Keep your positive attitude and start again.

Reevaluating Your Goals

It's important that your employer is aware of how you are doing on the job. It is just as important that *you* are aware of where you were, where you are, and where you are going.

You are the one who is in charge of your career. Remember the plan of action you developed in Chapter 6? You set

On a regular basis, you will need to review your career plan to see how well you are progressing toward your goals. Which goals should you expect to meet first, your long-term goals or your short-term goals?

your short-, medium-, and long-range goals. You wrote them down and set dates for meeting them.

On a regular basis, take out your list of goals and ask yourself, "How am I doing?" Of course, you'll want to look at your short-term goals more often than your long-term goals. As you reach your short-term goals, you'll be inspired to reach the long-term goals.

No plan is going to be perfect. You will have to make changes along the way so that the plan can still work for you.

If your goals work out pretty much on time, you can be pleased. If, however, you have to make a few changes, make them. Life will throw a curve ball once in a while. When that happens, even the best planners have to make adjustments.

As you review your career plan and goals, remember that one of the most important things you have going for you is your attitude. Keep it positive. Believing you can succeed really makes a difference. With a positive attitude, you will be able to see more easily how even a bit of bad luck can be turned to your advantage. You will keep trying, and if you are out there trying, you will be where things are happening. Then anything is possible.

REVIEW YOUR WORK

1. What is severance pay?
2. What is the difference between being fired and being laid off?
3. What is unemployment compensation?

Chapter Summary

- You will probably hold more than one job during your career. Every job you hold should give you opportunities to grow.
- As you grow in your job, you will be given more responsibility. Eventually, you should get a promotion.
- A promotion usually means an increase in pay.
- You can prove you are ready for more responsibility by helping other workers, working late, coming to work early, or doing things that nobody has asked you to do.
- When you think about a job change, be sure to keep your career goals in mind.
- You might find a new job through networking or through a transfer within your company.
- It is important to be fair to your present employer while job-hunting and to stay on good terms with him or her when you leave.
- Being fired means losing a job because the worker was at fault in some way. Being laid off means the worker loses the job through no fault of his or her own.
- Once in awhile you have to look at your career goals to see how you're doing.

Reviewing Vocabulary and Concepts

A. On a separate sheet of paper, write the numbers 1–8. After each number write the word from the word bank that best matches the definition.

Word Bank

promotion
giving notice
fired
severance pay
networking
letter of resignation
laid off
unemployment compensation

1. Money paid to out-of-work people from a fund that employers pay into.
2. The system in which you pass job information along to others as well as receive information from them.
3. A move to a job that is higher in rank than the one you had before.
4. Telling an employer you are leaving a job.
5. When a worker loses a job because he or she was at fault.
6. When a person loses a job for reasons other than being at fault.
7. This is a written statement of your intention to leave the company.
8. An amount of money an employee receives when the company he or she works for lets him or her go.

B. Write numbers 9–15 on the same sheet of paper. After each number write in the letter that best completes the statement.

9. Before you accept a promotion, you need to ask yourself if you _____ .
   a. can do the job
   b. are happy
   c. really want it
   d. will get more pay
10. Keeping your present job while looking for one elsewhere is _____ .
    a. really easy
    b. not easy
    c. a good idea
    d. not a good idea

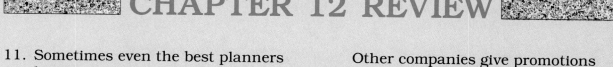

11. Sometimes even the best planners have to _____ .
    a. get fired
    b. get laid off
    c. give notice
    d. make adjustments
12. Jobs that people have when they are first joining the workforce are called _____ .
    a. entry level
    b. easy
    c. minimum wage
    d. short-term
13. Not losing benefits during a job change is one of the advantages of _____ .
    a. knowing the boss
    b. networking
    c. severance pay
    d. a transfer within the company
14. One good way to prove you can handle *more* work and responsibility is to do a job _____ .
    a. poorly
    b. sloppily
    c. before you're asked
    d. after you're asked
15. It's a good idea to look for _____ .
    a. dangerous working conditions
    b. opportunities to learn new skills
    c. new jobs
    d. ways to take time off work

Thinking Critically About Career Skills

Write your answers to the following questions on a separate sheet of paper.

1. Do you think you should be loyal? Why? Is loyalty more important for small businesses than it is for large companies? Why?
2. Some companies give promotions based on the amount of time a worker has been with the company. Other companies give promotions based solely on the worker's job performance and ability. Which system do you think is the most fair? Why?

Building Basic Skills

1. **Writing** Imagine that you were offered a new job that would pay $6,000 more a year. Write a letter of resignation that explains to your current employer why you are leaving. Remember that you want to keep your present employer's respect and friendship.
2. **Research** Find out what the laws in your state say about unemployment compensation. Present your findings to your class in a two-minute speech.

Applying Career Skills

1. Start networking right now. Make a list of all the possible sources to find out about job openings. Include such people as your parents, friends, teachers, counselor, and friends of your parents. Make a 3 × 5 card for each person with his or her name, address, phone number, and occupation. Each time you make contact with this person, update the card with a little note of the date and what the conversation was about.
2. Look at the ways you can prove you are ready for more responsibility on page 237 of your text. Make a list of ways you can apply these methods around your house.

CHAPTER 13

HEALTH
AND SAFETY
AT WORK

OBJECTIVES

In this chapter, you will learn about
- the dangers involved with the use, misuse, and abuse of controlled substances
- the steps business and industry are taking to fight substance abuse in the workplace
- the importance of safety in the workplace

Throughout this book, you have worked hard to assess your skills, learn to make good career decisions, find the right job, and work toward career goals. Now you will explore another vital area—your health and safety at work.

Each year, accidents happen on the job. Some of them are caused by human error due to substance abuse or as a result of unsafe working conditions. This chapter looks at both issues—substance abuse and the overall safety of your work environment.

What Is a Substance?

Alcohol, tobacco, and drugs are all called substances. You will find out just what they are and what they do to your body and mind. You will see how people abuse them. You will also look at the cost of each in terms of money, time, and potential injury on the job. Then you'll learn how industry is helping employees who are abusing these substances.

Alcohol

Alcohol *is a drug that is produced by a chemical reaction in some foods and has powerful effects on the body.* It is a controlled substance. *A* **controlled substance** *is one whose use is limited by law.* Alcohol consumption is illegal for those under 21 years of age.

The *mental* effects of alcohol on each person are different. For anyone who drinks it, however, the *physical* effects are much the same. Alcohol is a depressant. When drank, it enters the bloodstream and affects the nervous system. It slows a person's reaction time, causes slurred speech, impairs vision and judgment, and causes a loss of coordination. A person who has had too much alcohol is called *drunk, intoxicated,* or *under the influence.* Great quantities of alcohol consumed in a short period of time can cause death.

People who regularly drink alcohol come to need more and more of it to feel the desired effect. After a while, this increased use causes the drinker to form an alcohol addiction. *An* **addiction** *is a physical or mental need for a substance.* Such addiction to alcohol is alcoholism. **Alcoholism** *is a disease caused by a physical and mental need for alcohol.*

It is illegal for anybody to be intoxicated while driving a vehicle. It is also illegal for adults to give or sell alcohol to people under the legal drinking age, including their children.

The federal government now requires a warning label on all packaged alcoholic beverages sold in the United States. One of these reads: "Government Warning: According to the Surgeon General, women should not drink alcoholic beverages during pregnancy because of the risk of birth defects." Another reads: "Government Warning: Consumption of alcoholic beverages impairs your ability to drive a car or operate machinery, and may cause other health problems."

State laws dealing with driving under the influence of alcohol are becoming more strict. Many states now penalize a person convicted of drunk driving with a jail sentence, a fine, and the loss of his or her driver's license.

CAREER Q&A

ALCOHOL IS ALCOHOL

Q: A friend of mine tells me beer drinking is OK. He says only the "harder" stuff can get you into trouble. Is he right?
A: No, he is absolutely wrong. Like other forms of liquor, beer contains about an ounce of alcohol per 12-ounce can or bottle.

Tobacco

Tobacco use, whether it is smoked in a cigarette, pipe, or cigar, or used in smokeless tobacco products such as snuff, is a harmful and expensive habit. (People who smoke one pack of cigarettes each day could spend more than $500 in a year.) Like alcohol, tobacco is a controlled substance.

Tobacco use increases one's chances of getting lung disease, cancer of the mouth, and heart disease. A single puff of cigarette smoke exposes the body to more than 3,000 chemicals. Some are deadly. Almost all negatively affect the body.

Each cigarette package must have a health warning printed on it. For example: "Surgeon General's Warning: quitting smoking now greatly reduces serious risks to your health" or "Surgeon General's Warning: smoking by pregnant women may result in fetal injury, premature birth, and low birth weight."

There is as much concern about the dangers of secondhand smoke as there is about the danger of directly inhaled smoke. **Secondhand smoke** *is the smoke in the air from a tobacco product being smoked by others.* Inhaling secondhand smoke exposes nonsmokers to the same health risks as smokers. City and state laws now make it mandatory for businesses, industry, and such public places as restaurants to have designated areas for smoking. This reduces the possibility of nonsmokers being exposed to secondhand smoke. The airline industry also has controlled smoking on flights. There are designated seating areas for smokers and nonsmokers. By law, smoking is now prohibited entirely on many flights.

Drugs

A **drug** *is a substance other than food that changes the structure or function of the body or mind.* The word "drugs" has many meanings. It can mean *prescription drugs,* such as penicillin. It can mean *over-the-counter drugs,* such as aspirin, that are safe to use without a doctor's supervision. It can also mean *illegal drugs,* such as marijuana and cocaine. Whether illegal or prescribed, all drugs are controlled substances.

Some prescription drugs and over-the-counter drugs can cause side effects. **Side effects** *are reactions to a medicine other than those intended.*

Typical side effects of many drugs include nausea, dizziness, drowsiness, irrational thinking, poor judgment, slurred speech, mood swings, and irritability. All of these

Smoking damages the lungs' ability to work. What difference would that make to someone wanting to be a professional athlete?

side effects can lead to impaired work performance that may lead to accidents or injury in the workplace.

You should always ask your doctor about the possible side effects of any prescription drugs he or she prescribes for you. Most prescription drugs now also carry appropriate warnings on the labels about how to take the medicine (with food, for example) or about possible side effects. Over-the-counter drugs should list similar information.

Prescription drugs are taken to cure or treat an illness or other condition. Illegal drugs are taken with the deliberate intention of altering one's frame of mind. Usually, illegal drugs severely alter a person's ability to make judgments and rational decisions. Using them while at work, particularly when operating machinery, can lead to serious accidents, injury, or even death. All of this means that the employer pays more in sick time, disability payments, and higher insurance rates.

The use, possession, cultivation, selling, and handling of illegal drugs is against the law. There are federal, state, and city drug laws to prosecute offenders.

Substance Use, Misuse, and Abuse

Substance use *is using any substance for its intended purpose.* Examples of appropriate substance use include taking blood pressure medicine as prescribed by a doctor, or taking antibiotics to fight an infection.

Substance misuse *is using a substance in a way other than its intended use.* Examples include sharing your prescription with others and taking your own prescription medicine more frequently than prescribed.

Substance abuse *is any use of an illegal drug and excessive use of any other controlled substance.* If the use is heavy and/or continuous, substance abuse usually results in physical, mental, and/or social problems. It has serious consequences in the workplace.

Substance Abuse and the Workplace

The worker who is a substance abuser is frequently late or absent. He or she has impaired physical and mental functions and may be inattentive and have frequent temper outbursts. The employee's behavior is a reflection on the company. Would you want an employee working for you if he or she had a temper outburst with one of the customers? Would you want to shop where a sales clerk doesn't pay any attention to you?

Many companies have designated areas off-limits for smoking. Why do you think companies would take this step?

THANK YOU FOR NOT SMOKING

In the workplace alone, substance abuse costs more than $140 billion a year. This includes the costs for treatment programs provided by industry and government, inferior products and services, absenteeism, low productivity, accidents, high insurance rates, and replacement costs if the worker is released from the job.

Have you thought about the costs to the teen substance abuser? Similarities exist. The teen substance abuser has low grades, is absent a lot, is inattentive, and has trouble getting along with others. This makes it difficult for the student to find employment.

CASE STUDY Officer Anderson flashed her squad car light at the new luxury sedan. The driver pulled to the side of the road. Two other police units pulled alongside the driver. The officers discovered $20 worth of cocaine in the car. They arrested the driver for possession of an illegal drug.

After the suspect was taken away, Officer Anderson looked at the $35,000 car. This car may bring a lot of money to the department, she thought. Federal law now allows the police to take permanent possession of any vehicle used in a drug deal. Most of these cars are then sold, and the proceeds go to the police department. So, $20 worth of cocaine could cost this man a $35,000 car.

Thinking About the Case Study

1. Why was the man going to lose his car?
2. What other types of risks was the driver taking by buying and using drugs?

Help from Industry

Industry is doing its share to help workers who abuse alcohol, tobacco, and drugs. It is using several different programs to help substance abusers because it believes

- workers are valuable
- it is better to offer assistance to workers experiencing personal problems than merely to discipline or fire them
- recovering employees become increasingly more productive and effective

EAP. *One program designed to help workers who have a substance abuse problem is called the* **Employee Assist-**

ance Program *or* **EAP.** The program helps to identify and correct employees' substance abuse problems. With EAP, employers and employees both win.

Basically, the program operates like this. A worker doing poorly in his or her job is given the choice of entering the EAP or facing disciplinary action or even dismissal. The employee who chooses to enter the program gets a great deal of help in overcoming the substance abuse problem. He or she then returns to work and becomes a valued, productive worker.

Drug Tests.

Many industries are requiring drug tests at the time a worker is hired. **Drug tests** *reveal the presence of drugs in an individual's body.* In many cases, an employee who is found to have drugs in his or her system is referred to a program, such as EAP, for help. In other cases the employee is fired. This testing program costs money. The drug-testing industry brings in an estimated $300 million a year. Many employers and some unions have worked out their own standards for acceptable, responsible drug testing.

More and more companies are getting strict about their hiring procedures. An individual with drugs in his or her system will not be hired. In many cases, workers that are already employed in a company starting a drug testing program must be tested if they are suspected of using drugs.

Many employers will help pay the cost of sending workers that have problems with substance abuse to drug rehabilitation centers. Why do you think employers might be willing to pay this cost?

Electing the Right Career

"When I grow up, I'm going to be president of the United States of America!"

Many children make this prediction sometime during their childhood. The President of the United States is one of the most important people in the world, as well as one of the most visible.

The world of politics can be glamorous and exciting. It is also very competitive. Politicians must first win difficult and hard-fought elections. Then they must complete the job for which they were elected while working to insure that they are re-elected. All the while, politicians are in the public eye with seemingly every move they make analyzed by the media and the voters.

Elected officials, however, are not the only workers in the area of politics. For each elected official, there are many other workers away from the public eye with interesting and exciting jobs. If you are interested in politics, you might wish to be an administrative assistant to an elected official. This vital job includes handling many—if not all—of the administrative tasks associated with the elected official's job. Administrative assistants usually are involved with hiring other staff members, coordinating all staff work, scheduling appointments and appearances, and checking all speeches, press releases, and official documents.

If you would like to put your communication skills to work in the area of politics and public service, you might be interested in a position as a speech writer or press representative for an elected official. Duties include writing and issuing press releases, writing

speeches, and acting as a go-between for the elected official and the press.

If you like working with people, you might enjoy a job as a constituent representative. *Constituent* is another word for voter. Constituent representatives use the authority of the elected official's office to help voters with problems with other governmental agencies. Constituent representatives also help voters to get their messages regarding important issues through to the elected official.

Support workers, such as secretaries and clerks, are also very important to elected officials.

If you're thinking about casting your vote for a career in politics, see your guidance counselor today. He or she can help you plan your career strategy.

Quit Smoking Programs.   Industry is also helping with the smoking problem. Companies designate smoking areas to control secondhand smoke and help establish a safe work environment. Smoking is not allowed in areas where materials are stored that burn easily or can explode.

Various types of quit smoking programs are offered to workers. They range from one-hour sessions to ten-week sessions.

REVIEW YOUR WORK

1. What are the physical effects of alcohol?
2. What are the health risks associated with smoking?
3. What are the risks of using illegal drugs while at work?

Safer Working Conditions

Accidents at work can cost employers enormous amounts of money in medical expenses and insurance payments. Accidents also result in lost production time. So, businesses are concerned about providing a safe working environment for workers.

CASE STUDY

Tina is an underwater photographer. She loves the excitement of plunging in the water and photographing the mysteries of the ocean. There are dangers associated with her job, such as extreme water temperature, strong currents, and equipment failure. Tina takes special precautions whenever she works underwater. She uses only the correct equipment and thoroughly checks it before and after use. She continually watches weather and water conditions. As you can see, Tina is very concerned about safety on the job.

Thinking About the Case Study

1. Why do you think Tina is so concerned about keeping her equipment in good condition?

Safety Regulations at Work

Business and industry take many steps to create regulations to insure worker safety. Some of the regulations are

Surviving Pressure

Pressure surrounds us. Have you ever thought of all the pressure put on you? Commercials try to influence what you buy. Parents and teachers encourage you to make better grades. The clubs you belong to have rules you must follow. Some of your friends try to pressure you into "going along" with their actions.

Pressure from your friends is called **peer pressure.** Peer pressure occurs when your friends try to talk you into doing something—whether or not you want to do it. Most people feel peer pressure at some point in their lives.

You experience peer pressure when your friend talks you into going to the movie, even though you need to study for a test. Your date insists that you go to a party. However, you don't want to go because you know people there will be drinking alcohol. Your friend talks you into taking him to a shopping mall, even though this will make you late for work.

Peer pressure creates stress. You might worry that you won't have any friends if you don't do what they want you to do.

If it seems you cannot say "no" to your friends, don't be discouraged. **THINK POSITIVELY.** It is not as hard as you think to resist peer pressure. Start practicing saying "no." The first time you say "no," it might be difficult. You may be surprised that you did. However, you will be able to do what you want to do and still have friends.

Think about saying "no" to peer pressure as a way of getting the job you want some day. You are developing habits that will help you become a better worker. Each time you say "no" makes it easier the next time.

Ask your boss or supervisor about peer pressure at work. For instance, many workers will over-extend their break time. It takes a person who knows the difference between right and wrong to take only the required amount of time.

You will have to realize how important it is to say "no" to those situations that are wrong. By saying "no" to alcohol, smoking, and drug abuse, you will not harm your body. By saying "no" to extended breaks at work, you are proving that you are punctual. By following the dress and safety regulations required for the job, you are showing respect and contributing to a safe work environment.

Start practicing saying "no" to peer pressure so you will be a valuable worker. Valuable workers are hard to find.

easy for the company to enforce. Others require the employee's cooperation. Here are two examples.

* One state has just legislated that medical interns have a reduced work schedule. Prior to the state legislation, the interns often worked around-the-clock for three consecutive days.
* Bus drivers must come to a complete stop at all railroad crossings. This is done to insure that drivers are aware of any oncoming trains.

Protective Clothing

In many jobs, employees must wear protective clothing to lessen the chance of personal injury. Ear protectors, hard hats, safety shoes, gloves, arm protectors, and chest shields help protect the worker. These regulations can sometimes be difficult to enforce without close employer supervision. A worker can easily remove ear protectors, for example, which could result in a hearing loss over time.

Wearing proper clothing and following safety regulations become good habits that are applied to other areas of living. Jack and his three sons, for example, work on their trucks,

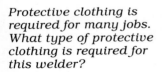

Protective clothing is required for many jobs. What type of protective clothing is required for this welder?

cars, and farm machinery in their spare time. When doing this, they all wear safety shoes and, if necessary, protective eye covering.

While teaching his daughter, Amy, how to use the power lawn mower, Mr. Chang made sure both he and Amy wore safety shoes, gloves, and slacks or jeans.

Work Environment

A safe work environment includes safety of the physical structure and surroundings of the business establishment. Most businesses strive to keep their plant, offices, and grounds safe. Government agencies assist in this effort by issuing a variety of regulations and guidelines.

Many building materials must be handled carefully to prevent workers from receiving high exposures to a number of dangerous articles. One example is asbestos, a building material. It is known that high exposures to asbestos cause serious lung problems. Building owners therefore follow government guidelines. They handle such materials carefully to protect workers' health.

Safety and Responsibility

As you can see, it is the responsibility of both employer and employee to maintain a safe work environment.

The employee must be ready for work. His or her system should be free of any substances that might affect job performance or safety. He or she should know, understand, and follow all safety regulations and wear all protective clothing required.

The employer must make sure that everything is being done to protect the safety of all employees and customers. He or she must make sure that one employee's irresponsibility, such as a worker's substance abuse, does not place others in danger. He or she must also enforce all safety regulations and make sure that the workplace is as safe as possible.

REVIEW YOUR WORK

1. Why are businesses so concerned with worker safety?
2. What can workers do to help promote a safe work environment?
3. What can employers do to help promote a safe work environment?

Chapter Summary

- A controlled substance is one whose use is limited by law. Both alcohol and tobacco are controlled substances.
- The word "drugs" has many meanings. It can mean prescription drugs, over-the-counter drugs, and illegal drugs.
- Substance abuse in the workplace causes serious problems for both the abuser and the employer.
- Industry is doing its share to help workers who abuse alcohol, tobacco, and drugs. This help includes Employee Assistance Programs, drug tests, and quit-smoking programs.
- Accidents at work can cost employers enormous amounts of money in medical expenses and insurance payments. Businesses are concerned about providing a safe working environment for workers.

Reviewing Vocabulary and Concepts

Write the numbers 1–14 on a separate sheet of paper. After each number, write the letter of the answer that best completes the following statements or answers the following questions.

1. For anyone who drinks alcohol, the _____ effects are much the same.
   a. mental
   b. physical
   c. social
   d. economic

2. It is legal for teens to consume alcohol _____.
   a. all of the time
   b. some of the time
   c. only under adult supervision
   d. none of the above

3. Alcohol and tobacco are examples of _____.
   a. an addiction
   b. a controlled substance
   c. an illegal drug
   d. an over-the-counter drug

4. A physical or mental need for a substance is called _____.
   a. tolerance
   b. EAP
   c. addiction
   d. a side effect

5. Typical side effects of many drugs include _____.
   a. nausea
   b. dizziness
   c. drowsiness
   d. all of the above

6. Any use of an illegal drug and excessive use of any other controlled substance is _____.
   a. addiction
   b. substance use
   c. substance misuse
   d. substance abuse

7. The Employee Assistance Program, or EAP, is designed to _____.
   a. help workers carpool to work
   b. help workers who have a substance abuse problem
   c. help workers make friends
   d. help workers with child care

8. To reveal the presence of drugs in an individual's body, many industries require _____.
   a. drug tests
   b. quit-smoking programs
   c. participation in the Employee Assistance Program
   d. honesty

9. In the workplace alone, substance abuse costs more than _____.
   a. $200 thousand a year
   b. $100 million a year
   c. $140 billion a year
   d. $600 billion a year

10. For an employee to be safe at work, he or she should _____.
    a. be free of any substances that might affect job performance
    b. know, understand, and follow all safety regulations
    c. wear protective clothing
    d. all of the above
11. Inhaling secondhand smoke exposes nonsmokers to _____.
    a. the same health risks smokers are exposed to
    b. a few of the health risks smokers are exposed to
    c. no health risks
    d. twice the health risk smokers are exposed to
12. Serious lung problems can be caused by high exposure to the building material called _____.
    a. drywall
    b. wood
    c. shingles
    d. asbestos
13. Using a substance in a way other than its intended use is _____.
    a. addiction
    b. substance misuse
    c. substance use
    d. substance abuse
14. Cocaine is considered _____.
    a. a safe drug
    b. a prescription drug
    c. an over-the-counter drug
    d. a controlled substance

Thinking Critically About Career Skills

Write your answers to the following questions on a separate sheet of paper.

1. Why is it important for the employer to assure that the working environment is safe? Why is it important for the employee to follow safety regulations?
2. Describe the problems that substance abuse can cause for a teen. How would substance abuse affect his or her time in school? at home with his or her family? at his or her job?

Building Basic Skills

1. **Refusal Skills** List two ways to say "no" to a peer who is pressuring you to try tobacco. List two ways to say "no" to alcohol. List two ways to say "no" to drugs.
2. **Research** Use news broadcasts on television and radio and reports in the newspaper to determine the types of accidents employees have while at work. For at least one instance, describe how the accident might have been avoided.

Applying Career Skills

1. Talk to two adults you know who are required to wear protective clothing at work. Ask them about the types of duties they have at work. How do they feel about wearing protective clothing and how does it protect them?
2. Go to the library and find books about alcohol, tobacco, or drugs. After choosing one substance, research the physical and mental effects of it. Write a 200-word report describing the effects and why it would be difficult and unsafe to work while using this substance.

OUR ECONOMIC SYSTEM

OBJECTIVES

In this chapter you will learn about
- how our economy works
- the meaning of free enterprise
- your role in our economy

Have you traveled to many different parts of the country? If not, perhaps you have seen TV programs showing life in the industrial cities, the suburbs, the small towns, and the farming areas.

Each of these areas is very different. The industrial cities have large factories and smoke stacks. The suburbs have offices, smaller factories, and shopping malls. The farming areas have miles of land where crops grow and cattle graze.

None of these areas could survive without the others. The cities, suburbs, and farm areas depend on each other. Each area adds something to the whole. Together these areas make up our country's economic system.

An **economic system** *is a group of people producing, selling, and using goods and services.* In this chapter you will learn how our economic system works. You will also learn how you will fit into the system. The more you understand about our economic system, the better your chances of reaching your career goal.

The Free Enterprise System

The economic system we use in our country is called the free enterprise system. *The* **free enterprise system** *is an economic system in which individuals and private business are free to organize and operate with little interference from the government. This is also known as* **capitalism.**

In a free enterprise system, individuals and businesses have a good deal of free choice. The government does not plan what or how many products will be available, as governments in other economic systems do. In free enterprise systems the government usually does not tell people where to work. The government usually does not tell producers what prices to charge.

Sometimes, however, the government *does* tell businesses what they must do. If customers or other businesses will be hurt by what a company does or fails to do, the government steps in. For example, government agencies regulate the cleanup of waste material.

Those who believe in free enterprise believe that most people want to improve their own lives. They believe that people are capable of making their own decisions. They also believe that if people make decisions that benefit themselves, these same decisions will benefit others.

To get a better picture of what free enterprise is all about, let's take a look at some of its more important elements. These include goods and services, consumers, profits, prices, competition, income, booms, and depressions.

In our country, the economic system is called the free enterprise system. What is the free enterprise system?

Goods and Services

Our economy is based on the production of *goods* and *services.*

Goods *are products that can be made.* Suppose you work for a company that makes computers. The computers that your company makes are goods.

You probably know what a service is. *A* **service** *is doing something to help someone else.*

Suppose you work behind the counter in a fast-food restaurant. Your job is to be courteous to customers, take their orders, and serve them the food. In doing your job you are providing a service to people. Babysitting, cutting and styling hair, cleaning clothes, and managing others' money are also services.

Consumers

When people buy and use goods and services, they are called consumers. *Everyone who spends money to buy goods and services is a* **consumer.**

As consumers we make decisions every day about how we will spend our money. Should we buy a new TV or have the old one repaired? Should we eat out or eat at home? Can we afford a vacation this year?

The choices we make as consumers determine what goods are produced and what services are provided. Every purchase you make is a vote for a product or for a business. On the other hand, if you and other consumers decide *not* to buy certain products, the makers of those products have three choices. They can either improve their products, lower their prices, or stop making those products.

What do you expect as a consumer? You want to pay fair prices. You want a wide selection of products from which to choose. You want products that are of good quality, and you want your purchases to hold up under use.

The buying decisions that consumers make determine which goods and services are produced. How are consumer decisions similar to voting?

Being a consumer may sound as if it's a lot of fun. You may feel as if you could spend money forever. The truth of the matter is that you do not have unlimited money to spend. Therefore, being a *wise* consumer is serious business.

You and other consumers make our economy work. Chapter 16, "Managing Your Money," will give you suggestions on how to be a wise consumer.

Profits

Our economy consists of thousands of large and small businesses. Large companies owned by groups of people produce food, clothing, and business machines. In addition, many people own and operate their own small businesses. Barbershops and hair styling salons, bakeries, meat markets, and restaurants are but a few of the many small, successful businesses.

All businesses, both large and small, must earn a profit to keep operating. In fact, the main goal of every business is to earn a profit. **Profit** *is the money left after the business pays its expenses.*

For example, the cost of producing a T-shirt includes the cost of the fabric and thread, sewing machines, workers' wages, building rental, utilities, and advertising. The price you pay for the T-shirt has to include all of these costs plus some profit. If a T-shirt costs $2 to make and the company sells it for $3, its profit is $1.

The need to make a profit is the major reason why businesses must operate with little waste. If the cost of materials, workers' time, and energy are kept low, more of the money brought in becomes profit.

All businesses, both large and small, must earn a profit to keep operating. What is a profit?

Less waste can also mean lower prices for consumers. For example, Company A makes T-shirts for $2, and Company B makes them for $1.75. On a T-shirt that sells for $3, Company A makes $1 profit, but Company B makes $1.25 profit.

One way Company B can increase sales is to lower prices. Since it is spending less to make T-shirts, it can sell its shirts for $2.75 and still make as much profit as Company A. This means that the customers buy T-shirts for less money. It also means that Company A must either trim its costs or go out of business.

Pricing and Competition

You have probably noticed that prices frequently change. Several factors cause prices to change. Understanding these factors will help you make wise buying decisions.

Supply and Demand.   One of the most important factors affecting prices is the law of supply and demand. *The* **law of supply and demand** *says that as the supply of goods and services goes up, the prices go down. As the demand for goods and services increases, so do the prices.*

CASE STUDY Wet Mop is a very popular rock group. Stores cannot keep their tapes and albums in stock. Manufacturers are working overtime to meet the demand for Wet Mop recordings. Wet Mop travels around the world performing sell-out concerts. People stand in line to buy T-shirts and autographed pictures of the group. These people pay high prices to buy Wet Mop products.

After a while, however, a new singing group called Leaky Bucket becomes very popular. Everyone is listening to Leaky Bucket now, instead of Wet Mop. No one wants to buy Wet Mop's recordings, T-shirts, and pictures, at any price. Therefore, the prices of Wet Mop products go down. Soon manufacturers stop making Wet Mop products and begin making Leaky Bucket products.

Thinking About the Case Study

1. What happened to the prices of Wet Mop products when the demand was high?
2. What happened to the prices of Wet Mop products when the demand was low?

Competition.   Businesses compete with each other for the customers' money. This competition affects prices. In fact, we depend on competition to keep prices reasonable. The government has laws regulating companies' actions to be sure competition exists.

For example, if there were only one shoe manufacturer, that manufacturer could charge any price it wanted. Can you imagine paying $1,000 for a pair of shoes? When there are many shoe manufacturers, however, they compete with one another to sell shoes. Consumers can shop around for the best price.

Income

Not everyone can afford to buy the same goods and services. What people can afford generally depends on the size of their income. **Income** *is spendable money.*

Income can come from different sources. Most people earn money for work that they do. Some people own stock in businesses and are paid a share of the profits. Some people receive income from bonds (promises to pay) and savings accounts. Such income is called *interest.* Other people might own buildings and property and receive rent, another form of income.

In general, people earn money by having something other people are willing to buy. Supply and demand are at work again. The more demand there is for the person's products or skill, the higher the person's income will be.

Booms and Depressions

Our free enterprise system is constantly changing. New businesses start and old businesses close. Some workers are laid off and others are hired. Every change eventually affects all of us.

As a result of all the changes, our economy goes through good and bad periods. During the good periods most people have jobs and most businesses are profitable. During the bad periods many people are out of work and many companies go out of business.

The periods during which consumers have lots of money to spend and production is high are called **booms.** During a boom period, spending increases and consumers look for more goods and services. Companies invest in new equipment and hire more workers in order to produce more.

When production is down and many workers are out of a job, the economy is in a depression. What are periods of high production and employment called?

Often during a boom, production cannot keep up with consumer spending. When the demand is greater than the supply, prices rise. *This rise in prices caused by increased demand or low supply is called* **inflation.** If inflation goes on a long time, some people are not able to buy even the basic things they need.

The low periods in our economy, when production is down, are called **depressions.** Because companies are not producing as much, they don't need workers. Many people lose their jobs. Without jobs these people have no money to spend, which means businesses can't sell their goods and services. *The resulting drop in prices is known as* **deflation.**

The amount of money people can borrow also changes during booms and depressions. When times are good it's easier to borrow money from banks. People borrow money in order to spend it on something like a house or car. Production goes up, and more jobs are created.

During bad times, banks are very careful about the amount of money they lend. They believe that many people who want to borrow won't be able to repay the loans. So the money is not spent, and the economy continues to slide.

Your Role

During your lifetime, you will be wearing many different hats. You will be a consumer because you buy goods and services. You will be a producer because in your work life you will provide goods and services for other consumers. You'll also be a voter helping to decide what policies the government will follow. Eventually, you may become a supervisor or company owner and will make decisions that affect others' lives.

How can you prepare now for the several roles you will play in the economy? You can do the following.

- Listen to people who know and understand our economic system.
- Be alert to items in the news that tell about how the economy is doing.
- Read newspapers and news magazines.

By learning more about what's going on, you will be able to make better decisions.

What part will you play as a worker? The answer to this question depends on what type of work you decide to do. No matter what job you hold, however, you are important. Each worker is important.

During your lifetime, you will fill many different roles as a part of our economy. How can you prepare yourself to best fill these roles?

If you continue to learn new skills and do well on the job, you will help the economy grow. Talented and enthusiastic workers help businesses to succeed. On the other hand, poorly trained and careless workers help businesses to fail. The success of the company you work for will add to the success of the economy in general.

REVIEW YOUR WORK

1. How would you define the free enterprise system?
2. How do consumers influence supply and demand?
3. Why are profits important in business? How do businesses figure out their profits?
4. How does competition affect prices?
5. Name three sources of personal income. How does supply and demand affect a person's income?
6. What happens to people and businesses during booms and depressions?

Labor Unions' Role

A **labor union** *is a group of workers who work at similar jobs or in the same industry.* The primary concerns of labor unions are to improve the earnings, hours, working conditions, and job security of members.

Unions often disagree with employers. The employers want to keep their costs low so that their profits will be high. Satisfying union demands usually increases the company's costs.

If a labor union and a company cannot agree to a contract, the labor union may call a strike. What is a strike?

When the two sides differ, they try to work out an agreement through bargaining. A union leader says what the union wants. The company then makes an offer that meets at least some of the union demands. A process of give and take goes on until the two sides can work out a compromise. When a compromise is reached, a contract is signed. Most contracts cover a two- to three-year period.

If the labor union and company cannot agree, the union may call a strike. *A* **strike** *occurs when all the workers stop working and leave their jobs.* The union goes on strike to stop the company from doing business until the company agrees to the union's demands. The union members must vote to decide whether or not to strike.

Strikes are more likely to be successful when the economy is doing well. They are less likely to be successful when the economy is poor and unemployment is high.

During strikes, workers do not get paid. The loss of income can be difficult for their families. However, many unions have a strike fund that provides at least some income for striking members.

If a company is a "union shop," new employees must join the union within a certain time or pay the union an amount equal to union dues. In this way, all employees, union and nonunion, pay for the gains made by the union. Many states, mostly those in the South, have laws banning union shops. These laws, called *right-to-work laws,* guarantee a person the right to work without joining or supporting a union.

Companies hiring both union and nonunion workers are called "open shops." Union members' dues are higher in open shops because fewer people share the costs.

The Economy and Your Future Career

The United States and world economies are very large. As one individual, you may feel a very small part of the economic scene. Still, you should be knowledgeable about what role you want to play in the economy, or you will drift along without direction. Knowing more about how the economy is developing will help you in making wise career choices and setting career goals.

Goods-Producing Economy

Years ago our country was mostly a goods-producing economy. *A* **goods-producing economy** *devotes most of its materials and efforts to manufacturing goods.* These goods are sold around the world.

A CAREER LESSON

Q: How would understanding the economy help me in my career?

A: Knowing how the economy works will help you understand why certain business decisions are made. You will be a part of the decision-making process one day. You may want to review your career choices in light of economic trends and job opportunities.

Our Economic System

Thinking about economics confuses many people because they don't understand it. The dictionary says economics is "a social science concerned chiefly with description and analysis of the production, distribution, and consumption of goods and services." Does that make sense to you?

If economics is so confusing, why bother thinking about it at all? Wouldn't we all be much happier if we just ignored economics?

The answer is no. You can't afford to ignore economics. The quality of your life is linked to the life of every other person in the world by economics. We all affect each other economically. You need to understand and think about economics, so you might as well **THINK POSITIVELY** about economics.

You can learn to understand our economic system. Reading this chapter is a good start, and your teachers will continue to help you find good books. You can learn economics just as you learn any other subject—one step at a time.

Understanding economics will help you improve your money situation. You'll know the best times to borrow money and the best times to save money. You'll see business opportunities that you would otherwise miss. You'll understand whether such actions as raising taxes and reducing government regulations would help you as an individual or hurt you.

So think positively about economics. You will be helping yourself and people throughout the world live fuller, richer lives.

The United States was the first country to mass-produce automobiles, thanks to Henry Ford. It was the first country to give consumers a choice of hundreds of home appliances. American businesses made money by manufacturing a large variety of items. Profits were high, and people's wages grew.

As time passed, our country's standard of living rose. **Standard of living** *refers to what items consumers are able to buy and how much they cost.* People have a high standard of living when they have money to spend and a variety of choices of goods and services.

In recent years, however, United States manufacturers have found it cheaper to produce parts or all of their goods in foreign countries. For example, read the labels on the clothing you buy. You will see "assembled in Dominican Republic, in Costa Rica, or in Taiwan." This is true for many other products you use every day.

In many foreign countries around the world, it costs less to produce goods because wages are lower. Other costs are lower as well. Manufacturers have felt it makes sense to produce goods at the lowest cost possible, so many do business abroad.

As a result, our country is producing fewer manufactured goods. We are importing more of our products from foreign countries. In many sections of our country, factories are closing due to high costs of manufacturing. In some cases, such technology as computers or robots, is replacing people on the manufacturing line. Although we still manufacture goods, we are not the large manufacturing country we used to be.

Service-Producing Economy

How does our economy keep growing if we manufacture less and less? We are moving toward a service-producing economy. *A* **service-producing economy** *sells a variety of consumer services.*

Advertising has created a great deal of interest in spending on services. People are doing fewer things for themselves and are buying services from others. For example, more people than ever before are eating in restaurants. They are traveling for business and pleasure. Motels and hotels offer discounts to businesspeople and special rates for families on weekends. These are all services.

Entertainment is taking a larger share of what Americans spend. People go to see films, rent videos, watch cable TV, go to amusement-theme parks, and attend sporting events. These, too, are services.

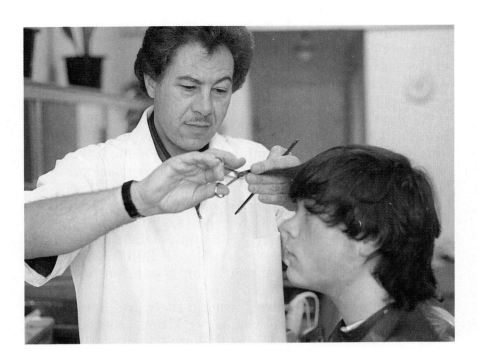

This person is having his hair styled. Is this an example of purchasing a good or a service?

People use real estate brokers to buy and sell homes. Stock brokers buy and sell stocks and bonds. Banks help people handle and save money. Insurance companies sell life insurance, as well as auto and home insurance. These are all services.

People are more health-conscious. Medical science has provided high-tech health care. Men and women of all ages are going to spas, gyms, and exercise classes. Helping people lose weight is now a big business. Veterinary care for pets is costly. These are all services.

Your Future Career Choices

What does the movement from a goods-producing to a service-producing economy mean to you? What does this signal to you in terms of your career selection?

More jobs will probably be available in the service sector than in manufacturing. More salespeople, office workers, technicians, and others providing services will be needed. Fewer people working on factory production lines will be required. Experts predict that by the year 2000, four out of five jobs will be in industries that provide services.

In order to qualify for good positions with chances for advancement, you will need more education. Technical education is especially important today. People specialize in more limited areas of work.

Music Hath Charms . . .

The house lights go out, and the crowd suddenly quiets. With a crash of noise, the stage lights erupt as the band launches full tilt into its latest hit. The crowd goes crazy as the concert of a lifetime finally begins.

The world of music offers many exciting and rewarding careers. For star performers, there is the glamour and thrill of performing before packed auditoriums filled with adoring fans. Many performers, however, never achieve star status. These are the people that sing in small nightclubs around the country or play backup guitar on a famous singer's album. Some others find themselves playing and singing songs for radio and television commercials.

There are, however, many careers in music other than performing. After all, not everyone who wants to work in the music business wants to perform in front of an audience.

There are many important and interesting behind-the-scenes jobs for people in the music industry. One such job is recording engineer. Recording engineers set up, monitor, and control much of the equipment used to produce the sounds we hear when we listen to the radio.

If you have both an interest in music and an interest in business, you might want to become a business manager for a musician or a band. As a business manager, you would see to all your clients' business affairs. You would help them make deals with record companies and promoters, and advise them in investing what they have earned.

Road managers and members of the road crew (sometimes called roadies) also work in the music business. These

are the perfect jobs for people who have an interest in music and who enjoy traveling. Road managers travel with a band and handle all the day-to-day business and travel arrangements that arise as part of a tour. Road crew workers handle the manual tasks associated with touring shows. They set up and tear down the stage. They also set up the lights and the sound system.

Like all businesses, the music industry also needs support workers. If you have secretarial or accounting skills, you might want to apply these to a job for a record company, a talent agency, or a radio station. An interest in retail and a love of music could lead you to a career as manager or owner of a record store.

As you can see, there are many careers available for people with an interest in music. If you think this might be the industry for you, talk with your guidance counselor today to start your career on a high note!

These people are shopping for toys for their grandchildren. Is this an example of purchasing a good or a service?

People are also finding out in many cases that salaries in service-related jobs are lower than in goods-producing jobs. Why? Many factors are involved. One major reason is that manufacturing jobs have been around longer than service-type positions. Labor unions have worked for many years to get higher wages for factory workers. Service-related positions are newer. They don't have the history of commanding more money.

This doesn't mean you can't earn a good income working in a service-related business. You can, depending on where you work and what skills you bring to the position.

Of course, what is most important is that the choice you make is the one that will satisfy you the most.

Entrepreneurship

Perhaps you have seen movies about pioneer families who built trading posts. Perhaps you have read about inventors, such as Thomas Edison, who turned their inventions into million-dollar companies. Perhaps you know people in your community who have started their own businesses.

All of the people described above are entrepreneurs. **Entrepreneurs** *are people who work for themselves.* They try to earn money by taking the risk of owning and operating their own businesses. If you work as a babysitter or mow the neighbors' lawns, you too are an entrepreneur. You will learn more about entrepreneurship in the next chapter.

REVIEW YOUR WORK

1. What do labor unions do? What is a strike?
2. How does the goods-producing vs. the service-producing economy influence your career choice?

Chapter Summary

- The more you know about our economic system, the better your chances of reaching your career goal.
- The economic system used in the United States is called the free enterprise system or capitalism.
- Our economy is based on the production of goods and services. Goods are things, such as clothing, cars, foods, and school supplies. Services are things that are done for people, such as baby-sitting, mowing lawns, and cutting and styling hair.
- People who buy goods and services are consumers.
- In order to exist, businesses must make a profit. Profit is the money left over after all the bills are paid.
- Our economy is affected by the law of supply and demand.
- Businesses compete with one another for the consumer's money. This competition affects prices.
- The economy is constantly changing and is subject to good periods called *booms* as well as bad periods called *depressions.*
- A labor union is a group of people who work at similar jobs or in the same industry who have joined together to improve their way of life.
- A strike is when all the workers leave their jobs at the same time and refuse to return until working conditions and/or pay are improved.
- Entrepreneurs are people who work for themselves.

Reviewing Vocabulary and Concepts

Write the numbers 1–16 on a separate sheet of paper. Beside each number, write the word from the word bank that best completes the statement.

Word Bank

strike	labor union
depression	inflation
supply and demand	capitalism
deflation	booms
profits	consumers
free enterprise	goods
income	entrepreneur
economic system	services

1. When a group of workers decides to walk off their jobs at the same time it is called a _____ .
2. Capitalism is also known as the _____ system.
3. An _____ works for himself or herself.
4. A group of people producing, selling, and using goods and services is a(n) _____ .
5. Under _____, individuals and businesses have a good deal of free choice.
6. Low periods in the economy are known as _____ .
7. When people earn money on savings accounts, it is known as interest _____ .
8. _____ have their members pay dues.
9. When you have clothes dry-cleaned and get a haircut, you are getting _____ .

10. _____ are active economic times when production is high and people can afford to spend money.
11. Earnings left after expenses are paid are called _____ .
12. _____ are people who buy goods or services.
13. When unemployment is high and people don't have money to spend on goods or services, our economy is suffering a _____ .
14. The law of _____ says that when the supply of goods and services goes up, the prices go down.
15. _____ are things that are produced to be sold.
16. When the demand for things is higher than production and prices go up, the economy is having _____ .

Thinking Critically About Career Skills

1. How do your consumer decisions act as a vote for or against a good or service? Use two recent consumer decisions you have made as examples in explaining your answer.
2. Explain what is meant by the statement, "the more demand there is for a person's products or skill, the higher the person's income will be"? How might this affect your career choice?

Building Basic Skills

1. **Writing** Write a 500-word report on one of the parts of our economic system that you read about in this chapter.
2. **Research** Go to the library and read about the Great Depression. Use at least two different resources. Write a 500-word report explaining the causes of the Depression.
3. **Mathematics** Calculate your total income for the year. Your salary is $14,500 a year. You earn $87.50 in interest from some bonds you own. You also collect $3,600 in rent (from which you must subtract $2,500 that you paid on the loan for the property you are renting). What is your total income?

Applying Career Skills

1. Ask your parents to tell you what they remember about the Arab oil embargo of 1973. Write a 250-word essay explaining how this example of low supply and high demand affected people on a personal level.
2. Using television commercials or magazine ads, examine how competition between businesses such as fast food restaurants or soft drink manufacturers affects their advertising. Summarize your observations in a 250-word essay.

ENTREPRENEURSHIP

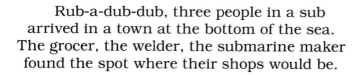

Rub-a-dub-dub, three people in a sub
arrived in a town at the bottom of the sea.
The grocer, the welder, the submarine maker
found the spot where their shops would be.

Does this rhyme sound silly to you? Who in the world would start a business on the bottom of the sea? Those who do, if communities are ever established on the ocean floor, will be the brave, risk-taking decision-makers of tomorrow. They will be the Henry Fords and John Deeres of the future.

Ford and Deere pioneered the auto industry and the farm machinery industry, respectively, many years ago. They were entrepreneurs of decades past. Their small shops have expanded into major corporations. Their products have been modified and improved. Their businesses now bring in millions of dollars annually.

What does it take to start your own business? As you learned in Chapter 14, entrepreneurs are the people who start and own the businesses that other people work for. This chapter will discuss entrepreneurship by telling you about small businesses and their importance in the economic system. You will explore the skills an entrepreneur needs, look at the types of jobs that can evolve into businesses, and examine some of the legal aspects of establishing and operating a business. You will also learn about the types of support agencies available for individuals wanting to start their own business.

You may decide being an entrepreneur is for you. Who knows? Maybe—just maybe—you will someday open a business in space or on the bottom of the sea.

Small Businesses

Compared to the big cities, the industrial giants, the massive government system, and the vast communication networks, the individual might seem rather insignificant. Small business might seem insignificant, too, when compared to the large corporations.

Fortunately, there are individuals who are willing to explore on their own instead of joining the industrial and commercial giants. They are the entrepreneurs, or small business owners.

What Is a Small Business?

A **small business** *is one that is independently owned and operated and not dominant in its field.* Kraft, Inc., which makes such dairy products as cheese, is a big business. Whoopie Cheese Store, which carries locally produced cheese, is a small business.

As a general rule, a service or retail business is considered "small" if the annual sales or receipts are $3.5 million or less. A manufacturing business is "small" if it employs less than 500 people. Most businesses are small. In fact, 99 percent of all businesses in the United States are considered small.

Importance of Small Businesses

Of course, the business giants are better known and have a more dramatic effect on our economic system. The importance of the small business to the nation's economic pros-

This market is an example of a small business. What is a small business?

perity, however, cannot be overstated. The small business owner is the foundation of our economy and the cause for economic change.

Many people do not realize that half of the work force is employed by small businesses. Most new ideas, goods, and service innovations come from new, small ventures. Nearly two out of every three new jobs are created by small business.

Risks

Because small businesses are so important to our free enterprise system and because there are so many of them throughout our nation, you might think it is always simple to start and successfully operate your own business. This is true only when the individual has done the necessary homework, has the necessary resources, and has the characteristics, skills, and interests needed.

Approximately 500,000 Americans try owning and operating a business every year. Unfortunately, thousands of businesses close each year. Many of these failures could be avoided by better planning, preparation, and management. There is no way to eliminate risk. However, success is more likely when the individual makes it a calculated risk and not a gamble.

This hair stylist is self-employed and, therefore, qualifies as a small business. Can you name any other small businesses in your community?

1. Explain how small businesses are considered the foundation of our country's economy.
2. Tell two ways to identify if a business is small.
3. Where do most of the new ideas, goods, and service innovations come from?

Skills Needed

Entrepreneurs create their own careers because they recognize unique relationships between society and its needs. Entrepreneurs are usually independent thinkers and doers.

CAREER Q&A

MORE ENTREPRENEURS

Q: My uncle is a welder, but he says he is also an entrepreneur. Is he right?

A: Many people, such as welders, cosmetologists, and writers, are self-employed and, therefore, are entrepreneurs. If you plan to enter one of these professions, you will need to understand how to make your small business work.

Looking Ahead

The thoughts you have about the following questions will help determine if you can plan for success when establishing your business.

- **Do I have what it takes to own a small business?** You need to be as objective as possible about your strengths and weaknesses. Are you a self-starter? How well do you get along with different types of people? How do you react to pressure? Are you emotionally strong? Do you make good decisions? Are you highly motivated? How well do you plan and organize?
- **How do I know what business to choose?** Usually, the business choice is based on a person's skills and interests. Along with skills and interests, you also want to consider the growth potential of the business in your area. Your chances for success are increased by matching your expertise to the needs of the local market.
- **To succeed, what do I need?** Few people start a business with everything needed. To ensure success, you'll need good planning, technical support, and sound management practices.

Specific Skills

In order for a business enterprise to succeed, there has to be a favorable economic environment. You can't control the overall economic environment. However, you can use the environment as an indicator to determine the establishing of business. You can try various techniques to find the right market for your goods or services.

CASE STUDY   Yvonne was a freshman in high school. Her parents and their friends had an abundance of tomatoes in their garden. Yvonne decided to set up a stand in the front of her house to sell the tomatoes. No one stopped to purchase the tomatoes. Yvonne obtained permission to operate her stand in a nearby shopping center parking lot. By the end of the tomato season, Yvonne had made $400.

Thinking About the Case Study

1. Why did Yvonne move her stand to the shopping center parking lot?
2. Why does Yvonne have the makings of a successful entrepreneur?

An entrepreneur must have *industry skills, management skills,* and *entrepreneurial skills* to use in a favorable economic environment.

Industry Skills.   **Industry skills** *relate to knowledge of an industry, product, or craft.* Obviously a person planning to start a business must have knowledge of its goods or

This independent gardener has the industry skills he needs to be successful. What are industry skills?

services. If it is a travel agency, the owner must know the travel industry. If it is a dry cleaning establishment, the owner must have knowledge and skills in the area of fabrics, cleaning methods, and cleaning solutions. Industry skills contribute to the quality of the goods and services.

Management Skills.   In order to maintain a business, management skills are essential. **Management skills** *relate to the handling of all financial aspects of a job or business.* They include handling a budget, operating accounts, and dealing with any other financial aspects of a business. Without financial knowledge, the entrepreneur may have difficulty handling the growth and development of his or her business.

Management skills also include handling people. An entrepreneur must choose employees, evaluate their performance, and handle schedules and deadlines. These management skills are essential for day-to-day operations.

Entrepreneurial Skills.   Decision-making and goal-setting were discussed in Chapters 5 and 6. These two skills plus the willingness to take risks are essential for the establishment of a business. The individual who wants to establish a business must also have a plan. This plan is similar to the career plan you put together in Chapter 6. (You will look at business plans later in this chapter.) The successful entrepreneur integrates the use of *entrepreneurial, management,* and *industry skills.*

Specific Characteristics

Successful entrepreneurs are a distinctive group of people. Three characteristics which distinguish successful entrepreneurs from others are *self-discipline, innovation,* and *human relations.* Having these characteristics contributes to an entrepreneur's success.

Self-discipline.   Successful entrepreneurs live their lives with purpose. They get things done. This often distinguishes them from other people who procrastinate and drift through life.

One quality most entrepreneurs share is self-discipline. **Self-discipline** *is the ability to regulate your behaviors and actions.* People with self-discipline get up and go to work, even when they don't want to. They don't waste a lot of time being upset over things that have gone wrong. Instead, they work to make things better.

No Place Like Home

Once upon a time when little girls were asked what they wanted to be when they grew up, many answered, "a mommy." They were basing their answer on the roles their own mothers played in the family: parent and home-maker. These roles required the skills needed to be a housekeeper, dietitian, cook, budget analyst, purchasing agent, seamstress, and child care worker. There was a time when most girls faced staying at home, being a parent and homemaker, whether they liked it or not. This is no longer true.

Today in the United States, more than half of all women of working age work outside the home. They hold down jobs in every sector of the world of work from architecture to zoology. Thus, men have had to learn to help out more around the house. Some men even choose to stay at home full-time to take care of their families.

Many women and men today are dis-covering that those same skills that make them successful homemakers are greatly in demand in the job market. There are many service-related jobs that require the skills that were once attrib-uted to "mommy."

Restaurants and caterers need cooks who can prepare delicious, nutritious food. Many large restaurants and cater-ing companies also require the services of a purchasing agent who can find the best bargains on the freshest and best groceries and supplies.

Cleaning and maintaining other peo-ple's homes have led many people from jobs as maids or housekeepers to suc-cessful businesspeople operating large cleaning services.

As the number of working parents begins to grow, child care workers are becoming greatly in demand. Live-in child care workers such as nannies make good salaries and save money on food and shelter. People with sewing skills can make a good living working out of their own homes.

If these jobs sound interesting to you, see your guidance counselor to find out more. The pace of American life has sped up a great deal, and many people are finding that they need help with do-mestic jobs. As this trend continues, there will be more and more need for experienced people to handle this work.

Self-discipline is the ability to regulate your behaviors and actions. Why is self-discipline an important quality for entrepreneurs?

Entrepreneurs are their own bosses, so they must have a great deal of self-discipline. Here are three ways you can work on your self-discipline.

- Do your chores without being asked.
- Make it a habit to double-check all your homework every night before you go to bed.
- Make yourself exercise at least 20 minutes every day.

Innovation.   **Innovation** *is applying original or borrowed ideas to situations in which they have not been used before.* Innovation usually occurs because a person asked the question, "Wouldn't it be helpful or easier, if. . . ?" This question has helped to produce the electric mixer, the shopping cart, the paper clip, and many other items on which we depend.

The innovator goes through three stages. First, the person has an idea. Second, he or she decides if the idea is worthwhile and fills a need in the market. Finally, he or she follows through with the idea and creates a good or service.

Try being an innovator. As you go through the three stages with an innovative idea, ask yourself these questions.

- Is it simple?
- Is it appropriate?
- Is it functional?
- Is it economical?

- Is it *safe?* There is nothing innovative about an idea that puts people's health at risk.

Human Relations.   In order for the entrepreneur to operate successfully, he or she must maintain good human relations. **Human relations** *means interaction with other people.* Chapter 10 discussed the importance of human relationships on the job from the standpoint of being an employee. Basically, those concepts also apply to an entrepreneur. He or she needs to maintain good relations with both employees and customers.

The entrepreneur's business is dependent on the quality of its human relations. Markets do not buy products, customers do. The customer is absolutely vital to the success of a business. The quality of human relations the entrepreneur needs is built by listening to customers and employees and responding to their needs.

CASE STUDY   Randi lives in a small town. She and her friends loved the only restaurant in the town. For them it was a place to meet, celebrate school victories, and get a quick meal. For older people, it was a place to get a good meal and see familiar faces. For local businesspeople, it was the perfect place to have a pleasant lunch or dinner while discussing business.

The restaurant owner died, and the restaurant closed. New owners reopened the restaurant, but it closed several months later. In fact, the restaurant changed ownership three times in three years. Each owner had failed by the end of the year.

Randi loves people and loves to cook. She wants to open the restaurant but doesn't want to experience failure. Yet, she knows the restaurant is needed and wanted by the community.

Thinking About the Case Study

1. What would you suggest to Randi to minimize the risk involved in opening the restaurant?

If the entrepreneur takes care of the customers and the employees, the market usually takes care of the entrepreneur. As an entrepreneur, don't lose contact with your employees and customers. Your business will suffer if you do.

In order for the entrepreneur to be successful, he or she must maintain good human relations. What does the term human relations *mean?*

REVIEW YOUR WORK

1. Identify three questions to ask yourself to determine if you can plan for success when establishing a small business.
2. Name the three specific skills an entrepreneur needs.
3. What is self-discipline?
4. List the three stages the innovator goes through to create a good or service.
5. Why must an entrepreneur maintain good human relations?

Establishing a Business

What type of business should an individual choose to establish? Usually, the best business is the one in which the individual is most skilled and has the keenest interest.

Sometimes it isn't just one person but two or several friends working on a project who generate the idea for opening a business. Sometimes a hobby expands into a business.

There are many different types of small businesses. What type of business is usually the best for an individual to establish?

Types of Businesses

Having an idea of the different kinds of businesses owned by entrepreneurs provides a better understanding of the entrepreneurial world.

A quick tour through the yellow pages of the phone book or the business community where you live helps identify small businesses started by entrepreneurs. Chapter 3 suggested that you tour your community. If you did this, you may have seen small businesses like these:

- Copenbarger's Oil Company: delivers fuel to farmers for use in the farming operations
- Johnson's Welding Services: in the shop or on-site welding services
- Goldfinch's Funeral Home: a family-owned mortuary
- Maria's Market: a small operation handling fresh meats, produce, and staple items such as bread and milk
- Wade and Jerry's Contractor Services: builds custom homes
- The Pool Center: sells and installs pools, saunas, and whirlpools, and carries a complete line of accessories
- The Elite: a "50s diner" known for its "good food with good friends"

Entrepreneurship

Perhaps you feel that it is "mission impossible" to become an entrepreneur. All of the homework required seems so time-consuming. There are so many successful entrepreneurs already. Maybe you don't want to develop a business plan, look at your skills and attributes, and further develop your industry, management, and entrepreneurial skills.

At this point, many individuals give up. They don't pursue the possibilities of becoming an entrepreneur any further. On the other hand, many people go ahead and establish a business without doing the necessary homework. Shortly thereafter, they face business failure.

If you really want to be an entrepreneur, don't give up. You can do it. **THINK POSITIVELY.** Yes, there are thousands of failures in small business, *but* there are many successes, too. Yes, it does take time and effort to do the necessary homework, but you shouldn't give up. A little time and effort now can mean you will become an entrepreneur—and a successful one. Besides, you might just discover you enjoy the homework involved with becoming an entrepreneur.

There are many advantages to doing the homework necessary for becoming an entrepreneur. By doing the homework, you will discover if you have the self-discipline you need to be a successful entrepreneur.

If you are really serious about being an entrepreneur, the homework only aids you in being a successful one by helping you minimize the risks in-

volved. You might also find that you make many important contacts that can help you after you open your business.

If you feel overwhelmed by all of the preliminary work required to become an entrepreneur, relax. Unlike other people who have failed, you know where to get assistance. This helps you find out if your idea for the business is good. By developing the business plan, you are checking to see if your small business is feasible.

Remember, everything discussed about being an entrepreneur contributes to you becoming more employable and being a better consumer.

Why give up before doing the homework necessary for establishing a small business? You have everything to gain from it.

Imagination and Confidence

The list of examples for the types of businesses is endless. Everyday, new businesses are being established. Individuals recognize a need, have a desire to fill the need, and are confident enough to start their own business.

Recognizing Need.   An entrepreneur may recognize a need because he or she experiences it. For example, the Starting Right Company came about because the Vice President, the mother of a six-year-old, needed tot-size frozen TV dinners. (This is an old idea applied in an innovative way.)

The need may also arise out of a request for the services and skills of the entrepreneur. For example, Bryan enrolled in the vocational education construction classes during high school. He started doing minor repair work on buildings in the area where he lives. His reputation as skilled craftsman grew. Today he has a three-person building repair crew, and his business continues to grow.

Confidence.   Future entrepreneurs must have confidence in the goods or services they have to offer. They must believe in their goods or services if they expect other people to believe in them. The success of Dart Messenger Service illustrates the importance of confidence.

The owner of Dart Messenger Service, Ms. Nuesbaum, quickly used all financial resources and still did not have the state license required to operate. This barrier seemed impossible, yet Ms. Nuesbaum remained confident that the service she had to offer was a good one. She made one last phone call and got the license. Today, her business employs 100 people. What is unique about her business? It will deliver anything legal from food to machine parts to exotic birds—and do so in costume if requested.

Entrepreneurs need to have confidence in the goods or services they provide. What is meant by confidence?

Developing a Business Plan

You have decided you have what it takes to own and manage a small business. You also have confidence and a belief in your good or service. Now you need to develop a business plan.

A **business plan** *defines your business and identifies its goals.* The plan includes how much you think it will cost to start the operation, the cost of running the operation, and expected profits. The plan is necessary for obtaining a loan to start your business.

You need to know where you want to operate your business and how much cash you will need. You also need specific information on employees (if you plan to hire them), vendors, and market possibilities.

Does this sound too involved and detailed for you? Don't let it discourage you. You can get some of the information needed for a business plan through class assignments. The owner of Federal Express, for example, devised the business plan for his company when he was a student. Though others said it couldn't be done, the owner believed in it. What a successful operation it is today!

The last two sections in this chapter provide information on legal aspects and available resources. This, too, can be integrated into your other courses.

REVIEW YOUR WORK

1. In what two ways can a need prompt an entrepreneur to start a business?
2. Why is it important for entrepreneurs to have confidence in their goods or services?
3. What is a business plan?

Legal Requirements

If you are interested in being an entrepreneur, you must realize that government regulates business. The local, state, and federal governments do so directly or indirectly. Here are some examples of government involvement.

Local governments have zoning ordinances that restrict the locations of businesses. State governments control the taxes on products sold. They also levy such other applicable taxation as property tax. The federal government regulates movement of goods and services out of state.

Needing a business license is an example of a government regulation that affects small business owners. Can you name any other examples of government regulations that affect small business owners?

Government Regulations

Governmental regulation of business is intended to balance the rights and needs of individuals with the rights and needs of business. A business may decide that a good way to sell a product is through a door-to-door campaign. This is legal; the business has a right to do it. A customer decides to buy the product, which is also legal. The customer also has the right to change his or her mind about a purchase and receive a refund. The government protects this right but sets a time deadline. This allows the consumer to change his or her mind about the purchase but insures the protection for both parties.

Laws attempt to achieve a healthy competitive environment for business and to guarantee the rights of the employees. Regardless of the type of business, the entrepreneur must adhere to government regulations.

Legal Approval

You might find you need some type of legal approval to operate your business. A simple way to determine if legal approval is necessary is to go through the imaginary process of operating a business.

That is what Ms. Boswell did. She and two friends decided to start a business manufacturing place mats. These were not ordinary place mats. They were designed in the shape of Texas. The three mastered the production, identified sources for supplies, priced the product, and checked both the need for the product and sources for distributing it.

Then they decided on a name for the company. The name had to be registered—the first need for legal approval. Ms. Boswell also realized that some restrictions applied to operating a business in her home, hiring employees, and posting a commercial sign in her yard.

The three friends anticipated advertising in catalogs and magazines. This meant doing business outside the state. They had general information about federal government regulations, but they needed special information regarding their own business.

Finally, the three friends realized they lacked information about taxes, reporting profit and loss, and anything else needed by the Internal Revenue Service. The threesome sought outside help. The following section discusses available resources.

Available Resources

Fortunately, Ms. Boswell and her two friends were avid readers. They believed that you can learn about a topic by reading about it. That is how they found out about the Small Business Administration, the Service Corps of Retired Executives, and other resources.

SBA

*The Small Business Administration, commonly known as **SBA**, is a federal agency established to assist and protect the small business.* It helps new businesses get started and helps established businesses grow. SBA has more than 100 offices throughout the nation.

The assistance provided by SBA focuses on business development, financial assistance, contract assistance, and advocacy. **Advocacy** *means representing small business interests before Congress and other federal agencies.*

SCORE

The Service Corps of Retired Executives is commonly known as SCORE. **SCORE** *is a nonprofit agency that has more than 13,000 volunteer business executives who provide free counseling and training to small business owners.*

Ms. Boswell and her two friends contacted SCORE. The volunteer explained the procedures used to register the company name.

The 400 SCORE chapters across the nation make the resource fairly accessible to individuals needing assistance. SBA sponsors SCORE as well as the Small Business Development Centers and Small Business Institutes. Contact your local library for the address and phone number of the SBA and SCORE offices nearest you.

Other Resources

SBA and SCORE are excellent resources. However, there are other resources for information on small businesses. Examples include:

- Chambers of Commerce (city and state)
- Public libraries
- Banks
- Local colleges
- Trade associations

The various chapters in this book have also suggested talking to others. Visiting with the business owners in your own community is an excellent way to learn more about operating your own business.

REVIEW YOUR WORK

1. How does each level of government regulate business?
2. Tell three things that need legal approval when it comes to starting a small business.
3. Explain the purpose of SBA.
4. Identify five resources for obtaining information on small businesses.

Chapter Summary

- Small businesses are very important to our economic system.
- Those who wish to start a small business should be aware that there are risks involved.
- Entrepreneurs need certain skills to assure their success in business. They must be objective in evaluating their strengths, weaknesses, and personality. The entrepreneur needs industry skills, management skills, and entrepreneurial skills.
- In establishing a business, the entrepreneur must recognize a need and have confidence in his or her goods and services. The entrepreneur must also have a business plan.
- Local, state, and federal governments regulate business. These regulations are intended to balance the rights and needs of individuals with the rights and needs of business.
- There are resources available to help entrepreneurs. Two important resources are the SBA and SCORE.

Reviewing Vocabulary and Concepts

Write the numbers 1–14 on a separate sheet of paper. After each number, write the letter of the answer that best completes the following statements or answers the following questions.

1. Entrepreneurs create their own careers because they recognize unique relationships between society and its _____.
   a. population   c. needs
   b. careers   d. laws

2. A business that is independently owned and operated and not dominant in its field is considered _____.
   a. unimportant   c. an industry
   b. small   d. innovative

3. Good planning, technical support, and sound management practices are needed to _____.
   a. work
   b. choose a business
   c. start a business
   d. succeed as an entrepreneur

4. Three characteristics that distinguish successful entrepreneurs from others are self-discipline, innovation, and _____.
   a. free enterprise
   b. human relations
   c. wealth
   d. good looks

5. A _____ defines your business and identifies its goals.
   a. business plan   c. license
   b. need   d. market

6. Regardless of the type of business, the entrepreneur must adhere to _____.
   a. innovation
   b. human relations
   c. personal skills
   d. government regulations

7. _____ relate to knowledge of an industry, product, or craft.
   a. Entrepreneurial skills
   b. Research skills
   c. Industry skills
   d. Management skills

8. Handling a budget, operating accounts, and dealing with any other financial aspects of a business are examples of _____.

a. industry skills
b. human relations skills
c. management skills
d. entrepreneurial skills

9. One who procrastinates and drifts through life does not have _____.
   a. innovation
   b. self-discipline
   c. confidence
   d. advocacy

10. The entrepreneur must listen to customers and employees and respond to their needs in order to maintain good _____.
    a. human relations
    b. self-discipline
    c. industry skills
    d. advocacy

11. A non-profit agency that has more than 13,000 volunteer business executives who provide free counseling and training to small business owners is called _____.
    a. SBA
    b. SCORE
    c. Chamber of Commerce
    d. a trade association

12. In the United States, _____ businesses are small.
    a. no
    b. some
    c. most
    d. all

13. _____ of the work force is employed by small businesses.
    a. None
    b. One-quarter
    c. One-half
    d. All

14. Along with his or her skills and interests, someone who wants to be an entrepreneur should also consider the _____ of his or her business.
    a. management skills
    b. growth potential
    c. innovation
    d. human relations

Thinking Critically About Career Skills

Write your answers to the following questions on a separate sheet of paper.

1. How are the business plan of an entrepreneur and the career plan of an individual similar? How are they different?

2. Self-discipline, innovation, and good human relations are three characteristics of a successful entrepreneur. Would these characteristics also be helpful for an individual who worked for others? Why or why not?

Building Basic Skills

1. **Writing** In a 75-word paragraph, explain how someone can turn a hobby or other interest into a small business.

2. **Mathematics** Calculate the total number of small businesses in a community if 90 percent of all business in the community are small and there are 210 businesses.

Applying Career Skills

1. Go to the library and find books about a successful entrepreneur. Write a 100-word report about how and why he or she was successful.

2. Interview a small business owner. Ask him or her to describe how he or she got started in business. What are the advantages of being a small business owner? Report your findings to the class in a two-minute speech.

MANAGING YOUR MONEY

Brian found the following notice on a school bulletin board. He talked to his friend, Tony, about it.

ATTENTION STUDENTS

FOOD WAREHOUSE 1780 Slide Road. Now hiring part-time help for grand opening in two weeks. Advance to $7.80 an hour. Minimum 4 hrs. per day. Contact Leon Washington, 555-3000.

"We could make $156 a week. Why, that's $624 a month. I could use that kind of money!"

"You wouldn't take home $156 a week, Brian."

"Yes, but the notice says $7.80 an hour."

"It says, 'advance to,' not 'start at.' Besides, taxes would be taken out first."

"Then I'll work overtime."

"You wouldn't get overtime pay until you had worked more than 40 hours."

"I think you'd better explain some of this stuff to me, Tony. I haven't even started work, and it sounds like I'm broke again!"

Brian is finding out there's a big difference between what you earn and what you get to spend. This chapter will explain how that happens. It will also give you some tips about how you can manage your money after you cash your paycheck.

Your Paycheck

For your own benefit, you should understand how to read your paycheck. You will want to know how much is taken out of your check and why.

Parts of a Paycheck

A paycheck contains two parts. One part is the check itself. The other part is the check stub. *The* **check stub** *shows how much you were paid and the different amounts deducted from your pay.* A check and check stub are shown on the next page.

In the example, Lawrence Bryant is the worker. He works for the A-1 Tent and Awning Company. The amount of his check is $186.69. The check was written on February 7. The company keeps its payroll money at the Dallas County Bank. J. G. Johnson signed the check.

Before you cash your check, you should tear off the stub. It's a good idea to keep your check stubs. As you can see from the example, they contain a lot of information:

- your social security number
- dates of the pay period
- the rate of pay
- total hours worked (if hourly rates are paid)
- any other pay, such as overtime
- **gross pay** (*total amount of earnings*)
- **net pay** (*take-home pay*)
- **deductions** (*money taken out for taxes, social security, and insurance*)

Many companies offer low-cost insurance to their employees. Usually, the company pays part of the cost, and the employees pay part. The employee's part is deducted from the paycheck.

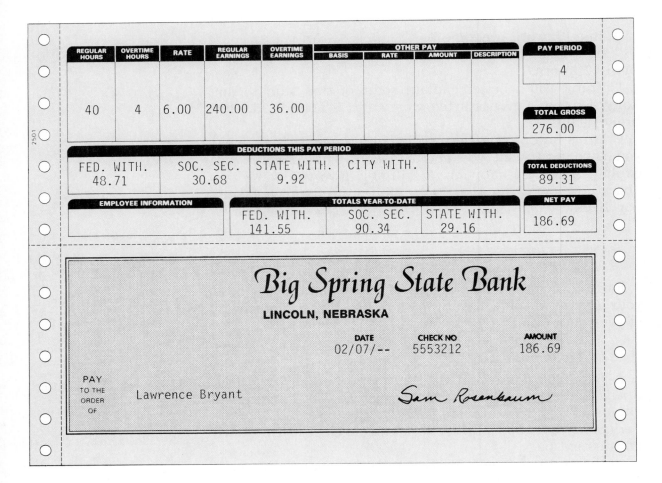

REGULAR HOURS	OVERTIME HOURS	RATE	REGULAR EARNINGS	OVERTIME EARNINGS	OTHER PAY				PAY PERIOD
					BASIS	RATE	AMOUNT	DESCRIPTION	
									4
40	4	6.00	240.00	36.00					

| | TOTAL GROSS |
| | 276.00 |

| DEDUCTIONS THIS PAY PERIOD | | | | | TOTAL DEDUCTIONS |
| FED. WITH. 48.71 | SOC. SEC. 30.68 | STATE WITH. 9.92 | CITY WITH. | | 89.31 |

| EMPLOYEE INFORMATION | TOTALS YEAR-TO-DATE | | | NET PAY |
| | FED. WITH. 141.55 | SOC. SEC. 90.34 | STATE WITH. 29.16 | 186.69 |

Big Spring State Bank

LINCOLN, NEBRASKA

| DATE | CHECK NO | AMOUNT |
| 02/07/-- | 5553212 | 186.69 |

PAY
TO THE
ORDER
OF   Lawrence Bryant

Sam Rosenbaum

Your paycheck and check stubs will probably look much like Lawrence Bryant's. How much money was withheld from his check for social security?

Income Taxes

The largest deduction from your paycheck will be for income taxes. Your employer will withhold these deductions from your paycheck and pay them to the government for you.

Income tax *is money paid from the income of workers to support the government.* When you first go to work, you have to complete a W-4 form for your employer. On this form you write your social security number and the number of **dependents** *(people who depend on your income to live)* you claim. If you are single and without children, you claim only yourself as a dependent. If your parents continue to support you, you claim no dependents.

Each year you must figure your income tax and report it to the government. It is not hard to figure your income tax if you use one of the simple tax forms. Form 1040EZ is the easiest tax form to complete. You can use this form if the only income you have earned is from your salary or wages.

You can get income tax forms from the post office, Internal Revenue Service (IRS) offices, and many banks and libraries. It's best to get two copies. Send one in to the IRS and keep one for your records. After you send in your first income tax return, the Internal Revenue Service automatically mails the same form to you the next year.

To complete your income tax return, you will need your W-2 form. The W-2 form is sent to you by your employer. It lists the total amount you earned, the number of dependents you claimed, and the amount of taxes withheld from your earnings during the year. You should receive a W-2 form from each employer you worked for during the year.

Read all the instructions on the tax form carefully. These instructions will tell you how to complete the form. If you need help, contact the nearest IRS office or call the toll-free number provided with the instructions.

Use the extra income tax form as a work sheet. After you have checked all your math, copy the figures onto your final form. Sign your name as it appears on your social security card and W-2 form and mail the form.

You must complete the tax form to find out how much tax you owe. Your employer will probably have deducted more than enough from your checks. If so, you will be entitled to a refund.

You will not receive your refund until you complete and mail your tax form. If you owe more tax, you will need to send a check with the form.

When you are first employed with a company, you have to fill out a W-4 form. What is the purpose of this form?

Form **W-4** Department of the Treasury Internal Revenue Service	**Employee's Withholding Allowance Certificate** ▶ **For Privacy Act and Paperwork Reduction Act Notice, see reverse.**	OMB No. 1545-0010

1 Type or print your first name and middle initial   *Allen W. Miller*   Last name | **2** Your social security number   *547-32-8901*

Home address (number and street or rural route)   *523 Heading Street*

City or town, state, and ZIP code   *Pekin, Illinois 61673*

3 Marital status   ☒ Single ☐ Married ☐ Married, but withhold at higher Single rate.
Note: *If married, but legally separated, or spouse is a nonresident alien, check the Single box.*

4 Total number of allowances you are claiming (from line G above or from the Worksheets on back if they apply)   **4** *1*

5 Additional amount, if any, you want deducted from each pay   **5** $ *— —*

6 I claim exemption from withholding and I certify that I meet **ALL** of the following conditions for exemption:
- Last year I had a right to a refund of **ALL** Federal income tax withheld because I had **NO** tax liability; **AND**
- This year I expect a refund of **ALL** Federal income tax withheld because I expect to have **NO** tax liability; **AND**
- This year if my income exceeds $500 and includes nonwage income, another person cannot claim me as a dependent.

If you meet all of the above conditions, enter the year effective and "EXEMPT" here   ▶ **6** 19 *— —*

7 Are you a full-time student? *(Note: Full-time students are not automatically exempt.)*   **7** ☐ **Yes** ☐ **No**

Under penalties of perjury, I certify that I am entitled to the number of withholding allowances claimed on this certificate or entitled to claim exempt status.

Employee's signature ▶ *Allen W. Miller*   Date ▶ *July 6* , 19 *— —*

8 Employer's name and address (**Employer:** Complete 8 and 10 **only if sending to IRS**) | **9** Office code (optional) | **10** Employer identification number

1 Control Number		OMB No. 1545-0008		

2 Employer's Name, Address, and ZIP Code	3 Employer's Identification Number	4 Employer's State Number

32-259784

5 Stat. Employee	Deceased	Legal Rep.	942 Emp.	Subtotal	Void
☐	☐	☐	☐	☐	☐

Snaps Fast Food
2305 15th Street
Amarillo, Texas 34552

6 Allocated Tips	7 Advance EIC Payment

8 Employee's Social Security Number	9 Federal Income Tax Withheld	10 Wages, Tips, Other Compensation	11 Social Security Tax Withheld
455-32-4703	1,032.04	9,540.98	938.23

12 Employee's Name, Address, and ZIP Code	13 Social Security Wages	14 Social Security Tips

16

Roberta E. Stone
7501 Detweiller Drive
Amarillo, Texas 34554

17 State Income Tax	18 State Wages, Tips, Etc.	19 Name of State
		TX

20 Local Income Tax	21 Local Wages, Tips, Etc.	22 Name of Locality

Form W-2 Wage and Tax Statement

36-2515832

Copy B To be filed with employee's FEDERAL tax return
This information is being furnished to the Internal Revenue Service

Department of the Treasury
Internal Revenue Service

At the beginning of each year, you will receive a W-2 form from your employer. What information is included on a W-2 form?

You may also have to pay state income tax. These taxes are always lower than your federal income taxes. State tax laws differ from state to state. Your W-2 form will show whether or not your employer has deducted state income tax from your checks.

Social Security

You will notice on your check stub that money has been taken out for F.I.C.A. These initials stand for *Federal Insurance Contributions Act.* The money taken out of your paycheck for F.I.C.A. is put into the social security fund. *The* **social security** *fund pays benefits to disabled workers and retired people.* Your employer must match your F.I.C.A. payments with an identical amount.

Signing Your Check

Before your paycheck can be cashed, you must endorse it. *To* **endorse** *means to sign your name on the back.* Your signature identifies you to the bank. An endorsed paycheck also lets the company know you cashed the check.

It's best to wait until you are at the bank before endorsing your check. Then sign your name on the back exactly the way it appears on the front of the check.

If you want to put the total amount of the check in the bank, write the words "for deposit only" above your signature. If you mail your check to the bank, this prevents any other person from cashing your check. The amount of the check is then placed in your account.

Some people do not use banks to cash their checks. Sometimes grocery stores, drug stores, and other businesses offer this service. Use caution. Many businesses charge a high fee for cashing your check. Not all businesses like to cash payroll checks. Also, identification is required. Don't endorse your check until you know for sure you can get it cashed.

REVIEW YOUR WORK

1. Name three paycheck deductions.
2. What is the simple income tax form called?
3. Name three things to keep in mind in completing income tax forms.
4. Why must a paycheck be endorsed?

Making a Budget

You've just received your first paycheck. What do you do next? Do you spend it all or save some? Do you have any bills to pay? Most people use a spending plan. *A **budget** is a spending plan that helps people manage their money.*

Right now you may not have much money to handle, so you may not have a spending plan. When you are working regularly and earning more money, you'll have to think about a budget. If you give some thought to one now, you'll be better prepared for later. In fact, you could even try to use a budget now to get started on the right foot.

Budgets really aren't hard to set up. The following guidelines can help you.

1. List your spending goals. Begin by writing down the things you would like to have. Your list might include a car, new clothes, savings, or more education.
2. Divide your goals into long-term and short-term goals. Long-term goals should be ones that take a year or more to reach. Now write down the amount of money each goal will cost. You may have to look at newspaper ads, make a few phone calls, or talk to people to get an idea of costs.

Buying a car might be a long-term spending goal for you. How can making a budget help you to meet this goal?

3. Think about which goals are most important to you. Number them in order of their importance. Your most important goal is number 1. The next most important is number 2, and so on.

    What you have just written will give you a basis for making some important decisions. You may have to give up or put off reaching some of your goals in order to meet another goal. For example, if you need a car to get to work, you may have to give up new clothes or a stereo.

4. Write down how much income you expect each month. Include everything, such as salary and tips.

5. Write down your expenses for each month. You'll have two kinds of expenses: *fixed* and *flexible.* Fixed expenses are paid every week or every month. The amounts are exactly or nearly the same each time. Rent, food, transportation, telephone, and school expenses are fixed expenses. Plan also for long-range fixed expenses that must be paid a couple of times a year. For example, you may pay automobile insurance premiums annually (once a year), semi-annually (twice a year), or quarterly (four times a year).

Flexible expenses don't come along as regularly as fixed expenses. The amounts may be different each month. Clothing, recreation, and medical costs are flexible expenses.

6. Subtract your total expenses from your total income. If you don't have money left over or you have run short, you will probably need to make some changes. Take a look at your flexible expenses. They are usually the easiest to change.

7. Keep records of your income and expenses, even small ones. The budget below is an example of one you can use. By keeping a record, you will find out where that money that seemed to just "disappear" actually went. You will also have a better idea where you can save.

Once you have some money left over each month, you can look at your long- and short-range goals. You can put aside a certain amount every month.

Remember, no budget is written in stone. Every once in a while you'll have to make changes. Nothing remains the same. Prices go up. You may get a raise which will mean more money for you. You may have an unexpected expense, such as a high medical bill.

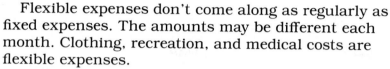

SAMPLE SPENDING PLAN

From _____ to _____

INCOME

Source	Estimated Amount	Actual Amount
Total		

EXPENSES

Fixed	Amount Set Aside	Actual Amount
Flexible		
Total		
Total income minus		
Total Expenses		
Balance		

You can use this sample spending plan in setting up your own budget. What is an example of a fixed expense?

By writing out a plan, you have a clearer picture of where your money is going. You will be more likely to reach the goals that are important to you. You will be able to get more value for your hard-earned money.

Checking Accounts

Opening a checking account will help you manage your money. Every day, people write checks to pay bills and make purchases. Writing checks is more convenient and safer than carrying around large sums of money. Your checking account will also help you keep track of how you are spending your money.

When you open a checking account, you receive a book of checks from the bank. In addition to the checks, the checkbook has a check register. The check register provides you with a place to record the amount of each check and any deposits (money put into an account).

You will also receive a card that allow you to get your money from automated teller machines, or ATMs. *An* **ATM** *is a machine that allows you to withdraw cash or make deposits to your account 24 hours a day.* Use caution when using an ATM. Because they are so easy to use, many people withdraw more money than they should.

It is very important to keep accurate records for your checking account. Simple addition and subtraction are all that is needed. Subtract the amount of each check or ATM withdrawal from the **balance** *(money you have in your account).* Add the amount of any deposit you make to the balance.

Never write a check for an amount that is more than your balance. The check will "bounce," and you will have to pay the bank a fee. A bounced check is a mark against you. If you write many bad checks, you will soon lose the privilege of being able to write checks. In addition, you have to pay a fee for a bounced check.

Always be sure you have enough money in the checking account to cover any service charges. Service charges vary from bank to bank. Many banks have a monthly service charge for handling your account. Banks may also charge you for each check you write or each time you use an ATM. Some banks provide free checks.

Your bank will send you a statement every month. The statement will list all the checks you have written, deposits you've made, and any service charges. Your cancelled checks (the ones that have been cashed) will also be included. You should save the cancelled checks as your proof of payment.

		RECORD ALL CHARGES OR CREDITS THAT AFFECT YOUR ACCOUNT							BALANCE	
NUMBER	DATE	DESCRIPTION OF TRANSACTION	PAYMENT/DEBIT (−)		√ T	FEE (IF ANY) (−)	DEPOSIT/CREDIT (+)		347	53
2902	10/7	United Insurance (for motorcycle)	39	72					307	81
401	10/12	Deposit					251	03	558	84
2903	10/15	Biehl's Cleaners	17	20					541	64
2904	10/22	S&K Chevrolet (October Payment)	205	95					335	69
2905	11/2	Harold's Sports	7	50					328	19
402	11/12	Deposit					275	00	603	19

Always check the bank statement against your checkbook records. Your figures and the bank's figures should agree. If the figures are not the same, try to find the error. Often it is a simple addition or subtraction mistake. The process of checking the statement with your checkbook record is called *balancing your checkbook.*

It pays to shop around if you are going to open an account. Charges for services differ from place to place. Compare interest rates, minimum balance requirements, check fees, and service charges. You will find wide differences.

Savings Accounts

Most people prefer to have their money work for them. They put their money in a savings account where it will earn the greatest amount of interest. **Interest** *is money paid to you for allowing a bank or savings and loan to use your money.*

When you open a savings account, you will get a passbook. The passbook is a record of your account. You will need your passbook when you put money into your account. You need it again when you make a withdrawal (take money out). You might also be able to use your ATM card to make deposits or withdrawals from your savings account.

The more money you have in your savings account and the longer it remains there, the more interest you will make. The interest your money has earned is added to your account.

Your check register will provide you with a place to record the amount of each check and each deposit for your checking account. Why is it important to keep track of your checking account balance?

If you put your money in a savings account, it can earn interest. What is interest?

For example, suppose you had $100 in a savings account for one year. The bank paid 5.5 percent interest annually. At the end of the year, you would have $105.50.

As you gain experience and earn more money, you will discover other ways to earn interest. A savings account is a good way for many people to begin a savings plan. As you become more experienced, you will also find other ways to invest your money.

REVIEW YOUR WORK

1. What part do goals play in developing a spending plan?
2. What is the difference between fixed and flexible expenses? How can you figure the amount of money you will have left over at the end of the month?
3. How can you prevent making an error in your checking account?

Consumer Credit

You probably know that many businesses allow you to use money, goods, and services before you pay for them. *Buying in advance of payment is called buying on* **credit.** The word *credit* comes from a Latin word meaning "trust". When you buy on credit, businesses *trust* you to pay them back.

Most people use credit at one time or another. If you have ever borrowed money from someone and promised to pay it back, you were using credit.

Not everyone can buy on credit. Usually you cannot get credit unless you have a job. Another requirement is that you be at least 18 years old and have an adult be responsible for the money you owe.

Consumers use credit to buy expensive products, such as cars, furniture, and large appliances. In this way they are able to use the goods while they are paying for them.

People also use credit to buy small, everyday items. Using credit for small purchases is a convenience. People can purchase items during the month and pay for them with one check at the end of the month.

When you apply for credit, you will need to provide a great deal of information about your money matters. Why do consumers use credit?

Obtaining Credit

You won't get credit by just asking for it. You have to apply for it. There are two ways you can begin.

- Apply to a local department store for a charge account in your own name. Make some small purchases you know you can afford. Pay your bill promptly each month. Doing so will give you a good reputation with that store.
- Open a checking and/or savings account in your own name at a bank. In the case of a checking account, be sure you maintain a good record.

Once you have obtained credit, you will have a credit rating. *A* **credit rating** *is a record of your credit behavior kept by a credit bureau.* The rating is used by those you wish to borrow from to determine your ability or willingness to pay your debts.

Credit bureaus are located thoughout the United States to provide businesses with information about credit ratings. In this way, the people who lend you money or sell you things are protected from those who don't pay their bills.

Are you a good risk? If lenders think you are, they will loan you money or issue you a credit card. How do lenders decide whether or not you are a good credit risk? They pay close attention to the following points.

- **Your ability to pay.** This is based on how much money you earn. Lenders also look for how long and how steadily you have worked. The better your work record, the better your chances for getting credit. It is best to work several months before applying for credit. In this way you will have time to build a good work record.
- **Your other debts.** You may have a big paycheck every week or month. However, if you also have a lot of debts to pay, it will be difficult for you to pay any additional bills. The people offering credit will want to know about your debts.
- **Your financial habits.** No one is going to question every penny you spend. However, having a checking or savings account is a sign of good personal money management. The lenders may have doubts about you if you can't demonstrate your financial responsibility.
- **Any past credit record.** Credit card companies and banks send credit information about their customers to the credit bureau. The reports show records of late or missed payments and other problems you may have had.

Sources of Credit

Credit cards are just one form of credit known as *sales credit or open-ended credit.* Another form of credit is known as *installment credit.*

Sales Credit.

Credit used for smaller purchases is called **sales credit.** It usually involves credit cards. There are three different types of credit cards: bank credit cards, store credit cards, and charge cards. Each type of card is used in a slightly different way.

Banks issue credit cards such as VISA or MasterCard. Currently, you have to make between $10,000 and $15,000 a year in order to get a card. Most banks charge a fee of $20 to $50, which you must pay every year. This fee covers some of their costs of handling your account.

You can use bank cards in a number of businesses, such as restaurants, retail stores, and mail order houses. Every month you will receive a bill showing the charges you have made. If you pay the bill in full, there are no adddtional charges.

If you only pay part of the bill, there is a finance charge on the unpaid balance, or the amount you still owe. Finance charges run about 1.65 percent a month, or a total of 19 to 20 percent a year.

Credit cards are a convenience for many consumers. Credit cards are an example of what type of credit?

A Career You Can Bank On

The world of finance is fast-paced and exciting, and many people are attracted to the prestigious job of running a bank. If you are interested in the world of finance, you should be happy to hear there are many different jobs available that will allow you to be a part of this world.

Bank officers include such positions as president of a bank, branch managers, loan officers, and operations officers. These jobs require a knowledge of banking as well as administrative and supervisorial skills. Almost all bank officers have a college education.

Other jobs in banks include customer service representative and teller. A customer service representative helps people to open new accounts and make the most of the bank's services. He or she must have strong people and sales skills. Bank tellers handle everyday banking transactions, such as deposits, withdrawals, loan payments, and transfers of funds. Tellers need math skills as well as people skills, and a pleasing personality.

If you would like to combine your interest in finance with your strong math skills, you might enjoy a job as a bank auditor. Auditors check on banks to make sure that all transactions are handled efficiently and accurately. Your data processing and filing skills might land you a position as a filing clerk. These workers are responsible for processing and filing checks, and for processing customer statements.

As banks, like almost businesses, become more automated, there is an increasing need for computer experts in the banking industry. These people set up and run complicated computing systems that automate banking transaction, thus saving both the bank and its customers time and money.

Additional support personnel in the banking industry include secretaries, security guards, and document couriers. Document couriers shuttle important documents between the individual branches of the bank and its administrative offices.

If any of these jobs interest you, talk with your guidance counselor. He or she can help you to plan your career today. You already know that there is money in banking; you might just discover there is more—your ideal career!

You will probably have to pay a minimum amount each month. The minimum is usually about $20.

If you have an unpaid balance one month, the next month the same unpaid balance appears along with your new charges. As you can see, unpaid balances and charges can pile up very easily.

Store credit cards are issued by most major stores. They are usually easier to get than bank credit cards. Stores do not charge you an annual fee for the use of their card. However, you still have to pay a finance charge on any unpaid balance. Finance charges are from 12 to 20 percent per year on the unpaid balance.

Charge cards are different from credit cards. Charge cards are only issued to people with excellent credit ratings. The reason for this is that charge cards do not offer you long-range credit. When your monthly bill comes in, you must pay it in full. You cannot carry the unpaid balance over to the next month. The fee for use of these cards is usually higher than the fee for bank cards. American Express is an example of a charge card.

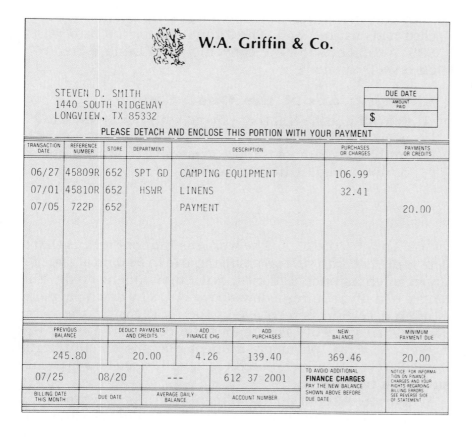

Buying on credit can cost a great deal of money. How much were Steven Smith's finance charges for the month shown?

The greatest advantage of credit cards is that they allow you to buy now and pay later. Even if you don't have the cash on hand, you can still take advantage of sales and good buys.

The disadvantage of credit cards is their cost, such as the fee for use of the cards and the interest you may have to pay. Many people are not careful about their use of credit. They run up large bills that they cannot pay. They get bogged down in bills and interest payments.

CASE STUDY Leslie loved her credit card. She didn't have to take time to write a check. She didn't have to worry if the check would bounce. If she saw a sweater on sale, she didn't have to pass it up just because she was a little short of funds. To her, using a credit card was like not spending the money at all. It was "painless."

At the end of the month, the bills came in. Leslie's credit card bill was always about $400. Since she had a good job, she was always able to pay about $200 of it. At the same time, however, she spent at least $200 more during each month. Her debt was growing.

By the end of the year, the interest on Leslie's credit card had cost her $40. The annual fee for the card was $35. A total of $75! The convenience of Leslie's credit card was expensive.

Thinking About the Case Study

1. Why did Leslie feel that paying with her credit card was "painless"?
2. In the long run, is it more expensive to write a check or use a credit card like Leslie?

Installment Credit.   The word *installment* means that a debt is divided into several smaller parts to be paid at specific times, such as once a month. With installment credit, the lender usually requires a down payment. The down payment is often a certain percentage of the total cost of the item, such as 10 percent. The higher the cost of the item, the higher the down payment. Interest charges usually begin immediately. Installment credit is usually used for big items, such as a house or car.

When you take out an installment loan, you have to sign a purchase agreement. The purchase agreement is written out by the lender. It states all the terms both parties agree to.

Make sure you read, understand, and are willing to accept everything in any purchase agreement before you sign it.

Most purchase agreements often include the following:

- names and signatures of buyer and seller
- date of the sale
- addresses of buyer and seller
- a description of the item or service being purchased
- cash sales price
- amount of down payment
- the difference between the down payment and the sales price
- balance of amount owed
- total amount of finance charges
- amount, number, and frequency of payments

Shop for credit the way you shop for anything else. Suppose you want to buy a car. After you decide on the type of car you want, you should shop around for the best price. Since a car is an expensive purchase, you will probably need an installment loan. You should also shop for the best loan interest rate. Not all interest rates are the same. Go to more than one place.

When you shop for credit, keep in mind the law requires that you be told these two facts:

- the *total cost* of the credit in dollars and cents
- *the true annual* percentage rate of interest

Remember that the total cost of credit must be added to the original purchase price to find out the real cost of an item.

How do you shop for credit? Some people are just interested in what the monthly payment is. However, if you want the most credit for the least cost, shop for the lowest *annual* percentage rate. Remember that the annual percentage rate is the total percentage of interest you would pay for the year.

Pretend the first car you buy is a used car. It costs $2,500. You saved $500 for a down payment. Therefore, you have to borrow the remaining $2,000.

You have several choices of where to go for the money. After shopping around, you find the following information based on a loan of $2,000.

- Loan from car dealer
  True annual percentage rate = 25%
  Total cost of credit = $574
- Loan from Bank A
  True annual percentage rate = 15%
  Total cost of credit = $327

- Loan from Bank B
  True annual percentage rate = 14%
  Total cost of credit = $307

From which source would you borrow the money? As you can see, it is to your advantage to compare annual percentage rates.

You, the Consumer

As a consumer you enjoy many privileges. You can buy a wide variety of products in a wide variety of stores. However, as a consumer you also have certain responsibilities. Reading labels, returning goods of poor quality, keeping records of

As a consumer, you have certain responsibilities. What are they?

your purchases, and promptly paying bills are your responsibilities as a consumer. By accepting these responsibilities, you will be more pleased with what you buy.

In order to get your money's worth when you shop, you need to become a skilled shopper. Skilled shoppers follow these guidelines:

- **Take your time about buying.** Sometimes you may want to buy something right now. If you don't have the cash, you will have to buy on credit. That costs you money. However, if you wait, you can save enough money to pay cash.

Skilled shoppers are always concerned with getting their money's worth. What guidelines do skilled shoppers follow?

- **Shop at sales.** Sales go on year around. Many so-called sales are not really sales at all. Some are simply a way to get you into the store. The store hopes you will buy products other than just the sale item. Also, items on sale may or may not be of the same quality as the store usually sells. When an item is truly on sale, it is offered at a price lower than its normal selling price. You need to decide if you are getting your money's worth.
- **Avoid impulse buying.** Impulse buying means that you buy an item even though you had not planned to do so. Buying on impulse occasionally is fun. Inexpensive items, such as a tube of lipstick or a tape, do not usually damage your budget. However, some items, such as electronic equipment or sporting goods, can be very costly. Try to shop with your budget in mind. If you stick to your budget, you can avoid impulse buying.
- **Look carefully at what you buy.** Even if you are not an expert, you can often tell when one item is better than another. As you continue to look closely, you will learn to see many differences in quality.
- **Study labels.** Look for labels and read them carefully. Labels describe what is inside of containers. They also describe the materials from which goods are made and how to use and care for them. A label can be a starting point for making a decision to buy. Think carefully about the information on the label.
- **Compare prices and services.** You usually have a choice of where to buy. Compare prices and services in different stores.

If you and other consumers are selective about what you buy, the makers and sellers will provide you with good quality merchandise.

REVIEW YOUR WORK

1. What is credit? What is a credit rating?
2. Name four points lenders look at when deciding whether or not you are a good credit risk.
3. What is the difference between sales credit and installment credit? What is the difference between a bank credit card and a store credit card?
4. Name six pieces of information included in a purchase agreement for an installment loan. Why should you shop around when looking for a loan?

Managing Your Money

Most people like to spend their money. They like going out to restaurants to eat. They enjoy buying new clothes. They especially enjoy the big purchases—a new car, a new television set, a new home. They feel good knowing that they can pull money out of their billfolds to buy whatever they desire. However, most people reach a point where they need to manage their money.

Managing money means saying no to yourself—not just once, but again and again. It means being patient—waiting months to buy something that other people might buy immediately.

Managing money also means being honest with yourself—admitting that there just isn't enough money for everything. It means planning—sitting down and carefully thinking through your financial situation. It means sacrificing, organizing, and persevering. Managing money isn't something that you do once and it's over. It's an ongoing process that requires constant attention.

Before you write off money management as something to avoid, think about this: the better job you do of managing your money, the more money you'll have to spend! This is why you should **THINK POSITIVELY** about managing your money. Each minute and each ounce of effort that you put into managing your money can mean extra dollars in your pocket. As the dollars add up, so will your peace of mind and your overall enjoyment with life.

Managing your money does not require any special talent or even a lot of money. As mentioned, it takes patience, planning, sacrifice, and perseverance. These are all qualities that you can develop.

Decide what's important in your life, and what's not. Plan how you will save the money you need to buy the things that you want most. Be patient—don't buy on impulse if you can buy for less later.

Use the techniques presented in this chapter, and think positively. The time and effort you put into money management will pay off.

Chapter Summary

- There is a big difference in what you earn and what you get to spend.
- A paycheck comes in two parts: the check and the check stub. The check stub includes a record of what you have earned and all deductions taken from your pay.
- Income tax is money we pay to support the government. Each April, every wage earner in the United States has to file a tax return.
- Social security is a fund into which you and your employer pay each pay period. The fund helps supplement your retirement income, or gives people who are disabled some income.
- Before a paycheck can be cashed, it must be endorsed on the back by the person whose name appears on the front.
- A plan for the way you intend to spend your money is also called a budget.
- Most people have checking accounts because it is more convenient than carrying around large sums of money.
- Savings accounts are a way to have your money earn more money. That happens when banks or savings and loans pay you interest on the money you deposit.
- Credit buying means you buy things with a promise to pay for them. Buying on credit costs money.
- Careful consumers take their time about buying, shop at sales, avoid impulse buying, look carefully at what they buy, study labels, and compare prices and services.

Reviewing Vocabulary and Concepts

Write the numbers 1–12 on a separate sheet of paper. After each number, write the letter of the answer that best completes the following statement.

1. The part of the paycheck that you cash or deposit is the _____ .
   a. check stub   c. net pay
   b. gross pay   d. check itself
2. The word *credit* comes from a Latin word meaning "_____ ."
   a. belief   c. promise
   b. trust   d. money
3. Buying on credit costs money because the lender charges _____ .
   a. half-price   c. interest
   b. double   d. the bank
4. A _____ is a record of your credit behavior kept by a credit bureau.
   a. checking account
   b. savings account
   c. personal budget
   d. credit rating
5. Gross pay is the amount you earn before _____ .
   a. net pay   c. deductions
   b. social security   d. income tax
6. When you _____ a check, you are signing it on the back.
   a. okay   c. balance
   b. endorse   d. write
7. A(n) _____ fund pays retirement and disability.
   a. welfare   c. insurance
   b. social security   d. income tax
8. _____ is money paid to support the federal government.
   a. F.I.C.A.   c. State tax
   b. Sales tax   d. Income tax

9. The amount on the check itself that you can deposit or cash is _____ .
   a. gross pay
   c. net pay
   b. credit
   d. a balance
10. The money left in an account is known as _____ .
    a. credit
    c. the balance
    b. savings
    d. a budget
11. _____ are people who depend on your income to live.
    a. Consumers
    b. Merchants
    c. Dependents
    d. Credit bureaus
12. A budget is _____ .
    a. net pay
    b. gross pay
    c. deductions
    d. a money management plan

Thinking Critically About Career Skills

Write your answers to the following questions on a separate sheet of paper.

1. Why do you think buying on credit has become so popular? What are the risks associated with buying on credit?
2. Should a person use gross pay or net pay when planning a budget. Why?

Building Basic Skills

1. **Writing** Write a simple spending plan you can use to manage your money for two to three months. Use a copy of the spending plan on page 305 or develop one of your own.
2. **Mathematics** Calculate your net pay if your gross pay was $287.56; your federal tax deduction was $72.86; your state tax deduction was $8.16; and your F.I.C.A. deduction was $28.98.

Applying Career Skills

1. Ask your parents to let you assist them the next time they balance the checkbook against the statement. Afterward, write a three-minute speech explaining the process of balancing a checkbook.
2. Obtain a credit card application from the lobby of your parent's bank. Read the application. Then, go back over the application. Mark an *I* beside each item that is designed to identify the applicant. Mark a *P* beside each item that is designed to show the applicant's ability to pay. Mark a *D* beside each item designed to show the applicant's other debts. Share your completed application with the class.

In the *Career Handbook*, you will find valuable information about 15 different career fields open to you after you graduate from high school. Thinking now about career fields that interest you gives you an opportunity to learn more about that area. You can talk to people in that field. You can take courses in school that will help you learn more about a career area. Perhaps you can find a part-time or volunteer job in a line of work that interests you. You can also learn more about your career options by going to the library and visiting your school guidance office.

Using the Career Handbook: The 15 occupational clusters covered are: Agribusiness and Natural Resources, Business and Office, Communications and Media, Construction, Consumer and Homemaking, Environment, Fine Arts and Humanities, Health, Hospitality and Recreation, Manufacturing, Marine Science, Marketing and Distribution, Personal Services, Public Services, and Transportation.

Included in each occupational cluster you will find the answers to these questions:

- **Description of Work.** What are some typical jobs in this career area? (The jobs described are only a few of the many possibilities in each area.)
- **The Working Conditions.** What are the work surroundings like? Is the work stressful? Is the work dangerous?
- **Training Required.** How do you prepare for a career in this field?
- **Personal Characteristics.** What kind of person is going to be successful in this field?
- **Job Outlook.** Will there be many job openings in this career area?

CAREER HANDBOOK

Agribusiness and Natural Resources

Occupations in the agribusiness and natural resources occupational cluster involve supplying consumers with raw materials for food, shelter, and clothing. *Agribusiness* means agriculture and businesses related to agriculture. This career cluster includes jobs in agriculture, forestry, land and water management, mining, petroleum production, and agriculture support services.

Agricultural workers raise crops and livestock. Forestry workers harvest trees used for housing materials and paper products. People in land and water management take care of public lands and water resources. Workers in mining and petroleum locate and remove raw materials from the earth. Workers in support services provide information and help to improve product quality.

Description of Work: Farm operators are either farm owners, tenant farmers (renters), or farm managers. The tasks they do depend on the size and type of farm. Operators of large farms have employees to do most of the physical work. Operators of small farms do much of the work themselves.

On crop farms, workers have to plan crop production, plant, fertilize, spray, cultivate, harvest, and sometimes even package products. Workers on livestock, dairy, and poultry farms must buy, feed, breed, care for, slaughter, and sell the animals. Farm operators must also make many business and management decisions that require careful planning and record keeping.

Other agricultural workers include groundskeepers, gardeners, animal caretakers, agricultural product graders, sorters, and inspectors. Product graders examine products such as eggs, meat, and vegetables to determine their quality and grade. Food inspectors inspect meat and poultry to make sure it is safe to eat.

Fish and game wardens patrol and protect public areas and wildlife. They enforce federal and state laws and help to promote safety outdoors.

Forestry workers help to manage forest lands to insure their future growth and to regulate current use for business and recreation. Loggers use chain saws to cut trees. Workers in sawmills cut logs into lumber to be sold for construction.

Workers in the mining industry include mining engineers who help to design and operate mines, and miners who extract, or take out, minerals from the ground. In the petroleum industry, petroleum engineers plan and manage the drilling for oil and gas. A variety of workers in different job classifications drill for oil and maintain equipment.

Agricultural scientists develop ways of improving the quality and quantity of farm crops and animals. Agricultural extension agents work for state governments to provide information and support to local farmers and ranchers. They help to solve problems, arrange meetings to share information, and develop helpful written materials.

Working Conditions: The majority of people in agribusiness and natural resources work outdoors. Farm operators and workers often work from sunrise to sunset. Crop farming is seasonal—from six to seven months a year. Livestock, dairy, and poultry farmers work all year. Operators of these farms rarely get a chance to take a vacation.

Agricultural scientists do most of their work in laboratories but often go out in the fields. They usually work regular office hours. Agricultural extension agents work in offices but are often out in the field talking to farmers and ranchers and helping to solve problems.

Training Required: Education and training needed to qualify for a position in agribusiness and natural resources vary with the type of job. Most laborers and miners have a short training period and learn on the job. Petroleum and mining engineers, however, have college degrees.

The fields of agriculture and forestry are becoming more scientific. In order to plan, harvest, and market products, good business judgment is required. A college education is becoming more and more important for people who own and manage agribusinesses and natural resources. People in this field also have to keep up-to-date on new developments.

Extension agents and scientists must have college degrees. Generally, a master's degree is a minimum requirement. Many scientists have doctoral degrees in their areas of specialty.

Personal Characteristics: Many of the jobs in the agribusiness and natural resources career cluster require physical work. Therefore, strength, stamina, and good hand-eye coordination are important. A large number of positions in this occupational cluster are located in rural areas that are not densely populated. So, workers should enjoy being alone or with few people for long periods of time. Scientists must be patient, observant, able to solve problems, and attentive to details. Engineers need strong math and science backgrounds.

Job Outlook: In general, agribusiness and natural resources is a career area of limited growth. As the population of the world gets larger, there is need for more food, clothing, and shelter. However, workers in agriculture, forestry, and mining have become very efficient in the way they work. They are able to produce more than ever before due to improvements in types of plants, fertilizers, breeding methods, feed, and all types of equipment. Most of the job openings will come because people are retiring or going to other jobs.

Farms can be passed down through a family. Buying a farm is very expensive. Equipment is also costly. The trend is toward fewer and larger farms. Larger acreage can be worked more economically, and many farms are now operated by big businesses. The small farmer is finding it harder to make a profit.

The number of positions in forestry, mining, petroleum, and land and water management are not expected to increase.

Other Considerations: Locations of work are generally limited. The type of land and climate determine what and where crops can be grown. Large acres are needed by livestock for grazing. Lumbering is done in forests, and mining can only be done where the minerals are located.

Business and Office

Occupations in the business and office occupational cluster focus on positions providing management and support services for companies. Jobs are in administration, management support, and administrative support.

Managers and administrators are in charge of planning, organizing, and controlling businesses. Management support workers gather and analyze data to help company executives make decisions. Administrative support workers do a variety of tasks, such as keeping records and operating office equipment.

Description of Work: Managers' and administrators' responsibilities are as varied as their titles. In a small, owner-operated firm, the owner makes all the management decisions. Large companies, such as automobile manufacturers or international banks, have several levels of management, including top-level, middle-level, and supervisory-level, or junior managers.

Top-level managers coordinate all of the divisions of a business so the company can run smoothly. In this category are people with the titles of chief executive officer, president, and vice presidents of large divisions, such as manufacturing, marketing, and sales.

Management support occupations are the second level of managers and administrators. These people collect, process, and analyze data needed by top-level administrators to make decisions. For example, accountants and auditors interpret financial records and give advice on money matters. Loan officers of banks approve or deny applications for mortgages and other loans. Personnel specialists help to recruit, select, place, and train employees. These and numerous other positions exist in middle management in large numbers of companies.

Administrative support workers perform a wide variety of tasks in many types of businesses. Workers in this group prepare and keep records, operate office machines, make reservations, and collect, distribute, and account for money, material, mail, or messages.

Administrative support jobs include bookkeepers who keep financial records and bank tellers who receive and pay out money to customers. Secretaries are also administrative support workers. Secretaries take dictation, type, schedule appointments, give information to callers, and handle other office functions. Legal and medical secretaries have special knowledge of legal and medical terms. Some other administrative support job titles include personnel clerk, clerk-typist, file clerk, shipping and receiving clerk, receptionist, and messenger. Among support workers, the amount of responsibility varies widely.

Working Conditions: A large number of people in the business and office cluster work a regular eight-hour day, five days a week. However, many workers in this area work longer and/or shorter hours depending on their companies. For example, tax accountants work long hours during tax season in order to meet pressing deadlines. People in charge of large computer systems must be on call 24 hours a day in case the system breaks down.

Office work lends itself to flexible working arrangements. Many workers hold part-time or temporary jobs. Some are in job-sharing arrangements in which they share their job duties with another person.

The majority of offices are clean, well-lighted, and well-ventilated. Depending on the position held, office surroundings vary. Top executives usually have spacious offices and private secretaries. Lower-level managers may have desks in large rooms and share secretarial services with others. Workers doing clerical tasks may work in large, somewhat noisy rooms.

Clerical work may involve sitting for long periods of time. Some workers spend long hours in front of computer terminals and may experience eye and muscle strain.

Training Required: Education and training vary depending on the type of work and the amount of responsibility handled. People in upper- and middle-management positions are almost all college graduates. People in highly technical work, such as computer programmers, need master's degrees to increase their chances for promotion to good jobs. Certified public accountants (CPAs) who often specialize in tax work must take classes and pass a set of examinations in order to be certified.

People in responsible business positions often begin by working as an assistant to others. If they do well, they can move up to positions with more authority, but they must prove themselves in their current jobs.

Many companies, especially large ones, provide company training programs to upgrade workers' skills. In many occupational areas, continual training is important.

People doing secretarial and clerical work must be high school graduates with good office skills. High school vocational programs offer secretarial training, business schools offer one- and two-year programs. Vocational-technical institutes and community colleges also train people for secretarial work. Beginning clerical workers generally receive some on-the-job training. Many executive and administrative secretaries have college educations.

Personal Characteristics: People in top- and middle-management positions should show determination, confidence, motivation, organizational skills, and be able to make good decisions. They must be able to get along well with others.

In general, people in business need to understand business systems. They should be patient and able to concentrate for long periods of time. Accuracy and attention to detail are important. They must be able to get along with others. Finally, they should have good written and oral communication skills.

Job Outlook: On the whole, management and management support are growing areas of employment. Some positions within the management area, such as accountants, auditors, and computer specialists, are especially in demand.

The number of jobs involving clerical and lower-level administrative support work are decreasing. Automated office equipment enables fewer workers to do more work. Therefore, the need for more workers is not as great.

Other Considerations: Many business operations have been revolutionized by technical improvements in computers. As a result, the way people do their work has been altered. Adaptability and education are key ingredients to success in the business world.

Communications and Media

Occupations in the communications and media occupational cluster deal with organizing information and communicating it to people. Included in this cluster are jobs in radio and television broadcasting, journalism, motion pictures, the recording industry, and telecommunications (telephone, telegraph, and satellite systems).

People in radio and television broadcasting prepare and present radio and television programs. Workers in journalism write, edit, and produce newspapers, books, and magazines. Workers in motion pictures and the recording industry make movies, records, and tapes. Workers in telecommunications design and maintain equipment that allows people to communicate by telephone, *facsimile* (printing words via telephone), and telegraph.

Description of Work: Many of the jobs in the communications and media career cluster are glamorous and exciting. All jobs in the cluster, however, are important and require hard work.

Work in television and radio varies depending on the job and the size of the station. In small stations employees may be asked to do many different jobs including announcing, operating control boards and cameras, selling commercial time, and writing advertising and news stories. In larger stations each of these jobs is handled by specialists.

In journalism, reporters gather information and write stories about local, state, national, and international events. When covering a story, they may do background research, locate public records, and interview a variety of people. On large newspapers, editors make assignments and coordinate activities of general assignment writers, foreign correspondents, feature reporters, columnists, and editorial writers.

Other workers on a newspaper take photographs, write headlines, paste up pages, obtain advertisements, sell subscriptions, and do general office work.

Technical writers who write about specialized areas may work for firms manufacturing aircraft, chemicals, computers, and other products.

People write and edit for book publishers, magazines, broadcasting companies, advertising agencies, and the federal government. Freelance writers are paid for the individual articles, books, and scripts they write.

Producing motion pictures and recordings involves the work of people who have broad responsibilities, such as producers and directors. Producers coordinate writers, directors, and editors, and obtain money to produce movies and recordings. Directors guide cast and crew members during rehearsals and filming. Camera operators, lighting technicians, sound mixers, and editors are other jobs involved with motion pictures and the recording industry.

Telecommunications, a fast-growing technical area, employs people to design and maintain telephone, satellite, and laser communications. (Satellites above the earth receive and send signals, speeding up communication.) Skilled engineers design systems that change the way people communicate.

Other employees who help to service and maintain telecommunications systems include telephone operators, telephone installers, and line inspectors.

Working Conditions:

Broadcasters at radio and TV stations usually work in well-lighted, air-conditioned, soundproof studios. If reporting from outside the studio, conditions may not be ideal. Often they work under the pressure of rigid deadlines.

Newspaper and magazine reporters usually have hectic schedules and work under pressure to meet deadlines. Newsrooms are frequently crowded and noisy. Working hours vary depending on the job. For example, reporters for morning papers work late afternoon until midnight. People responsible for printing and distributing papers work throughout the early morning hours.

Motion picture and recording company workers have varied hours. People involved in the production of a film or recording may work irregular hours in order to meet scheduled deadlines.

Telecommunications workers often work on different shifts for scheduled work hours. In emergencies, they may have to work overtime. People installing and repairing equipment often have to work outdoors in both good and poor weather. Sometimes the work can be dangerous.

Training Required:

Radio and television are very competitive fields. People in broadcast news need a college liberal arts or humanities degree. Experience working at a school radio station and on school publications and summer work at local stations and newspapers is helpful. In order to work for stations in bigger broadcast markets, several years of successful working experience are needed.

Most newspaper editors have a bachelor's degree in journalism, including liberal arts courses. It is helpful to be familiar with word processing equipment.

People working behind the scenes in radio and TV need a high school education and often train on the job. In some cases, technical training is important.

In telecommunications, engineers must have a bachelor's degree in their area of specialty. Technicians working in satellite communication need technical training. Telephone installers and operators receive on-the-job training.

Personal Characteristics:

Working in the media requires creativity, talent, and the accurate use of language. In journalism, being observant, thinking clearly, and seeing the significance of events are important. Announcers must have good voices, excellent speaking skills, and a well-developed personality style. Ability to work under pressure is also important.

People involved in engineering and technical work need math skills and ability in handling detail and solving problems.

Job Outlook:

The number of positions for radio and TV announcers and reporters is limited and highly competitive. Radio stations are more likely to hire beginners than TV stations. Broadcasters must prove they can attract large audiences.

Writing and editing, though not a growing area of employment, continue to have competitive job openings. The best opportunities are in writing for trade publications.

Job opportunities in telecommunications are good for engineers working in highly specialized areas and for their trained support staff. Telephone operators and installers have limited job opportunities due to technical improvements that have reduced the need for workers in these two areas.

Construction

Occupations in the construction occupational cluster involve building, repairing, and modernizing homes and other kinds of buildings. Work is also done on a variety of other projects, such as airports, mass transportation systems, roads, recreation facilities, and power plants.

Construction workers are grouped into three general areas: structural, finishing, and mechanical workers. Structural workers include bricklayers, carpenters, concrete masons, ironworkers, stonemasons, and construction machinery workers. Finishing workers include drywall installers and finishers, carpet installers, *glaziers* (those who work with glass), insulation workers, marble setters, painters, paperhangers, plasterers, roofers, and tilesetters. Mechanical workers include electricians, pipefitters, plumbers, and sheetmetal workers. Each area is very specialized.

Description of Work: Bricklayers and carpenters are structural construction workers. Bricklayers build walls, floors, partitions, and fireplaces using brick, cinder, and concrete block. They spread *mortar* (a cement mixture) with a *trowel* (a flat, metal tool), put bricks on the mortar, and tap them into place. Leveling the bricks, fitting them in around different openings, and smoothing out the work also have to be done.

Carpenters build the framework for houses or other buildings, frame the roof and interior, and install doors, windows, flooring, cabinets, wood paneling, molding, and trim. In order to do their job, they have to read blueprints and know local building codes. They cut and shape wood using hand and power tools and join materials with nails, screws, or glue.

Carpet installers and drywall workers are finishing construction workers. Carpet installers lay carpets in homes, offices, restaurants, and stores. They have to measure and plan the layout since most carpet comes in standard widths. Their work involves rolling, measuring, and cutting carpet. They use hammers, drills, staple guns, rubber mallets, and other tools designed for their work.

Drywall installers and finishers use drywall board (thin layers of plaster covered with heavy paper) to cover walls and ceilings. They have to measure and cut drywall to fit around windows and doors. Then they glue, nail, or screw the panels into place. Finishers work with a trowel to apply a special mixture called drywall compound used to finish corners and rough edges.

Electricians and plumbers are mechanical construction workers. Electricians install electrical systems that operate heating, lighting, power, air conditioning, and refrigeration units. They read blueprints in order to install wiring inside walls and to put in switches and outlets. Wiring must be connected to circuit breakers and transformers. Electricians spend a great deal of time inspecting equipment to locate problems before breakdowns occur.

Plumbers build and repair the water, waste disposal, drainage, and gas systems in homes and other buildings. They also install plumbing fixtures (bathtubs and sinks) and appliances (dishwashers and water heaters). They work from blueprints and fit the piping into the building. To put a system together, they have to cut and bend lengths of pipe using saws, pipe cutters, and pipe-bending machines. When piping is in place, plumbers install fixtures and appliances and then connect the system to the outside water and sewer lines.

Working Conditions: Construction work often involves long periods of time standing, bending, and working in small spaces. Work is often done outdoors or in partially enclosed areas.

Workers use many sharp tools and do their jobs surrounded by piles of building materials. As a result, they have the highest injury rate of any industry. Builders stress the use of safety equipment, such as hard hats, steel-toed shoes, safety belts, and protective glasses.

Training Required: Construction trades offer good opportunities for people who are not planning to go to college but are willing to spend several years learning a skilled occupation.

Employers prefer high school graduates with courses in math and mechanical drawing. Some workers learn their skills through on-the-job training. However, authorities recommend formal apprenticeship training as the best way to learn basic skills. Most apprenticeship programs are supervised by joint committees composed of local employers and trade union representatives.

Apprenticeship programs require supervision on the job (usually for three to four years) by a skilled construction worker plus 144 hours or more of classroom instruction. In areas where joint committees do not exist, the apprenticeship agreement is between the apprentice and the employer.

In many states, some construction workers (mostly electricians and plumbers) are required to have a license. To obtain a license, workers must pass an examination showing their knowledge of the trade.

Personal Characteristics: Since a great deal of construction work requires lifting heavy materials, physical strength and stamina, or energy, are needed. Construction work requires a team effort, so the ability to get along well with others is important to workers in this field.

Manual dexterity (the ability to work with one's hands) is needed to work quickly and accurately with tools and equipment. The ability to solve mechanical and structural problems is important. Construction workers must also be precise, have an eye for detail, and be able to picture objects from blueprints.

Job Outlook: Job growth in the construction industry is about average. The best employment opportunities exist in the more populated areas of the country.

The state of the nation's economy affects the rate of construction and remodeling. When the economy is healthy and expanding, more construction jobs will be available. When the economy slows down, jobs are harder to find.

Other Considerations: Weather influences the number of days many workers can work. Rain slows down construction, and cold weather can bring outside building to a halt.

In general, construction workers can find jobs in all parts of the country. They have better opportunities to open their own businesses than workers in other skilled occupations. About one out of four skilled construction workers is self-employed.

Consumer and Homemaking

Occupations in the consumer and home-making occupational cluster involve developing, producing, and managing goods and services that improve the quality of home life. Jobs in this cluster center around areas such as food, housing and household equipment, textiles and clothing, family relations and child development, and the extension service.

People who work in the area of food help to provide food and food information for consumers. Housing and household equipment workers design and evaluate home interiors and home equipment. People in the textiles and clothing field design and promote the sale of fabrics and clothing. Workers in child development work to improve family relations and child growth. Employees of the extension service help to educate homemakers and youth in subjects such as the selection and care of clothing, food preparation, child care, and the management of family finances.

Description of Work: People who work in the area of food include dietitians and nutritionists, consumer service specialists, and food journalists. Nutritionists work with people to help them understand how food affects the body and to help improve their eating habits. Dietitians are nutritionists who may work as administrative dietitians or clinical dietitians.

Administrative dietitians manage large-scale meal planning and preparation in company cafeterias, schools, and other large institutions. They supervise the planning, preparation, and service of meals. They hire and train kitchen workers and are responsible for purchasing food, equipment, and supplies.

Clinical dieticians usually work in hospitals, nursing homes, or clinics. They evaluate patients' nutritional needs and develop diets or eating plans.

Consumer service specialists are employed by large food packaging companies and supermarkets. These specialists look into what consumers want and help food companies develop new products. They also prepare informational materials that encourage consumers to use the company's products.

Food journalists are employed by magazines, newspapers, and radio or TV stations. They create and test recipes for publication or broadcast.

Housing and household equipment workers may be employed as home service directors and interior decorators. Home service directors work for equipment manufacturers and utility companies such as gas and electric companies. They promote the use of their company's equipment or utility by answering customers' questions, writing booklets, developing recipes, and giving presentations to groups.

Interior decorators may work for a decorating firm, builder, or home furnishings store, or they may be self-employed. They help clients plan and decorate their living and office spaces by selecting and placing furniture and equipment. They also work out color schemes and help select accessories such as pictures and floor coverings.

Textiles and clothing workers are employed as fashion coordinators, fashion journalists, and consumer service specialists. Fashion coordinators work for department stores, clothing retailers, and fashion mail-order companies. They present fashion shows and organize displays and advertising to encourage customers to purchase the latest fashions.

Fashion journalists work for magazines, newspapers, and radio and TV stations. They report on fashions and accessories.

Consumer service specialists represent a company to the public. They work for fabric manufacturers, sewing machine companies, and accessory manufacturers such as thread companies. It is their job to promote the use of a company's products.

Child development specialists may work as nursery school teachers and day-care program coordinators. Nursery school teachers work with young children before they

enter kindergarten and elementary school. Day-care program coordinators work with businesses to establish in-house day care for the children of employees.

Extension service workers are employed by the extension service in each state. They provide information for consumers and families about nutrition, home furnishings, child development, and money management. They present community programs, work with youth groups such as 4-H Clubs, write bulletins and newspaper columns, and appear on radio and TV programs.

Working Conditions: Almost all people in the consumer and homemaking area work in pleasant offices and work areas. In general, they have a standard work week. People working with clients such as interior decorators may have to hold meetings at the clients' convenience. Extension service workers often have to attend meetings at night and on weekends. Journalists, consumer service specialists, interior designers, and extension agents usually have to travel on the job.

Training Required: Consumer service specialists, dietitians, journalists, nursery school teachers, and day-care program coordinators all have college degrees. Registered dietitians must also serve a 6- to 12-month internship. Family relations counselors usually have a master's degree.

Fashion coordinators and interior designers may be college graduates or have post-high school training in a professional or vocational school.

Personal Characteristics: People working in the area of foods, especially dietitians, should have some background in science. They need organizational skills, the ability to understand consumers' needs, and good communication skills.

People in fashion and interior design should be artistic and have a strong color sense, an eye for detail, and good communication skills. Child development specialists need patience and the ability to develop good relationships with others. They also need to be observant and creative. Extension agents need to be well organized and have good communication skills.

Job Outlook: Dietitians and nursery school teachers have the best opportunities for employment. Limited growth is expected in the other positions in the consumer and homemaking area.

Environment

Occupations in the environment occupational cluster (our surroundings) involve the protection of natural resources and the population. Jobs center around pollution prevention and control, disease prevention, environmental planning, and resource control.

Pollution prevention and control workers attempt to measure and control water, soil, and air pollution. (*Pollution* is the result of chemicals or waste materials being released in water, air, and soil.) Disease prevention workers try to control organisms that cause disease. Environmental planning workers look ahead to future population growth and increased demands on natural resources. Resource control workers regulate the use and care of natural resources.

Description of Work: Environmental Protection Agency inspectors are an example of workers concerned about the prevention and control of pollution. The Environmental Protection Agency (EPA) is an agency of the United States government that works to protect the environment from pollution. EPA officials establish and enforce regulations to limit pollution. EPA workers also clean up hazardous waste dump sites.

Consumer health inspectors who specialize in consumer safety visit firms that produce, package, and market food, drugs, and cosmetics. They look for anything in products that would be harmful to those who use them and examine the labeling to be sure it is truthful. They use testing kits and instruments and collect samples to be sent for analysis.

Other workers involved in pollution prevention and control include chemical engineers who specialize in pollution control in the manufacturing process, and chemists who analyze water in water purification plants. People work and supervise in the areas of testing and collecting garbage and sewage disposal, all of which helps to keep the environment clean and safe.

Workers in the area of disease prevention include entomologists, epidemiologists, and exterminators. *Entomology* is a specialized area in which scientists study insects and how they affect plants and animals. They help in controlling and eliminating pests that destroy crops or spread disease. Epidemiologists investigate the organisms that cause food spoilage and food poisioning. Exterminators use chemical sprays and gases to eliminate pests in buildings and surrounding areas.

Urban and regional planners and landscape architects are some of the people involved in environmental planning. Urban and regional planners help local officials make decisions about the future growth of cities and towns. They look at a region's long-range needs for housing, education, transportation, and business sites. Planners must be familiar with laws and zoning codes, as well as how much the proposals will cost.

Landscape architects plan the best use of land for projects such as parks, airports, highways, shopping malls, and housing developments.

The sciences of ecology and zoology are concerned with natural resources. For example, ecologists might study the way organisms and the environment react with one another. They investigate the way pollutants, rainfall, temperature, and altitude affect living things.

Zoologists study animals. They examine the way they develop, their behavior, diseases, and life stages. Other workers in the area of natural resources include aquatic biologists who study plants and animals living in the water and the conditions that affect them. Wildlife biologists study and work with wildlife (animals and birds) to learn more about them and to ensure their future safety.

Working Conditions: EPA inspectors travel and make on-site inspections of manufacturing plants, dump sites, and other facilities. Their work surroundings vary from location to location, and their hours may be long and irregular.

Chemical engineers, entomologists, ecologists, and zoologists generally work regular hours in offices and labs. These scientists sometimes work with dangerous organisms or *toxins* (poisons). They may also have to make field trips, some of which could involve physical activity and primitive living.

Urban and regional planners and landscape architects do most of their work in offices, although they have to make on-site visits. They need to work cooperatively with others.

People whose work involves garbage collection, sewage disposal, and extermination of pests work in a variety of locations. Some of the surroundings may be unpleasant. Exterminators handle dangerous chemicals.

Training Required: Education and training vary with the job. EPA inspectors usually have a college education with a degree in environmental health or physical or biological science. Engineers must have at least a bachelor's degree in their area of specialty.

Scientists (entomologists, ecologists, and zoologists) with a master's degree can do *applied research* (solving practical problems). A doctoral degree is required to do more complicated research and go into administrative positions.

Entry-level positions for urban planners generally require a master's degree in urban/regional planning. Landscape architects should have a Bachelor of Architecture degree. Almost all states require architects to be registered (licensed) in order to practice. This means a person must have a bachelor's degree and have worked in an architectural office for three years.

Workers in garbage collection, sewage treatment plants, and extermination receive on-the-job training.

Personal Characteristics: In almost all positions dealing with the environment, people must use a cautious, scientific approach to their work. Being observant and attentive to details is important. People should be able to work independently or as part of a team. They should also be able to communicate their findings clearly.

Urban and regional planners and landscape architects should have good math and drawing skills.

Job Outlook: In almost all positions in the environmental area, expect job growth to be slow. Many of these positions are involved in working for or in cooperation with federal, state, and local governments. The government often takes a long time to agree on and pass regulations and may have limited money to spend on enforcing laws and regulations.

Fine Arts and Humanities

Occupations in the fine arts and humanities occupational cluster involve developing, promoting, and preserving the arts and social values. Jobs center around areas such as performing arts, visual arts, writing, religion and *theology* (study of religious belief), history, and museum work.

People in the performing arts present theatre, music, and dance productions. Workers in the visual arts produce various forms of art. Writers create fiction and nonfiction books, magazine articles, and poetry. Religious and theological professionals prepare worship services and provide religious guidance. Workers in museums preserve and study the records and materials of the past.

Description of Work: People in the performing arts include actors, dancers and choreographers, musicians, and workers providing support services. Actors portray roles in television, movies, and theatrical productions.

Dancers perform alone, with a partner, or in groups. They may perform in ballets or do modern or acrobatic dances. Choreographers create dance steps and routines for performances and instruct dancers.

Musicians include instrumentalists, vocalists, and conductors. Instrumentalists play one or more musical instruments as members of an orchestra, band, or other musical group. Some compose and/or arrange music. Musicians study and rehearse musical scores.

Vocalists sing classical, opera, religious, folk, pop, rock, or rap music. Conductors lead bands and orchestras. They audition and select group members, select music, and direct rehearsals and performances. Other people working in the performing arts include stage directors, theatre managers, costume designers, and drama coaches.

People working in the visual arts include those in graphic and fine arts and the applied arts. Fine artists (painters and sculptors) create art works that are appreciated for their beauty. Applied artists design objects that are both practical and attractive.

Graphic art is also known as commercial art. Graphic artists work as illustrators who draw pictures for books, magazines, newspapers, record albums, and films.

Designers working in applied art usually specialize in one type of product or activity. They may design automobiles, clothing, furniture, home appliances, industrial equipment, movie or theatre sets, packages, or make floral arrangements.

Writers or authors create original works of fiction or nonfiction for books or magazines. Often they specialize in such areas as historical novels, humor, romance, science fiction, or mysteries. Playwrights write plays to be produced as live theatre. Poets compose different types of verse.

People doing religious work may be members of the clergy serving in churches and synagogues. They may work in educational institutions or act as chaplains in the armed forces or prisons. Others may serve at hospitals or on college campuses. Many people do religious work as missionaries or in social welfare agencies.

Archivists and curators do most of their work for public and private museums. They search for, obtain, assemble, catalog, exhibit, and maintain items of interest. These items may have artistic, historical, and/or cultural value.

Working Conditions: People in the performing arts often work long, irregular hours. Travel is often required. Conditions on location may vary from spacious and well equipped to small and poorly equipped. Meeting schedules and long rehearsals can be stressful and tiring.

People in fine arts usually have their own studios, and their working conditions and hours vary. Artists in applied and graphic arts often work in well-lit and comfortable offices during regular working hours. If deadlines have to be met, they may have to work overtime.

A large number of writers do freelance work and set their own hours. People doing religious work often have regular office hours but are "on call" for emergencies.

Curators' and archivists' surroundings vary depending on the type of work they do. They often work alone on identification and classification of material and keep regular working hours.

Training Required: Formal education and training for the fine arts and humanities vary. Musicians and singers often spend years in intensive training and practice before appearing professionally. Actors might work in school and community theatre. Formal acting training in drama schools is helpful, though some actors have succeeded without formal training.

Ballet dancers must begin serious training by at least age 12. Modern dance does not require as many years of training (although many modern dancers do begin training at a young age).

Many professional musicians begin studying an instrument at an early age. Classical musicians need long periods of training. Popular musicians can have successful careers without much formal training; however, classical work is helpful.

In the visual arts, a good *portfolio* (a collection of work samples) is sometimes more important than formal education. Educational needs vary. Floral designers learn on the job. Industrial designers must have a minimum of four years of college. Fashion designers and those in fine art usually have some type of specialized training in a professional school.

Writers often have a broad liberal arts education. The training for religious workers varies. Most denominations require education at a theological school. People working as archivists and curators usually have graduate degrees and a lot of practical working experience in their areas of specialty.

Personal Characteristics: In the fine arts and humanities, people must be talented in order to be successful. Devotion to one's work is also important.

Job Outlook: In the performing arts, the number of talented people far exceeds the number of positions available. It is difficult to find full-time employment, and performers usually have to add to their income by holding other jobs.

Painters and sculptors often find it difficult to support themselves through the sale of their work and frequently need to hold other jobs. Although work in design is competitive, good positions are available. Graphic artists enjoy good employment opportunities due to the importance of advertising.

The need for religious workers varies. Employment opportunities for curators and archivists are limited.

Health

Occupations in the health occupational cluster involve providing services to meet people's physical and mental health needs. Jobs in this cluster center around areas such as health and mental health, diagnosing and treating practitioners, nurses, pharmacists, therapists, health technologists, and technicians.

Health practitioners diagnose, treat, and try to prevent illness and disease. Nurses, pharmacists, and therapists care for the sick, help the disabled, and give advice about ways to improve and maintain health. Health technologists and technicians operate medical equipment and perform tests used for diagnosis and treatment of various illnesses.

Description of Work: Health practitioners include a number of doctors specializing in different areas of medicine. Physicians perform medical examinations, diagnose illnesses, and treat people who are sick. They may be in general practice or specialize in a certain field of medicine, such as psychiatry, family medicine, general surgery, *obstetrics* (delivering babies), or *pediatrics* (care of children). Most medical doctors are specialists.

Dentists are practitioners who examine teeth and mouth tissue, fill cavities, repair or take out fractured teeth, and help people keep their mouths healthy. Most dentists practice general dentistry, but some specialize in areas such as oral surgery and *orthodontics* (straightening teeth).

Chiropractors treat people by massaging muscles and manipulating bones, especially the spine. They do not prescribe drugs or perform surgery. Optometrists examine people's eyes, diagnose vision problems, and prescribe eye glasses or contact lenses.

Registered nurses, pharmacists, and therapists work as part of the medical team. Most registered nurses work in hospitals where they care for patients, assist in surgery and in diagnosis, train and supervise other staff members, and provide health education for patients. Nurses also work in nursing homes, rehabilitation centers, clinics, physicians' offices, and in people's homes.

Licensed practical nurses (LPNs) help to care for the sick. They work under the direction of physicians and registered nurses but do not have the extensive education and training registered nurses do.

Pharmacists generally work in hospitals or community pharmacies where they provide drugs and medicines that are ordered by doctors.

Therapists use a variety of techniques to help patients who have physical injuries or emotional and mental problems. Physical therapists use exercise and other treatments to help people increase their strength and ability to use parts of their body which have been injured. Occupational therapists help people with physical injuries to care for themselves and learn how to do everyday tasks again.

Health technologists have more complex jobs and more responsibility than health technicians. However, both technologists and technicians work in all areas of medical care. Radiation therapy technologists operate equipment used to treat cancer patients. Radiologic technicians operate X-ray machines that produce X-rays of the brain and other parts of the body. Dialysis technicians operate kidney machines.

Dental hygienists work under the direction of a dentist. They provide care such as cleaning teeth, taking and developing X-rays, and explaining proper care of the mouth.

Working Conditions: Many health care providers work in offices and laboratories that are clean, comfortable, and well-equipped. Physicians, nurses, and some medical technologists work under stressful conditions when a patient's life is in danger.

Physicians who practice general medicine often work long, irregular hours. Surgeons performing complicated operations can be in the operating room for hours at a time. Many other health care professionals work

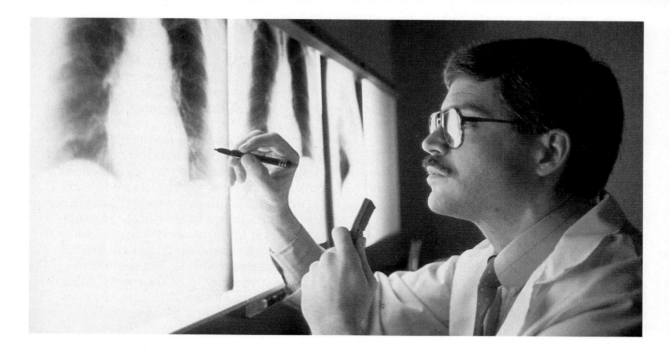

a 40-hour week, although they may work different shifts in hospitals. Caring for people who need medical care can be an emotional and physical strain.

Training Required: Each state has laws regulating the training accepted and the tasks that many health care professionals, including physicians, dentists, nurses, and pharmacists, can perform. Medical doctors, chiropractors, optometrists, dentists, and nurses must pass state medical examinations before they can practice.

Medical practitioners have the most extensive training of any professional group. Physicians have three to four years of medical education after college plus a one-year residency in a hospital. If they specialize, they must spend several years in training after residency.

Chiropractors and optometrists have two years of college plus a four-year program of study. Dentists have two to four years of college plus four years of dental school.

Therapists have a four-year program of study in their specialty. Pharmacists study in a pharmacy program lasting five years beyond high school. Registered nurses study from two to five years after high school. Medical technologists usually study for four

years, and medical technicians have training that ranges from on-the-job training to two-year programs. Licensed practical nurses study for one year.

Personal Characteristics: People in health care must have a strong desire to help the sick and injured. Emotional stability and the ability to make decisions in emergencies are important. Those who work closely with sick people must be sincere and trustworthy.

Workers who are under the supervision of other health professionals must be able to follow orders and pay attention to details. Nurses and therapists need physical and emotional stamina in order to do their work.

Job Outlook: Most of the people interested in health care careers have good to excellent chances for employment, with the exception of pharmacists and some clinical laboratory technicians.

Other Considerations: The health care system is undergoing a great deal of change, mostly due to rapidly increasing health costs. More emphasis is being placed on *outpatient* care (not in the hospital), in-home care, and community health services rather than on patient care in the hospital.

Hospitality and Recreation

Occupations in the hospitality and recreation occupational cluster involve helping people make travel plans and participate in leisure-time activities. Jobs center around such areas as travel agencies, transportation, and public and private recreation.

Workers in travel agencies help people make travel plans. Workers in the transportation industry help to provide services for travelers. People in public and private recreation perform and/or arrange recreation and entertainment activities.

Description of Work: People working in travel agencies include travel agents and travel counselors. Travel agents help their clients make the best travel arrangements, keeping in mind people's tastes, budgets, and other requirements. Travel agents use a variety of sources for information on departure and arrival times, fares, and hotel accommodations. Most travel agents use computers for information about fares and schedules.

Automobile clubs employ travel counselors who plan trips for club members. Using a road map, they show the best routes to take. They also indicate mileage, points of interest, restaurants, and hotel accommodations along the way.

People working in transportation services include reservation and transportation ticket agents, flight attendants, tour conductors, and tour directors. Reservation and ticket agents are employed by airline, railroad, bus, and steamship companies. They help customers by answering questions, making reservations, and writing and selling tickets. When passengers leave for trips, agents check baggage, direct them to departing gates, and help them to board.

Flight attendants provide assistance, safety information, and refreshments to airline passengers. Tour conductors point out interesting and historical locations to tourists and answer their questions. Tour directors accompany groups on trips, taking care of all arrangements and handling any problems that arise.

Workers in the area of recreation include recreation workers, athletes, and entertainers. Recreation workers plan, organize, and direct activities that help people enjoy their leisure hours. Employment opportunities include working in parks and wilderness areas, health clubs, community centers, camps, sports and entertainment centers, tourist attractions, and hotels and resorts.

Participants in sporting events and entertainment include a large variety of people. Professional athletes participate in competitive sporting events, such as football, basketball, baseball, soccer, hockey, tennis, golf, and a number of other sports. Athletic teams have managers, directors, trainers, and equipment handlers. Umpires and referees make sure the rules of the game are enforced. Sports instructors, such as golf pros and ski instructors, teach others to play and enjoy sports. Circus entertainers work as clowns, acrobats, and animal handlers. Other entertainers include comedians, magicians, and puppeteers.

Working Conditions: Employees in hospitality and recreation work in a variety of settings and in very different surroundings. Many people in this occupational area work irregular hours because leisure activities are enjoyed around the clock.

Travel agents work in offices and usually have a 40-hour week. During busy travel periods, they are under pressure to help customers. They use the telephone a great deal of the time.

Reservation and ticket agents work different shifts because transportation facilities operate 24 hours a day. Poor weather, labor strikes, and holiday rush periods that cause scheduling problems often make the work stressful.

Recreation workers usually have a 35- to 40-hour week and often spend long periods outdoors. Recreation workers are generally physically active.

People who participate in entertainment and sporting events work in a variety of surroundings both indoors and outdoors.

Professional athletes work under a great deal of physical and mental stress and risk serious injuries. Most circus work is both dangerous and strenuous.

Training Required: People working as travel agents may begin by working part-time at a travel agency. Travel courses are offered by a number of educational centers and are helpful in learning all aspects of the business.

Reservation and ticket agents often have some college work, although that is not a requirement for the position. Some agents learn on the job. Many larger employers offer training programs that last from one week to a month or more.

Recreation workers have a variety of backgrounds. Many summer jobs in the area of recreation can be filled by those with a high school diploma. However, people with a bachelor's degree from college have a better chance for advancement. Many colleges offer major courses of study in recreation or physical education. People wanting administrative positions will probably need a graduate degree in recreation.

The most important requirement for athletes and entertainers is skill. Most athletes have natural athletic ability and instincts. However, proper training along with dedicated practice are essential. Athletes have to be in top physical condition to be successful.

Personal Characteristics: Travel agents and reservation and ticket agents should have pleasant personalities, good speaking voices, telephone skills, and be able to handle details. Recreation workers should like people, be creative and resourceful in planning activities, be in good health, and have physical stamina.

Athletes need a great deal of stamina to perform. They also need mental and physical discipline to achieve success in sports. The ability to accept criticism about their performance and to be able to concentrate are important.

Job Outlook: Travel agents have good job opportunities. However, the travel business can be affected by a poor economy when people usually spend less money on leisure travel. Reservation and ticket agents have limited job opportunities because computers are widely used.

Recreation workers have good employment prospects due to the growing number of people who have leisure time. Athletes and people in entertainment do not have a great deal of job security. The people with the best talent and ability do not have difficulty finding employment. Most professional athletes are under 40 years of age. Younger athletes usually have more stamina than older players and can play for longer periods of time.

Manufacturing

Occupations in the manufacturing occupational cluster involve the design and assembly of products ranging from huge earth-moving equipment to the microminiature parts of an electronic instrument. Jobs center around such areas as management, scientific, engineering, technical, skilled, semi-skilled, and unskilled work.

Management workers supervise manufacturing plants. Scientists do basic research on products and manufacturing methods. Engineers design working products and systems. Technicians handle specialized manufacturing operations. Skilled, semi-skilled, and unskilled workers carry out tasks ranging from those requiring high levels of ability to those requiring mostly physical effort.

Description of Work: Generally, the management of a large manufacturing company includes people holding positions such as president, vice president, and managers of various divisions. The president is in charge of developing and overseeing all of a company's programs and progress. Manufacturing plants may have one or more vice presidents who report to the president. A vice president may be in charge of purchasing, sales, manufacturing, engineering, or finance.

Division managers carry out the policies set out by the president and vice presidents. They coordinate the activities of departments such as production, distribution, engineering, maintenance, personnel, and sales.

Scientists, such as chemists and physicists, solve problems in developing new products and technology. Chemists have developed new and improved fibers, paints, adhesives, drugs, electronic components, lubricants, and other products. Mathematical research done by physicists has contributed to such advances as the flights of the space shuttles, improved medical instruments, and increased automobile safety.

Engineers (electrical, industrial, and mechanical engineers) apply scientific theories to solve practical problems. They design industrial machinery and equipment for manufacturing, heating, and air-conditioning systems, automobiles, home appliances, and electronic home entertainment equipment.

Engineering, science, and electrical technicians assist scientists and engineers in research and production. In research, technicians do routine design work, set up equipment, prepare experiments, and organize results. In production, they prepare plans for parts of the manufacturing process and conduct tests to maintain product quality.

Skilled workers include tool designers, die makers, tool makers, and machinists. They use detailed instructions to produce goods that must meet quality standards. For example, tool makers may make such tools as guides for drill presses that must be accurate enough to produce thousands of the same part. Tool makers read and follow the blueprints produced by the tool designer.

Semi-skilled workers control and monitor machines and equipment during the manufacturing process. They have titles such as metal-working and plastic-working machine operator.

Unskilled workers are also known as laborers. They perform various jobs requiring close supervision.

Working Conditions:
People in management positions work in offices. The types of offices and the assistance they receive depend on the level of their position. Problems such as strikes, economic downturns, and increased competition can cause considerable stress.

Scientists usually work regular hours in offices and labs. Some are exposed to health or safety hazards when handling certain materials. The risk is small if proper procedures are followed.

Some engineers work at a desk in an office most of the time. Others work in research labs or industrial plants. Most technicians work regular hours in labs, offices, and industrial plants.

Skilled, semi-skilled, and unskilled workers have regular shifts. Most factories are well-lighted and well-ventilated. However, powerful, high-speed machines can be dangerous if all safety rules are not strictly followed.

Training Required:
People in management are usually college graduates, many with majors in business, engineering, or finance. Scientists have graduate degrees in their areas of specialty. Engineers have undergraduate and perhaps graduate degrees in their areas of interest.

Technicians usually need some type of post-high school training. This can be obtained at a technical institute or community college. Some technicians receive their training from the armed forces or through on-the-job training. Some highly trained technicians attend four-year colleges.

Apprenticeship programs are considered the best way to become a skilled worker. These programs combine both work and classroom experience or supervised instruction. Some skilled workers learn a trade informally on the job, but workers from apprenticeship programs are preferred. Most semi-skilled and unskilled workers learn their jobs through on-the-job training provided by their employers.

Personal Characteristics:
People in management need good communication skills. They should be able to see the broad picture as well as the details and be able to plan and make decisions.

Scientists need to be able to work with their hands building scientific equipment and performing experiments. They should be able to see projects through to the end, concentrate on important details, and work independently.

Engineers should be able to work as part of a team. They need to be creative, able to solve problems, and remember details. They must be able to express themselves orally and in writing.

Technicians have to follow directions, have technical and math skills, and be attentive to details. Skilled and semi-skilled workers should be able to follow directions and be able to work carefully. Unskilled workers need strength and stamina.

Job Outlook:
The positions available will vary from industry to industry depending on new technology and foreign competition. Few new management and research scientist positions will be created. Engineers and technicians have excellent job prospects. In general, the need for skilled and semi-skilled workers will be more limited than in the past due to automation in the workplace and the importation of foreign-manufactured goods.

Marine Science

Occupations in the marine science occupational cluster involve discovering, developing, improving, and harvesting marine life. The word *marine* means things related to the sea or ocean. Marine science jobs are in areas such as research, fishing and aquaculture, and marine engineering and technology.

Marine research workers explore and study the oceans and seas. Fishing occupations involve harvesting fish, and aquaculture occupations center on cultivating marine life for harvest and sales. Marine engineering and technology workers deal with the design, construction, and operation of ships and underwater structures.

Description of Work: Marine researchers include geological oceanographers, physical oceanographers, geochemical oceanographers, and aquatic biologists. *Oceanography* means the study of the environment in the oceans, including the water itself, water depths, water beds and rocks, and the plants and ocean life.

Researchers in oceanography usually specialize in one area of interest. Geological oceanographers study the ocean bottom. They collect information using sensing devices aboard ships or sometimes from underwater research craft. Some explore for possible oil and gas reserves below the ocean floor. Physical oceanographers study such things as ocean currents and how the air and atmosphere affect them. Geochemical oceanographers study the chemical makeup of oceans.

Aquatic biologists study the aquatic plants and animals along with the conditions that affect them. The word *aquatic* refers to growing or living in or upon the water. Aquatic biologists may specialize in an area. Marine biologists study salt-water life. Scientists who study fish are called *ichthyologists.* Marine botanists study aquatic plant life, and marine zoologists study aquatic animal life.

Fishing and aquaculture workers include line fishers, fish farmers, and shellfish growers. Line fishing workers catch fish with hooks and troll lines. Fishing may be done from the land or from a vessel. Lines must be put out with hooks, bait, and sinkers attached.

Fish farmers raise fish such as trout, catfish, and salmon in stock ponds. A fish farmer may supervise the processing and marketing of the fish. Shellfish growers cultivate and harvest beds of clams, oysters, mussels, shrimp, and other shellfish. Water areas must be staked out and seeded with young shellfish called *spat.* After the shellfish are harvested, they must be sorted and packed in containers for shipment.

Marine engineering and technology workers include marine architects, marine engineers, commercial divers, and scuba divers. Marine architects design and oversee the building and repair of marine craft such as ships, tugs, and submarines. Marine engineers design and oversee the construction of *propulsion* (driving) systems and heating and cooling systems for marine craft.

Commercial divers work below the surface of water. They inspect and repair docks, ship bottoms, ship propellers, and bridge structures under the water. They work with tools and sometimes use explosives below the water.

Scuba divers are sometimes called salvage divers. They dive to locate and recover wreckage below the water. Some specialize in underwater photography.

Working Conditions: Most research workers divide their time between the office or laboratory and fieldwork. Their fieldwork may carry them to remote areas where they spend long periods of time at sea. The fieldwork can be more dangerous than working in an office or laboratory.

Fishing and aquaculture workers spend most of their time outdoors in various weather conditions. Their work is physical, especially in line fishing. Whenever poor weather conditions occur at sea, it can be dangerous.

Marine architects and marine engineers spend part of their time in offices working on design problems. They also make on-site visits to inspect and supervise repairs and construction.

Divers and scuba divers can be involved in dangerous work, handling equipment underwater, and facing unknown conditions. Safety often depends on equipment being in good condition.

Training Required:
Marine researchers need at least a master's degree in their area of interest to qualify for a good position and promotion. It is helpful to have a strong background in science and mathematics. A doctoral degree is needed for most research positions. Marine researchers usually are certified scuba divers.

Workers who fish get on-the-job training and have often grown up in areas where fishing is important to the economy. People in aquaculture are involved in a very scientific field and have to continue to keep up-to-date as new developments occur. They must have good business judgment in order to plan, harvest, and market their product.

Marine architects and marine engineers must be college graduates with strong mathematics backgrounds. Many people in these fields do a considerable amount of work with computers.

Commercial divers must attend vocational diving school programs that last about one year. All divers must be certified scuba divers. Certification is earned by attending short courses and passing written exams and open-water dive tests.

Personal Characteristics:
Marine research workers need to be able to work as part of a team. They should be curious, able to concentrate on detail, and communicate well. When doing fieldwork, physical stamina is important.

Fishing and aquaculture workers need patience, strength, and stamina. Marine architects and marine engineers should be able to communicate well with others, handle details carefully, and be able to solve problems. Divers need to be in good physical condition, have strength and physical stamina, and excellent coordination.

Job Outlook:
People interested in working in most positions in marine science have good career opportunities. Line fishing jobs are limited due to the closure of fishing areas in some places.

Marketing and Distribution

Occupations in the marketing and distribution occupational cluster involve forwarding goods from the manufacturer to the consumer and influencing the consumer to purchase the products. Marketing and distribution jobs center around areas such as marketing, purchasing, sales promotion, and selling.

Workers in marketing plan the sale and distribution of goods. Purchasing agents buy materials and equipment, often for resale. Sales promotion workers create a demand for products. People engaged in selling help customers make buying decisions.

Description of Work: All types of products—from such raw materials as oil and cotton to such finished products as automobiles and breakfast cereals—are marketed. People who market products include sales managers, wholesalers, retail store owners and managers, and market research analysts. Sales managers handle a variety of tasks. They direct the sales staff, set sales goals, give advice on promoting sales, and analyze sales results.

Wholesalers manage businesses that buy large quantities of merchandise from manufacturers and then sell this merchandise to retail stores. Retail store owners own and operate private businesses that sell goods to customers. If the store is small, the owner is usually also the manager. Managers hire and train salespeople, plan work schedules, price merchandise, and promote sales.

Market research analysts work for large companies that sell goods to people or for independent agencies whose main job is to survey the marketplace. Analysts conduct studies of market conditions by using surveys and research. They summarize and analyze the data to predict or forecast what future sales will be.

People in purchasing include purchasing agents or buyers, assistant buyers, brokers, and importers. It is the job of purchasing agents and buyers to purchase the best merchandise at the lowest prices. This merchandise, in turn, is made into a product or sold to the consumer. For example, a purchasing agent for an automobile manufacturer may buy steel to be used in building cars. A buyer for a department store attends fashion shows and meets with manufacturers to buy the clothes sold in retail stores.

Brokers bring sellers and buyers of merchandise together. For example, a food broker who represents producers of frozen fruits and vegetables will sell these products to supermarkets. Importers bring in or import merchandise from foreign countries to be sold in this country.

Sales promotion work includes package designers and window dressers. Package designers design containers for products, taking into consideration convenience, handling, customer appeal, and cost. Window dressers plan and arrange commercial displays to attract customers' attention.

Salespeople sell a variety of products, such as furniture, appliances, automobiles, clothing, cable television service, and insurance. In addition to selling, most retail sales workers make out sales checks, receive cash and charge card payments, and give change and receipts. Well-trained salespeople help make the businesses that employ them more successful.

Working Conditions: People in marketing usually work in offices. Retail store-owners and managers may spend most of their time in the store, doing such things as talking to salespeople and customers, setting up displays, and checking stock. Many sales managers and wholesalers travel to visit customers in their businesses.

Purchasing agents and buyers, brokers, and importers work in offices and may spend several days a month traveling. Buyers are often under great pressure because sales are very competitive, and they frequently work more than 40 hours each week.

Product and package designers generally work in well-lighted and comfortable offices. Window dressers work in stores and store windows.

Some salespeople work in stores. Although they usually work a 40-hour week except for holiday periods, they often have to work nights and weekends, depending on the store's hours. Other salespeople, such as those selling goods to manufacturers, spend most of their time traveling by car or airplane. Travel may take them away from home for long periods of time.

Training Required: People in marketing come from different backgrounds. Some go into the family business with training on the job. Others go into business after high school and college. Sales managers are usually college graduates with degrees in business or liberal arts. They often go through company-sponsored training programs. Market research analysts are college graduates with majors in marketing, including work in *statistics* (a branch of mathematics).

Most buyers begin their careers by selling merchandise. Some are college graduates. Others attend vocational schools and community colleges offering training.

Many package designers attend art institutes or major in art in college. Some window dressers take post-high school design programs; others learn on the job.

Training requirements for salespeople are as varied as the work itself. Most employers look for high school graduates to sell routine items, such as cosmetics, shoes, and clothing. Large retailers offer short training programs. However, in selling more complex products such as computers, people need college backgrounds and technical training.

Personal Characteristics: Personality characteristics are more important in marketing and sales occupations than in almost any other area of work. People should be outgoing, enthusiastic, and persuasive. Success in sales takes initiative, energy, self-confidence, and self-discipline.

Packaging designers and window dressers must be creative problem-solvers who have an eye for color and design. They must be self-disciplined and able to communicate ideas visually. People's tastes change frequently. So, people in the design field need to be open to new ideas and influences.

Job Outlook: Marketing and sales offer good employment opportunities since people are continually buying new products and replacing old ones. The field of design also offers good job possibilities.

Personal Services

Occupations in the personal services occupational cluster involve providing services that help people care for themselves and their possessions. Jobs in this cluster center around areas such as domestic services, lodging services, barbering and cosmetology, dry cleaning and laundry services, domestic animal training and care, and food and beverage preparation and service.

Domestic service workers provide services for their employers and their employers' guests. Lodging service employees provide general services to people staying in hotels and motels. Barbering and cosmetology workers help to improve people's personal appearance. Domestic animal care workers care for and train pets and other domestic animals. Food and beverage preparation and service workers prepare and serve food and drinks for customers.

Description of Work: Domestic service workers include day workers, housekeepers, cooks, gardeners, and chauffeurs. Day workers clean, make beds, and do other tasks in private homes. Day workers are self-employed or work for home cleaning services. Housekeepers perform a variety of tasks and often live with their employers and their families. Cooks plan menus and prepare meals in private homes. Gardeners take care of lawns and flower gardens. Chauffeurs drive automobiles for the owners and care for their cars.

Lodging service employees include hotel managers and assistant managers, housekeepers, bellhops, and maintenance supervisors and workers. Managers are responsible for efficiently operating hotels and motels. They manage the front desk, housekeeping, food service, recreational activities, marketing and sales, and security. Managers working for large chains may be assigned to organize new hotels or motels, or reorganize those that are not operating successfully.

Hotel/motel housekeepers must be sure rooms are clean and orderly. Bellhops help guests to their rooms, handle luggage, and provide information about hotel services. Maintenance supervisors and workers care for the buildings and grounds.

Barbers and cosmetologists care for people's hair and perform other related tasks. Barbers cut, trim, shampoo, and style hair. Cosmetologists are also known as beauty operators, hairstylists, and beauticians. They shampoo hair, cut hair, style hair, and advise patrons on hair care. Cosmetologists may give manicures, scalp treatments, facial treatments, and provide makeup analysis.

Dry cleaning and laundry workers include supervisors, spotters, and cleaners. Laundry supervisors oversee workers who receive, mark, wash, and iron clothing and linens. Dry cleaners operate dry cleaning equipment and pressing machines. Spotters working for dry cleaners identify stains in fabrics and apply chemical solutions to remove them. Furniture and rug cleaners use chemical solutions and equipment to clean rugs and furniture.

Domestic animal care workers include dog groomers, dog trainers, horse trainers, and people who own and operate kennels and pet shops. Dog groomers wash dogs and clip their hair and nails. Dog trainers train dogs to obey and perform tricks. People owning and operating kennels care for dogs and cats while they are at the kennel. Pet shop owners and workers care for the pets that are for sale and sell pet food and animal grooming equipment.

Food and beverage workers include chefs, cooks, and food servers. Chefs and cooks work for restaurants, schools, hospitals, and cafeterias. (Chefs are more highly trained and skilled than cooks.) Typically, the chef or cook prepares food with the help of others. In exclusive restaurants, each chef or cook has a special job creating only desserts, sauces, meat, or fish. Head chefs plan, purchase, and oversee all kitchen work.

Food servers take customers' orders, serve food and beverages, make out checks for the customers' meals, and sometimes

take customer payment. In small restaurants, they may have to set up and clear tables and carry dirty dishes to the kitchen.

Working Conditions: The surroundings and difficulty of work vary with each position in the personal services occupational cluster. In general, domestic work is physical and requires bending, stooping, and moving objects. Hotel managers should have initiative and be able to organize and supervise the work of others. The work may involve covering night and weekend shifts.

Barbers and cosmetologists spend long periods of time standing on their feet. People in dry cleaning and laundry work also spend many hours standing. The shops they work in are often hot, and the work is physical. People working with animals should like them and be patient. Horse trainers usually spend a great deal of time outside.

Employees in food and beverage service have to work together as part of a team, often during busy, stressful periods. They are continually on their feet and may have to lift heavy objects. Working hours in restaurants may include late evenings, holidays, and weekends. Food servers should be well spoken, neat, and clean. A good memory is also helpful. Chefs and cooks need to be creative, have a keen sense of taste and smell, and be well organized.

Training Required: Workers in domestic service, dry cleaning and laundry services, and food service usually learn their work on the job. Barbers and cosmetologists must be licensed by the state and be a graduate of a state-approved vocational school. Dog groomers can learn their trade on the job, but many also take vocational courses.

Many chefs and cooks begin as kitchen helpers. Some serve an apprenticeship with a well-known chef. An increasing number of chefs attend culinary institutes with two-year programs.

Hotel managers should have a bachelor's degree in hotel and restaurant administration or attend a junior college or technical institute offering courses in hotel work.

Personal Characteristics: People working in the personal services occupational cluster must enjoy working with other people. Almost all jobs in this cluster require patience and understanding from the worker. A pleasing, friendly personality is also important.

Job Outlook: In almost all of the positions in personal services, with the exception of barbers, the job outlook ranges from good to excellent. Many people are now buying services rather than doing things for themselves.

Public Services

Occupations in the public service occupational cluster involve supplying services to the public, many of which are supported by tax money. Jobs center around areas such as city and town services, protective services, the armed services, postal services, public utilities, education, and social services.

City and town administration employees are involved in policy making, licensing, regulating, and record keeping for the city or town. Protective service workers enforce laws that protect citizens and help to prevent loss of life and property. Postal service workers transport and deliver the mail. Public utility workers maintain the equipment that produces and/or distributes water, electricity, and gas. People in educational occupations help to educate the public. Social workers help people facing personal and family problems.

Description of Work: A city manager works in city and town administration. The manager has a staff and coordinates all the operations of the city/town, studies problems such as housing, and helps to plan for future development.

Protective service workers include police officers, fire fighters, and members of the military or armed forces. Police officers in smaller communities have duties ranging from controlling traffic to investigating crime. In large police departments, officers are assigned to a specific type of duty such as neighborhood patrol, traffic duty, or work on a mobile rescue team. State police officers patrol highways and enforce laws that govern the roads.

Firefighters respond to fires and handle other emergencies. They operate equipment, rescue victims, give emergency medical aid, ventilate (air out) smoke-filled areas, and help save the contents of buildings.

People in the armed services (also called the military services) serve in the Army, Navy, Marine Corps, Air Force, and Coast Guard. Together they provide our national defense. The military services are the largest employer in the country. They offer a wide range of employment and training opportunities in managerial and administrative jobs, clerical work, skilled construction trades, motor vehicle repair, occupations in electronics, and many other specialties.

The United States Postal Service employs workers in a number of jobs, the majority of which are mail carriers or postal clerks. Most mail carriers travel planned routes delivering and collecting mail. They also collect money for cash on delivery (c.o.d.) items, get signed receipts for registered mail, and help to sort mail. Postal clerks may sell stamps, weigh and stamp packages, register and certify mail, separate and sort mail by hand, feed letters through stamp-canceling machines, and operate electronic letter sorting machines.

Workers in public utilities supervise and/or operate equipment that supplies water, electricity, and gas. People in this area work in a variety of jobs. For example, a water treatment plant operator regulates the motors, pumps, and valves that purify drinking water. A load dispatcher in the electric company controls the flow of electricity throughout an area.

Educational professionals are employed as teachers, librarians, and counselors. In addition to teaching, teachers prepare lessons, grade papers, attend meetings, serve on committees, and often supervise school activities.

Counselors help people handle personal, social, educational, and career problems. They might serve as school and college counselors, helping students understand themselves and their abilities. They might serve as employment counselors, helping people make wise career decisions. They may also serve as rehabilitation counselors, helping handicapped or injured people.

Librarians work in user or technical services. Those in user services work directly with people to help them find information. Librarians in technical services obtain and catalog books and materials.

Social service workers help individuals and families whose lives are affected by poverty, alcoholism, drug abuse, behavior problems, or illness. Social workers may specialize in family services, child welfare, medical social work, mental health, or aging. They counsel people and refer them to other helpful services.

Working Conditions: The working conditions of public service workers vary widely. City and town managers do most of their work in offices and have an average-length work week.

Protective service workers often work on varying shifts since police and fire fighting services are needed 24 hours a day. Some fire fighters, for example, are on duty 24 hours and then off for 48 hours. Police officers and firefighters face a higher risk of injury than most people.

Armed service personnel lead a disciplined life. Hours, working conditions, and danger vary depending on assignments.

Mail carriers must begin work very early in the morning in order to sort mail and organize it for deliveries. Carriers spend most of their time outdoors and must deliver mail in all weather conditions. Postal clerks work indoors under varying conditions, de-

pending on whether labor-saving equipment is used.

Public utility workers work both indoors and outdoors depending on their responsibilities. Indoor work may range from quiet to noisy when large equipment is involved.

Educational work is done mostly indoors. Classroom teachers stand a great deal of the time and often attend meetings and prepare their work after school hours. Librarians also work indoors and may have to work some evenings and weekends, depending on library hours. Social service workers are in offices and may have to do some traveling to visit clients.

Training Required: People in city administration, education, and social service work need college educations. Public school teachers and social workers must get state certification. Many states require teachers to earn a master's degree within a certain period of time. College and university teachers and professors have master's and doctoral degrees.

Police officers and firefighters must have a high school education. An increasing number of police positions require college work. People in protective services have a training and probationary period.

People in the military service range from high school to college graduates. They have a 6- to 11-week basic training period. Most receive on-the-job training.

Utility workers have a training period. Some may need post-high school technical training.

Personal Characteristics: City and town administrators must be well organized and work well with people. Protective service employees need to be physically fit, have a sense of fairness and honesty, and use good judgment. Educational professionals should be able to motivate people, make and keep good relationships with people, and be creative. Social workers should have basic concern for others, objectivity, and the ability to work well with people.

Job Outlook: Employment opportunities in public service work are good. Fewer job opportunities will be available in the postal service and in libraries.

Transportation

Occupations in the transportation occupational cluster involve the movement of people and goods from one place to another. Jobs center around areas such as highway transportation, airborne transportation, and rail transportation.

Workers in highway transportation move people and goods by bus and truck. Employees in airborne transportation fly people and freight to their destinations. Railroad workers transport freight and people by rail.

Description of Work: Inter-city, local, and school bus drivers pick up and discharge passengers at bus stops or stations. Inter-city drivers operate buses traveling between towns or cities. Local drivers operate within one city. School bus drivers have a route within one school district. On most runs, drivers collect fares, issue transfers, and answer questions. Drivers must follow their time schedules and be alert to prevent accidents.

Truck drivers usually pick up goods from factories and deliver them to warehouses, terminals, or stores. Long-distance deliveries can take a day, a week, or longer, depending on the distance. Drivers must check their trucks to be sure they are operating safely. When driving they must be alert to prevent accidents and drive trucks efficiently.

Route salespeople deliver their firm's products to stores. They may stock shelves, set up displays, and sell products.

Pilots, copilots, engineers, and air traffic controllers are all responsible for airline safety. Most pilots transport passengers, cargo, and mail. Others spray crops with fertilizers or insecticides, test aircraft, and take aerial photographs. Helicopter pilots are involved in firefighting, police work, weather station operations, and rescue efforts.

Before departure, pilots must make their flight plans and check their planes to be sure the engines, controls, and instruments are operating safely.

Air traffic controllers keep track of the planes flying in the air. They regulate the flow of air traffic in and out of airports and make certain that planes are flying a safe distance from one another. They work in teams, telling pilots of local weather conditions and observing planes' flight paths on radar screens.

Rail transportation workers include locomotive engineers, locomotive firers, and conductors. Engineers are in charge of the operation of the locomotive. They operate machinery, interpret signals, and are responsible for the safety of the train. The firer is an assistant to the engineer. Conductors handle communication, paperwork, and passenger tickets.

Working Conditions: Bus drivers often have to drive through heavy traffic while dealing with passengers. Though not physically difficult, driving is stressful. Local and inter-city drivers work different shifts in order to provide day and night service. School bus drivers usually work about 20 hours a week when school is in session.

Local truck drivers usually work 48 hours or more a week, often through heavy traffic, which can be stressful. They frequently load and unload their own trucks and have to lift, carry, and walk.

By law, long-distance truck drivers cannot drive more than ten hours without being off duty at least eight hours. Drivers on long runs must remain alert for long periods of time. Although many drivers work during the day, night travel is common because roads are less crowded then.

By law, airline pilots cannot fly more than 100 hours each month. Most pilots fly about 80 hours a month and work an additional 80 hours a month on non-flying duties. The majority of flights involve layovers away from home. Work schedules are irregular because airlines operate flights all day and night.

Flying does not involve much physical effort. However, the mental stress of being responsible for the safety of the plane and people can be tiring. Pilots must be alert and quick to react if anything goes wrong. Air traffic controllers also operate under a tremendous amount of stress in making sure the airways are safe.

Rail transportation workers work different shifts in order to provide service around the clock. In general, the work is not dangerous if safety procedures are followed. Engineers must be alert to any danger on the tracks and to signals indicating rail conditions.

Training Required: Most bus companies prefer hiring high school graduates. Drivers must have a chauffeur's license (commercial driving permit) or a special school bus license. Drivers must pass a physical examination and vision test. Intercity bus training programs are two to eight weeks of classroom work and behind-the-wheel instruction. School bus drivers are instructed for one week.

Truck drivers must have a chauffeur's license which usually includes passing a vision test and physical exam. Employers prefer applicants with good driving records and some previous truck driving experience. Truck drivers often start as dock workers, loading and unloading goods. A small number of private and public vocational schools offer truck driving courses.

Pilots must have a commercial pilot's license. Helicopter pilots must have a commercial license with a helicopter rating. Strict physical, vision, and written examinations must be passed. Airline pilots must pass additional licensing tests.

Most airlines require pilots to have at least two years of college, but they prefer college graduates. Flying can be learned in the military or in civilian flying schools. All new pilots receive several weeks of intensive training.

Air traffic controllers must pass difficult examinations. Job applicants should have three years of general work experience, four years of college, or a combination of both.

Railroad transportation workers are usually high school graduates and must pass physical and written tests. Training classes are five weeks or more.

Personal Characteristics: The ability to understand and follow complex operating rules, procedures, and instructions are important. Coordination and manual dexterity, good health, good vision, and good color perception (recognition) are necessary. Varying amounts of mechanical aptitude are needed to fix parts of a vehicle not operating correctly.

Job Opportunities: Good job opportunities are available in all areas of transportation for qualified people. Positions as railroad engineers and air traffic controllers are competitive.

GLOSSARY

A

Academic achievement tests. Tests that measure your knowledge and skills in reading, science, math, and social studies. (p. 32)

Addiction. A physical or mental need for a substance. (p. 251)

Advocacy. Representation of small business interests before Congress and other federal agencies. (p. 297)

Alcohol. A drug that is produced by a chemical reaction in some foods and has powerful effects on the body. (p. 251)

Alcoholism. A disease caused by a physical and mental need for alcohol. (p. 251)

Alternative. A choice. (p. 85)

Application form. A form that asks for information about you, your education, and your work experience. (p. 143)

Apprentice. Someone who learns an art or a trade by working for a set period of time in that field. (p. 103)

Aptitudes. The skills you can learn quickly; ability. (p. 26)

Attitude. A way you think and feel about certain topics or life in general; your general outlook on life. (p. 153, 226)

Automated teller machine. (ATM). A machine that allows you to withdraw cash or make deposits in your account 24 hours a day. (p. 308)

B

Balance. An amount remaining after a withdrawal or payment, such as in a checking account. (p. 308)

Body language. The message people deliver through their mannerisms; the way a person walks, sits, stands, or speaks. (p. 152)

Booms. Periods during which consumers have lots of money to spend and production is high. (p. 269)

Budget. A spending plan that helps people manage their money. (p. 305)

Business plan. A statement or report that defines your business and identifies its goals. (p. 294)

C

Capitalism. An economic system; a free enterprise system in which individuals and private businesses are free to organize and operate with little interference from the government. (p. 265)

Career. Time spent in one type of job or area of interest. (p. 13)

Career interest areas. Categories of jobs that are similar according to interests. (p. 43)

Check stub. Part of a check that shows how much you were paid and the different amounts deducted from your pay. (p. 301)

Classifieds. Newspaper ads that list many different kinds of advertisements for such things as items for rent or sale. (p. 117)

Commission. Payment based upon a percentage of the money you bring in for a company. (p. 174)

Communication. Getting your message across to others. (p. 213)

Compromise.   To give up something in order to come to an agreement. (p. 194)

Computerized guidance programs. Programs on personal computers that provide information about the job world. (pp. 71–72)

Constructive criticism.   Criticism designed to be helpful. (p. 203)

Consumer.   A person who spends money to buy goods and services. (p. 266)

Controlled substance.   A substance whose use is limited by law. (p. 251)

Cooperative education programs. Programs for students to go to school and work at the same time. Part of the day is spent at school and part of the day is spent on the job. (pp. 76–77)

Cost-of-living increase.   A raise given to help workers keep up with rising prices and costs. (p. 185)

Credit.   A means to buy in advance of payment. (p. 310)

Credit rating.   A record of your credit behavior kept by a credit bureau. (p. 312)

D

Decisions.   Situations requiring you to make a choice. (p. 82)

Deductions.   Money taken out of a paycheck for taxes, social security, and insurance. (p. 301)

Defensive.   Not accepting responsibility for what you have done, or getting upset about a kind of criticism that is not important. (p. 204)

Deflation.   A resulting drop in prices from a depression in the economy. (p. 270)

Dependents.   People who depend on your income to live. (p. 302)

Depressions.   Low periods in the economy when production is down. (p. 270)

Destructive criticism.   Criticism that focuses on just the bad things and gives the person no help. (p. 202)

Downtime.   Any time during which workers can't work, for whatever reason. (p. 173)

Drug.   A substance other than food that changes structure or function of the body or mind. (p. 252)

Drug tests.   Tests to reveal the presence of drugs in an individual's body. (p. 256)

E

Economics.   A social science concerned with the description and analysis of the production, distribution, and consumption of goods and services. (p. 11, 274)

Economic system.   A group of people producing, selling, and using goods and services. (p. 265)

Emotions.   Feelings. (p. 190)

Employee Assistance Program (EAP).   A program to help identify and correct employees' substance abuse problems. (p. 256)

Employment agency.   An organization that helps people find jobs. (p. 120)

Employment trends.   An indication of whether the need for certain work will grow or shrink over the next several years. (p. 58)

GLOSSARY

Endorse. To sign your name on the back of a check to identify you to the bank cashing a check. (p. 304)

Enthusiasm. Eagerness and interest. (p. 159)

Entrepreneurs. People who work for themselves. They try to earn money by taking the risk of owning and operating their own businesses. (p. 278)

Entry-level position. A job at the beginning level. (p. 170)

Evaluate. To judge the worth, quality, or goodness of something. (p. 85, 93)

F

Fee. An amount of money or percentage of your salary paid to an employment agency for matching people with jobs. (p. 121)

Fired. Loss of a job because a worker was at fault. (p. 246)

Free enterprise system. An economic system in which individuals and private business are free to organize and operate with little interference from the government; capitalism. (p. 265)

Full time. A work schedule of 40 hours a week. (p. 6)

G

G.E.D. Certificate. A General Educational Development certificate that says you have learned the things that are needed to get a high school diploma. (pp. 100–101)

Giving notice. Telling your employer you'll be leaving. The usual notice is two weeks. (p. 243)

Goals. The things you want to accomplish. (p. 105)

Goods. Products that can be made. (p. 265)

Goods-producing economy. An economy that devotes most of its materials and efforts to manufacturing goods. (p. 273)

Gross pay. Total amount of earnings. (p. 301)

H

Human relations. Interaction with other people. (p. 289)

I

Identity. The way we see ourselves in our minds and the way we think others see us. (p. 12)

Income. Money earned from work or from other sources, such as stocks, bonds, or savings accounts; spendable money. (p. 269)

Income taxes. Money paid from the income of workers to support the government. (p. 302)

Industry skills. Skills that relate to knowledge of an industry. (p. 285)

Inflation. A rise in prices caused by increased demand or low supply. (p. 270)

Initiative. The quality of doing what needs to be done without being told. (p. 178)

Innovation. Applying original or borrowed ideas to situations in which they have not been used before. (p. 288)

Interest. Money paid for allowing a bank or savings and loan to use your money. (p. 309)

Interest inventory. A questionnaire that indicates your strongest interests. (p. 25)

Interests. Things you enjoy doing or thinking about. (p. 21)

Interview. A get-acquainted meeting between the job seeker and the employer. (p. 147)

J

Job. A certain kind of work. (p. 13)

L

Labor union. A group of workers who work at similar jobs or in the same industry. (p. 272)

Laid off. Loss of a job that was not the worker's fault. (p. 246)

Law of supply and demand. In a free enterprise system, as the supply of goods and services goes up, the prices go down. As the demand for goods and services increases, so do the prices. (p. 268)

Letter of resignation. A written statement of your intention to leave a company. (p. 245)

M

Management skills. Skills that relate to handling all financial aspects of a job or business. (p. 286)

Merit increase. A pay raise given because an employee has done the work well. (p. 185)

N

Negative attitude. A way of looking at the world and only seeing the bad side of things. (p. 227)

Net pay. Take-home pay. (p. 297)

Networking. Learning about opportunities through people you know. (p. 239)

Nonverbal behavior. What a person does rather than what he or she says. (p. 152)

O

Objectively. Seeing or viewing a problem without emotions. (p. 190)

Occupational clusters. A group of occupations that are related in some way. (p. 46)

Outcome. The result of a decision; what happens after a decision is made. (p. 85)

Overtime. Work beyond the regular hours. The pay is usually one and one-half times the regular pay. (p. 175)

P

Part-time job. A job in which you work a portion of the full-time work week. (p. 79)

Peer pressure. Pressure from friends to do something. (p. 259)

Personality. The outward sign of your inner self; the total result of your attitudes, environment, and way of looking at life. (p. 36)

Personnel department. People who handle matters such as hiring new employees and arranging for employee benefits. (p. 152)

Piecework.   A set amount of money for each piece completed. (p. 174)

Positive attitude.   A general way of looking at the world that makes life more enjoyable for you and everyone around you. (p. 226)

Probationary period.   A training and evaluation period at a job. (p. 160)

Procrastinator.   A person who puts things off. (p. 98)

Profit.   Money left after the business pays its expenses. (p. 267)

Promotion.   Getting a job higher in rank than the one you already have. (p. 236)

Pronunciation.   The way you say your words. (p. 215)

R

References.   People who know you and know the kind of work you do or the kind of person you are. (p. 133)

Resume.   A summary of all the important information about you. (p. 145)

S

Salary.   A set amount of money paid by an employer for a certain period of time. (p. 174)

Sales credit.   Credit used for small purchases, usually with credit cards. (p. 313)

SBA.   Small Business Administration. A federal agency established to assist and protect small business. (p. 296)

SCORE.   A nonprofit agency that has more than 13,000 volunteer business executives who provide free counseling and training to small business owners. (p. 297)

Secondhand smoke.   Smoke in the air from a tobacco product being smoked by others. (p. 252)

Self-discipline.   The ability to regulate your behavior and actions. (p. 286)

Service.   Doing something to help someone else. (p. 265)

Service-producing economy.   An economy that sells a variety of consumer services. (p. 275)

Severance pay.   Cash amount given by the company to help make up for losing the job. (p. 246)

Side effects.   Reactions to a medicine other than those intended. (p. 252)

Skill.   The ability to do something. (p. 26)

Small business.   A business that is independently owned and operated and not dominant in its field. (p. 282)

Social Security.   A fund that pays benefits to disabled workers and retired people. (p. 304)

Standard of living.   Refers to what items consumers are able to buy and how much the items cost. (p. 275)

Stress.   The effect that pressure often has on people. (p. 207)

Strike.   Workers stop working and leave their jobs. (p. 273)

Substance abuse.   Use of an illegal drug and excessive use of any other controlled substance. (p. 254)

Substance misuse. Using a substance in a way other than its intended use. (p. 254)

Substance use. Using any substance for its intended purpose. (p. 254)

T

Technology. The use of ideas, processes, tools, and materials to get things done. (p. 8)

Temporary job. A part-time or full-time job that lasts only for a couple of hours, weeks, days, or months. (p. 79)

U

Unemployment compensation. Money paid to you from a fund that employers pay into. (p. 246)

V

Volunteer. A person who works without pay. (p. 79)

W

Wages. Pay figured by the hour or by the piece. (p. 174)

INDEX

INDEX

INDEX

INDEX

Photo Credits

Adamsmith/Westlight   338
American Airlines/Photo Edit   51
Apple Computers/INCO   9
William Atherton   15, 64, 84, 91, 140, 191, 215, 228
Craig Aurness/Westlight   347, 353
Robert Brenner/Photo Edit   5, 282
Paul Buddle   60
Tom Campbell/Westlight   270, 348
R. Cash/Photo Edit   158
Steve Chenn/Westlight   343
Cleo   78
Creative Slides and Advertising   48
Mary Kate Denny/Photo Edit   66, 156, 271
Department of the Navy   223
Laima Druskis   xvi, 77, 88, 102, 111, 212, 233, 265
Eric Dusenbery   149
David R. Frazier   27, 172
Tony Freeman/Photo Edit   11, 55, 71, 130, 155, 221, 222, 226, 244, 247, 253, 254, 287, 288, 318
Richard Fukuhara/Westlight   45
General Motors   58
Jeff Greenberg   73, 160, 236, 256, Inset 295
Julie Habel/Westlight   327
Richard Hutchings/Photo Edit   165, 178, 300
Walter Hodges/Westlight   335, 351, 355
Robert Landau/Westlight   330
Stephen McBrady   37
P. McCarten/Photo Edit   240
Robert McElwee   21, 49, 184
Felicia Martinez/Photo Edit   209
Mary Messenger   40, 126, 260, 293, 311
Warren Morgan/Westlight   341
John Neubauer   41
Chuck O'Rear/Westlight   333, 344
Alan Oddie/Photo Edit   264
Photo Edit   192, 314
Princess Cruises   42
Mark Richards/Photo Edit   16, 142, 175, 272
Will & Angie Rumpf   xvi, 3, 57, 281, 291
Jan Shaffer/Photo Edit   224
David Simpson   23, 214
D. Strickler/Strix Pix   107
Walter Urie/Westlight   329, 336
U.S. Army   176
Dana White   2, 6, 7, 10, 12, 14, 20, 24, 29, 30, 31, 33, 34, 35, 44, 50, 56, 63, 67, 69, 70, 75, 82, 83, 90, 93, 94, 97, 99, 100, 104, 114, 116, 117, 121, 122, 133, 135, 138, 139, 147, 150, 162, 163, 167, 170, 173, 179, 180, 183, 185, 186, 189, 194, 196, 197, 198, 200, 201, 203, 205, 206, 207, 218, 219, 229, 230, 234, 238, 239, 242, 250, 257, 259, 274, 277, 278, 283, 285, 290, 292, 295, 306, 310, 313, 319, 321.
Ann Wright   153
Duane Zehr   47, 53, 85, 105, 118, 125, 164, 220
Anna E. Zuckerman/Photo Edit   267